THE
BURGOYNE
DIARIES

Editorial Note: The spelling of place names in the original text is not always consistent. (The spelling of those names might anyway vary, depending on the source material.) The author also tended to alternate in the spelling of such words as 'Head Quarters'. The publishers, by and large, have left these words unaltered.

THE
BURGOYNE
DIARIES

THE FIRST WINTER
AT YPRES WITH THE
ROYAL IRISH RIFLES

GERALD ACHILLES BURGOYNE

Pen & Sword
MILITARY

First published in Great Britain in 1985 by Thomas Harmsworth Publishing.

Reprinted in this format in 2015 by
PEN & SWORD MILITARY
An imprint of
Pen & Sword Books Ltd
47 Church Street, Barnsley
South Yorkshire
S70 2AS

ISBN 978 1 47382 758 5

A CIP catalogue record for this book is
available from the British Library

Printed and bound in England
By CPI Group (UK) Ltd, Croydon, CR0 4YY

Pen & Sword Books Ltd incorporates the Imprints of Pen & Sword Aviation,
Pen & Sword Family History, Pen & Sword Maritime, Pen & Sword Military,
Pen & Sword Discovery, Pen & Sword Politics, Pen & Sword Atlas,
Pen & Sword Archaeology, Wharncliffe Local History, Leo Cooper,
Wharncliffe True Crime, Wharncliffe Transport, Pen & Sword Select,
Pen & Sword Military Classics, The Praetorian Press, Claymore Press,
Remember When, Seaforth Publishing and Frontline Publishing

For a complete list of Pen & Sword titles please contact
PEN & SWORD BOOKS LIMITED
47 Church Street, Barnsley, South Yorkshire, S70 2AS, England
E-mail: enquiries@pen-and-sword.co.uk
Website: www.pen-and-sword.co.uk

Introduction to 2015 Edition

The diaries cover a short period – so far as the Front is concerned – from 10 December 1914, when the 2nd Battalion Royal Irish Rifles (7 **Brigade, 3rd Division, II Corps**) was serving east of Kemmel, to the time when Burgoyne was wounded during an abortive attack at Hill 60 on 8 May 1915. Burgoyne was, for much of this time, the officer commanding D Company.

Internal evidence suggests that the diaries were written up and then pages regularly sent home – whether to his first or future wife it is not clear. On rare occasions they read almost as letters. He also took numerous photographs, but these, alas, seem to have been lost; his papers – presumably all the relevant military ones – were deposited by his daughter from his second marriage, and the editor of this volume, with the IWM.

This book, when combined with John Lucy's Great War classic *There's a Devil in the Drum* (1938), provides the outstanding account of a battalion from pre-war days and then through the agonies of Mons and the Retreat; the horrendous casualties of the Marne and the Aisne; the desperate struggles at La Bassée and First Ypres; and the tremendous task of the rebuilding of a battalion into the late spring of 1915 – a battalion that was twice reduced to not much more than a platoon between August and the end of November 1914. The period can be seen through the eyes of a regular, pre-war junior NCO (who went on to be commissioned) and Burgoyne, a reserve officer and company commander who came to the battalion at its lowest ebb, in early December 1914, and struggled with the twin realities of a miserable winter in the new phenomenon of trench warfare, and of the effort required to restore it to effective fighting fitness.

Gerald Achilles Burgoyne was born in 1874 in Chiswick, the son of Peter Burgoyne, a well-known wine merchant whose chief claim to fame was to establish the place of Australian wines in the UK. 'Achilles' came from his mother's side of the family (she was born in Germany). Gerald was born into a very well-off family and followed a classic career path for one of his background. He studied law and was called to the Bar, but never practised. He was a member of the Middlesex militia and then saw service with 3rd Dragoon Guards in the South African War, resigning his commission in 1910 and transferring as a special reserve officer to the Royal Irish Rifles that year. He was a gentleman of leisure and a keen huntsman (several references in the diary), with homes at one time or the other and sometimes, apparently, simultaneously, in Ireland and in the south west of England, as well as a base in London. He was married and had a son, Peter, born in 1900.

At the outbreak of the war he was a member of 4th Battalion Royal Irish Rifles. Under the Haldane Reforms (a man for whom Burgoyne had little time), the introduction of the Territorial Force did not apply to Ireland; so the 4th and 5th battalions remained as extra reserve battalions.

A few months were spent in training and some coastal defence duties; it was quite soon established that the battalion was going to be used as a drafting battalion. On 30 November he was selected to take a draft to the Front; he went off with a hundred men from the 4th Battalion, added another hundred from the 5th (he being the only officer) and, on the boat in Dublin, added another fifty men from the 3rd Battalion, under the command of Second Lieutenant Calverley.

The reality is that nothing much exciting happened to the battalion in the months recorded in his diary – no major action (until the counter attack in which Burgoyne was wounded;

some twenty died in the seven days around the attack in May in that fighting), not even any significant raiding; and yet the casualties that it suffered were very high – over a hundred killed and probably at least four times that number wounded or sick over the period of Burgoyne's trench service. This was very significant damage caused by what came to be known as 'trench wastage'; the scale of this was higher than was to be the norm as the war progressed. This situation needs explanation, something that the diary entries provide and which are supported by Lucy's account.

The diary is a unique account of the rebuilding of a traumatised battalion – in particular of one of its companies (D). It required a massive influx of reinforcements at the end of First Ypres to make it into a viable unit, let alone an effective fighting one. Most of this period was spent in the trenches forward of Kemmel or slightly to the north; and we are fortunate to have another classic memoir, written by a pre-war journalist, H.S. Clapham's *Mud and Khaki* (1930). He was a member of the 1st/1st Honourable Artillery Company, in the same brigade as the 2/RIR (from 9 December 1914) for the period of Burgoyne's service. Between these three books, written by highly literate men, it is possible to get a real feel of what the infantry endured in the trenches during that first, terrible winter of the war.

The key difference between these works (apart from the fact that Lucy and Clapham were 'other ranks', though both commissioned during the course of the war) is that the other two were memoirs written well after the war; and Burgoyne's is a diary, which he seems to have last touched in August 1915 after he had recovered from wounds received at Hill 60 that May but was still suffering from what now would be called post-traumatic stress disorder – he never returned to the Front. It would appear that there were very few changes from what was originally written apart from some footnotes.

When I first read this book, at the time of its publication in 1985 and at the recommendation of the highly knowledgeable Great War expert Tony Spagnoly, I would have to admit that I was put off by how almost shockingly unsympathetic he was towards his men. Examples of this abound; when carefully reading through the diaries I find that I took over twenty pages of notes, at least a couple of pages of which referred to this aspect of his character.

Incidents ranged from the attempted suicide of a draft member (not his regiment, in this case) on board a transport to his persistent desire for a death sentence to be imposed on a soldier caught sleeping at his post in the trenches (probably Rifleman Hurley – he received ninety days Field Punishment No 1). He rages about ineffectual NCOs (as, indeed, does Lucy); he is not against direct action – at least twice he vigorously struck soldiers (in one case possibly the only solution) and encouraged NCOs on one occasion to deal with an issue by beating up an offending soldier: *give him a good hammering*. He records the incidence of executions, often with little sympathy – and makes the observation that firing parties were found from defaulters within the brigade (again, Lucy substantiates this). He is forever cursing his men as curs and being almost animal in their instincts – but is far more impressed with the drafts of what he calls Kitchener men who begin to arrive in early 1915.

On reflection, and with a good number of years since my first reading, one can understand – if not condone – his attitude. The battalion was in a terrible, mauled state. Drafts initially came from the reserve system and seem to have been of, generally, poor quality. There was a chronic shortage of capable NCOs and the quality of officers was not much better. The battalion was on active service in a fairly precarious part of the line in ghastly weather conditions for much of the account. The brutality seems to have been directed to survival – harsh treatment seemed to be the only way to bring immediate results, in getting soldiers to adopt a sensible trench discipline and to start acting as soldiers. One can debate the rights and wrongs of it, of course, but in my opinion this certainly was not either gratuitous violence or the consequence of a sadistic streak.

For he can also show a real concern for the welfare of his men (*my poor, careless boys*) and can empathise with their situation: *At about 2.30 this morning I heard a poor devil moaning and crying outside my dugout. Bitter frost and I knew and felt with 'em all. I was cold in my dugout with a fire. He was crying, 'Oh, God, take me out of this; oh, God, take me out of this.' Got him to the fire, but as he said his feet were frost bitten, I sent him over at once to the dressing station. I believe he was a decent young fellow...* There are numerous examples of his efforts to improve conditions for the men as best he could; whilst, as the diary proceeds, there is almost a clinical interest in following the deleterious effects of his existence and responsibilities on his own state of mind.

There are wonderful pieces of information that are lacking in other memoirs of this type: there are several pages describing a *'typical' tour of the trenches*; there is a most illuminating parade statement on a given day of his company's manpower deployment; the problems of dugout construction, trench maintenance and the disposal of old cadavers all receive attention; the state of the Germans opposite is described; he reports only rumours of a Christmas Truce – communications must have been very poor because there was a well-documented one only a mile or so to the right of his battalion's position; he records burials – amongst others, the very early ones in what is now Kemmel Chateau Cemetery – and his one leave; his rather bitter attitude towards the staff, an attitude, which is emphatically reinforced by a coda at the end of the diary.

Burgoyne celebrated his forty-first birthday in the trenches; he was quite an old man. He had seen something of life, admittedly from his very privileged standpoint; and had considerable experience as a soldier, both in an earlier war and in peace time. He is not afraid to admit his squeamishness when recovering remains for burial or trying to retrieve identity discs. Rapidly buried corpses in or near the trenches were a continuous issue as they resurfaced: *Cleaning out a drain we came across what looked like a bit of the brain and a face of a man, I didn't stay to investigate it – I fled.* The entries give clear insights into his operation as a company commander and also into his reactions to the miserable conditions that he endured in the trenches, which evidently continually sapped at his morale.

He gives a full description of the incident that resulted in his wounding (part of the prolonged tug of war with the Germans for the possession of Hill 60); apart from the confusion and half heartedness of the attack, by then he had come to take a real pride in his company.

He was never to return to the Front. It is quite clear that his own nerves were becoming increasingly frayed by the conditions (*It really is rotten walking up to the trenches and it gets on one's nerves*) at the Front and the stress of making anew an efficient company in such a badly damaged battalion. He notes on 24 February, that the battalion came out with 1,100 men and had since received twenty-five drafts of reinforcements, which he calculated as a total of 3,100 and the battalion then had a present strength of 900 – that is some 3,300 casualties in six months.

Relatively little is known of his life after the war; he remarried in 1922 and a daughter, Claudia – the editor of the diaries – was born in 1924. He was Cork Pursuivant of Arms; and at the time of his death he was living near Taunton, Somerset. Probably the first time he came to public attention was when he was killed at the age of sixty-two by Italian bombers whilst commanding a Red Cross mule convoy in northern Abyssinia (Ethiopia) in 1936 during Mussolini's shameless campaign. He went out to that country in November 1935 to offer his services in this humanitarian capacity (and perhaps this throws another light on his complex character). The incident certainly caught the attention of the international media.

The Royal Irish Rifles are blessed with fine histories; the much-respected military historian Cyril Falls wrote its regimental history (*The Royal Irish Rifles in the Great War*), though only about a page relates to the period covered in Burgoyne's diaries. Much the same amount of coverage of this phase of the war is provided in the much more recent and excellent James Taylor's *The Second Royal Irish Rifles in the Great War*. This rather goes to underline the point about how this period is regarded as relatively uninteresting – understandable, of course, given the significant battles in which the battalion would be involved in the three-and-a-half years of war that followed Burgoyne's departure from the Front. Yet it was a crucial time, a period of enforced and rapid reaction to the sorry state to which it – and many other battalions – had fallen by the winter of 1914.

Taylor's volume has a number of superb appendices – full biographical data on most of the officers, excellent casualty rolls and also a full listing of court martial cases. Since Burgoyne probably never considered the publication of his diary, he gives names of people freely (though, like many of his place names, not always accurately spelt). When this information is combined with the clear indication of the location of the various villages of significance to the battalion, of different headquarters and sections of trench occupied, the end result is a comprehensive guide to the part of the line occupied by 2nd Royal Irish Rifles, an area that, fortuitously, has been largely undisturbed by the march of progress over the last century and is still largely rural. It is possible to stand in places familiar to Burgoyne – for example near the replacement of Alston House, in the cemetery attached to Irish Farm and looking up towards Wytschaete, in Burgoyne's 'little cemetery' that is now Kemmel Chateau Cemetery, or in the square at Westoutre, where the battalion had its transport lines. It makes for an evocative trip, with Burgoyne as your *vade mecum*; and armed with the diaries and copies of Lucy's and Clapham's books, a visitor will be well equipped to acknowledge the forgotten men of the winter of 1914–15.

Nigel Cave
October 2015

PREFACE

These are the Diaries that my father, Gerald Achilles Burgoyne, wrote from the trenches just south of Ypres while he was with the Royal Irish Rifles in the Great War.

When he wrote them I had not been born, and when he died, aged 62, bombed by the Italian Air Force while he and his mules were convoying a Red Cross unit in Ethiopia in 1936, I was only 12.

I found the Diaries in a trunk full of personal effects when my mother died. I showed them to a long-standing friend who immediately suggested their publication.

Despite conditions of all-pervading mud, bitter cold and wind, let alone the bursting shells and the 'sipping' bullet, my father dispassionately recorded and drew what he saw. And these vivid accounts, written on pages of a notebook, were almost daily sent back to his wife. Each day is a gem of interest, from the very first entry in November 1914, to the last in May 1915.

The diaries end as abruptly as they begin. In May 1915 my father was wounded and sent back to England, after a gruesome and abortive attack on the notorious Hill 60.

Claudia Davison.

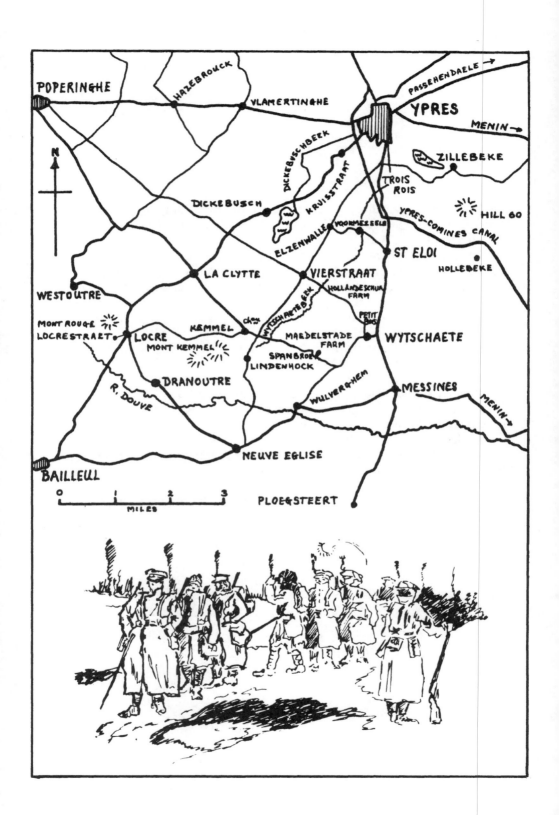

1914

I had completed my annual training with the 4th Battalion, and after a three weeks' course of instruction on the Lough Swilly Defences, at Buncrana (Donegal) I joined the 3rd Battalion, at the Kinnegar on July 27th for their training, and a recruiting march they were to make throughout County Antrim.

At the end of the week there were rumours of War, the recruiting march was abandoned, and War was declared on Monday, August 3rd. The following day all Battalions of the Special Reserves were ordered to mobilise and the 4th Battalion commenced mobilisation at Newtownards, marching into Holywood Barracks on the evening of August 6th under Colonel Findlay. I joined them from the camp at the Kinnegar the following day, on which date the 3rd Battalion left for Dublin, the 5th Battalion having mobilised at Downpatrick, came into Victoria Barracks, Belfast, and with the 4th Battalion and a Battalion of the Irish Fusiliers encamped at Carrickfergus formed the guard for the Belfast Lough Defences. We were first put to entrenching certain positions east of Grey Point: guarding the Port War Signal Station (telegraph) at Orloch Hill, and then settled down to recruiting and training men, as instead of using extra SR Batts as units in the field as was the original intention, we were to be used as drafting Battalions for both Officers and men in the same way as the Special Reserve Battalions.

November 30th

At 'Office Hour' the adjutant came out of his office with a telegram in his hand and asked if I minded going to Flanders. Told him I would certainly go with pleasure, if I were sent. 'That's all right then,' says he, 'For the War Office have wired in your name to accompany our draft this week.'

December 3rd

The draft of 100 men of the 4th Battalion paraded at 1 pm, and headed by our Pipes and our Band, we entrained at Holywood. At Belfast we boarded trams, and I had some difficulty in keeping the women who surrounded us from passing the men bottles of stout and whiskey.

In some half dozen trams we crossed the city to the Great Northern Station where a further draft of 100 men of the 5th Battalion met me, and I took the 200 men, with no officer to assist me, to Dublin. On board the boat I found awaiting me 50 men and young Calverly of the 3rd Battalion, who are quartered at Dublin. Colonel M'Cammon, Jack Curran, and several other officers of the 3rd Battalion were at the quay to wave their 'Au Revoirs' to us.

December 4th

Detrained at Southampton. The men behaved awfully well on the journey and gave me no trouble; a couple of hours with my Father and Mother and we embarked on the Transport 'Novian'. I believe some 3,000 to 4,000 troops are to cross with us, in several transports.

As there was a tail end of a gale on, we lay alongside all night, with the gangway drawn up. At dinner a man rushed in to say a soldier had just cut his throat on the Fo'c's'le – I was in command on board, so I rushed out. Found the starboard side of the Fo'c's'le running with blood and a man of the Northumberland Fusiliers lying in it. Amid cries of 'He's gone',

2

'No he ain't', 'Ah! poor fellow, 'es dying' and other cheery remarks, I forced my way into the crush around him. Had a horrid jag in his throat, in which I could see his windpipe, but that wasn't severed. The drizzling rain eventually brought him round and he was carried off the ship crying for his mother. Did it with a Government Jack Knife. Probably have succeeded if he'd used a steel blade! Jolly start for Active Service, and on a Friday too!

December 5th

Left the docks early in the morning and anchored off the Wight to await the other transports and our convoy, and we eventually sailed in the afternoon. Couldn't go over nine knots as the other transports were so slow, but we slowly forged ahead, and accompanied by our TBD escort we reached the Havre early.

December 6th

Sunday morning. Half of the drafts on board were disembarked, but the Irish Rifles, Gordons, and 5th Lancers and some others, go on this boat to Rouen tomorrow. Later we were all disembarked and bivouacked in the dock sheds, and as there was no boat ready for us we had to go and sleep there. Three or four of us officers got into a tiny office inside the shed to sleep. Rotten hanging about the dirty wharves.

December 7th

No orders, and we were kept still hanging about. Food scanty. I got one meal at the Club in Havre which struck me as being as uninteresting a place as Southampton. Received orders to embark; did so, and then heard we were not to move until about 8 pm so Calverly and I went down a rope ladder (all the gangways pulled up) and dined in the town, and we had to run to get back in time. Two or three men were absent at the embarkation and turned up, under Police escort, as we were leaving the quay.

A wretched cargo boat; cabins for four officers and there were eighteen of us on board, and no food for us. However, we got the steward to give us coffee and biscuits next morning. I slept in the pantry with my nose unpleasantly close to the steward's greasy towels; one man slept on the cabin table, several on the floor. We lost the beauties of our trip down the Seine by sailing by night, and on December 8th about 6 am we reached Rouen; a very pretty picture from the river. We disembarked at 8.30 and a guide led us up to the camp, close to Rouen Race-course, on which now stands a huge Canvas Field Hospital among the huts of which flit the Army Nurses in their bright scarlet capes.

Mud everywhere, and ankle deep near camp, and our camp wasn't fit to walk in without gum-boots. Put our men 14 to 15 in a tent. Calverly and I got a tent to ourselves, and found a rough, very rough, mess there, for which we were charged two francs a day, robbery, as we were only in a Government hospital tent, ate off a rough deal table, with the commonest of cutlery, and not enough of that either, and put up with rations. Someone was making a bit, but no one could complain as so few officers ever stayed there more than a night or so. On arrival I was told to prepare a draft of 190 men for the front (2nd Battalion) at once, and a nice job I had equipping them.

My own 4th Battalion draft had only the underclothing they were wearing; the spare shirts etc, having been taken from them before they left; the drafts from the 3rd and 5th Battalions had most of them spare underclothing, though several had sold their spare kit. All men had to get issued, as far as possible, with a second shirt, etc. I had to pay them, a long job, as each man had to sign for his money in his pay book. Each rifleman received 5 francs, and all NCO's 10 francs. They are putting up wooden huts in the Camp for, I hear, Kitchener's army, and though men are overcrowded in wet leaky huts, and lying in the filthy mud, the authorities will not allow us to put men in the eight or ten

4

huts which are completed, and which would each take fifty men. 'Pon my word it's extraordinary how frightened the British officer is of taking a little responsibility. So, because our Camp Commandant, or the District GOC, had no special orders men had to be out in wet tents and get pneumonia and kindred ills.

December 9th

No definite orders to move, so walked into Rouen. A most interesting old place, saw the Cathedral and the old Clock Arch, and then to tea at the only decent place, where I also had a bath. But had to go out and buy a cake of soap first, as they don't provide soap in the hotel bedrooms. Suppose the guests in France steal it!

Heard some of our troops had been looting a bit on the Aisne, but that is put down with an iron hand, and six men of a certain Corps, caught looting and 'other things' at the base, have been shot. At Havre some English troops broke open a lot of cases lying on the quay, Xmas gifts for the troops, and looted eighty plum puddings.

December 10th

At 11.30 I received orders to march out of camp at 1.30 with 190 men! No ammunition issued, men not all paid, no sergeants I can trust. Of course we were the last draft to parade. At 1 pm I went down to their lines to turn them out, and found the lines empty; no sergeants, no men. To the Canteen, and found the NCO's trying to chase the men back to their lines. The Camp Commandant hadn't the 'Savvy' to close the Canteen a couple of hours before a draft left, until I suggested it to him for future occasions. Got 188 men on Parade somehow, Lord knows how I got so many. Marched to the station, but one man was surprised when I snatched a beer bottle from his hand and smashed it on the pavement. I left Calverly with the 62 remaining over behind, and I was the only officer with my draft.

A draft of Gordons went up with us. Each two officers had one compartment of a corridor coach and we were quite comfortable, and six men in each carriage. Our troops in the train behaved awfully well, and gave little bother at the few halts we made.

I hear 'brain strain' has accounted for a few suicides among our officers. One poor old dug-out reached Rouen, where he found he simply couldn't face the idea of going to the front, and he 'went sick'. After being in hospital a few days the doctors sent him away, as they could find nothing wrong with him, so he shut himself up in a lavatory and blew his brains out. An officer in the ASC did the same thing, over-strain in his case. But I hear it's far more common in the German Army.

December 11th

Arrived at Bailleul where we detrained. A guide met us who seemed uncertain about the way. Over awful cobble stones we marched 6 miles to Locre; there I heard the 2nd Battalion were in the trenches, and I was sent a further 2½ miles to some huts at West Outre. Arrived there in the dusk, fagged out all of us. My NCO's not of great use, except one Sergeant whose name I forget; harangued them on discipline; told them I could not be bothered with petty crime, they must make the men obey them, how I did not care; and that I would back them up in all they did. Ten minutes later a miserable corporal runs up to me, 'Please Sir, Rifleman X has his rifle loaded and he won't unload it, and all the men's afraid of him'. I went back to Rifleman X, and without a word punched him twice under the jaw, told him luridly to unload his rifle, and the thing was done. Result, no more worry of any kind.

Owing to no orders on the subject and no transport, the remaining rations we should have had with us were left at Bailleul, and so on arriving at West Outre we were starving. However, in the pitch dark I at last found a supply officer, who in his own motor brought up supplies and some rum to camp for us, and the Divisional Supply Officer whom I met took me to his house and fed me; and I wanted it badly. Plenty of clean dry straw in the huts. I had one to myself, and my 'fleabag' arriving, I soon huddled down comfortably and slept well, though we heard the booming of the guns, and now and again a rattle of musketry to inform us we were close to the front. I was told that Smith Dorrien, in a speech to some troops, said all serious fighting would be over by April, even if the war is not over by then, and the general opinion is that the war will be over by the end of the summer. The march from Bailleul is a nightmare; seven or eight miles over these damned roads. The centre third of the roads is all round cobbles, greasy with mud and pitted by heavy traffic, the outside thirds are just quagmires into which one sinks over one's ankles; and the marching was made very tedious by the constant passage of motor cars and lorries and horse vehicles, for all of which we poor 'footsloggers' had to get into the mud.

Hear poor Allgood is dead:* killed while serving with the 1st Battalion.

These huts are penthouses, sunk about 18 inches into the ground, with a certain alley-way another foot deeper, and about two feet broad. The headroom inside about eight feet, room for thirty men. An awful night, soaking and very dark.

December 12th

Took the draft for a route march today, to see a bit of the country. Very like parts of Kent or Sussex; undulating folds, covered with small copses, and with hop fields. Our Howitzers are keeping up a constant cannonade and to us newcomers it seems rather warm.

The Battalion comes out of the trenches tonight and I join them tomorrow.

---

* He was killed by a stray bullet one night, as he was taking his company to the trenches.

All the staff I've run up against so far are charming, and go out of the way to help a poor stranger in a strange land, so we are getting along quite comfortably. I hear the worst part of some of the trenches where one division, the 3rd is, is the number of dead bodies, and bits of bodies, of Frenchmen that float about in them. The French had a big charge over the Kemmel country some weeks ago and lost very heavily. Otherwise I hear trench life is merely very tedious and very dirty.

On our route march I met two French Dragoons, their brass helmets in khaki covers, their horsetails hanging down. They were driving before them two miserable beings, whom they told me were 'suspects'; doubtless they'll be shot within a few hours. Hang dog looking brutes: men who have so low intelligence that they'd see no harm in selling their country for a few bits of silver.

The country is alive with English and French troops, and though the peasantry are going on with their farmwork as if there was no war at all, horse and foot cross the fields as if they were not there. In many places the fields are better than the roads.

December 13th

Took the draft a short march to St Jean Cappella just over the Belgian border. A message has just come ordering us to join the 2nd Battalion at Locre after we have had our dinner.

Captain Whelan was hit in the chest yesterday and died in about two hours. He was out scouting round with a dog and a rifle. I hear he walked right in rear of the German trenches, and returned safely, and he was hit whilst walking about behind his trench, and in full view of the Germans.

Our big 9.2 gun, drawn by a traction engine, is banging away about a mile from us.

I am told that one Company of this Battalion on the Aisne was surrounded and were all shot down. The last to go was a Sergeant who put up his hands to surrender, but though he was hit in three places, the brutes bayoneted him. A body of some

400 Germans tried to surrender in a body about this time and some regiment turned a machine gun on them; the next day they had to tell off a fatigue party to bury their bag, so we got a bit of our own back.

Joined the 2nd Battalion in the afternoon; found Major Alston in command, with Major Festing acting as second in command. The last three days in the trenches the Battalion lost some twelve men killed and wounded altogether, but Alston says three parts of the casualties in the trenches are entirely the men's own fault.

Took over command of 'C' Company from Norman (a Lieutenant) who has just returned from being wounded on the Aisne.

We are billeted in a tiny wayside inn about half a mile from Locre, and our men are in sheds and lofts around us.

December 14th

We are 'standing to' in Locre, as the 7th Brigade (ours) is in Reserve, the 8th Brigade is making an attack with the 9th Brigade in support. The attack is on Wyschaete, which the French immediately on our left are to take, their attack being directed on the convent. Our fellows attack Petit Bois and try to take the woods west of the town. Our artillery commenced their bombardment of the German trenches at 7 am and now (8.30 am) there is a heavy cannonade going on. My Company is halted just below a small hill to the north of Locre, on which stands a windmill; this hill is the observation station for the district, and commands the present battlefield, some five miles to the east. From the top I could see the towers and the spires of Ypres distinctly. The Prince of Wales with Colonel Stanley Barry, General Smith Dorrien, General Haldane commanding the 3rd Division in which we are, and other 'brass hats' were all up there. Met Colonel Boyle up there too.* Used to know him in

* I met him about 24th March, 1915, when I found him commanding a Brigade.

SA. In the distance we could see heavy shells bursting over the attacking troops, and a shrapnel burst in front of us, sufficiently near to hear the whistle of the bullets. Away to the north of Ypres, on the horizon, heavy shells are bursting, and we wonder whether our Navy are shelling the coast line. Little flickers of red betoken burning houses, but of the attacking line I could see nothing. It's all rather like a big sham fight at Salisbury, with spectators on top of the most prominent hill.

A few nights ago there was a heavy scrap over some French trenches. Our fellows could see the flashes of their rifles. It lasted an hour and at 1 am all was silence. The Germans had taken the trenches. At 3 am a further rattle broke out again, lasting till 6 am; then suddenly not a sound. The French had made a successful counter-attack, and retaken the trenches together with 200 prisoners.

Hear the Royal Scots have captured 40 Germans in a trench close to Petit Bois.

From 3.30 to 4.15 pm the French and our artillery bombarded Wyschaete and the German lines round them. In the growing gloom the gun-fire burst out below us and about a mile or rather less to our front; over Wyschaete and all along the ridge to the south of it, there is a cloud of little white puff balls, each burst heralded by a flame like the spark which comes from the top of an electric tram arm occasionally. I hear the Gordons are hung up on the right, and that we are waiting for the French attacks to be pushed home.

December 15th

We had to 'stand to' at 7 am. Like getting up in the middle of the night; dark as Hades and wet. Everything perfectly beastly, and everyone in a hopeless sort of state, carrying on as if there's nothing else to do. Very dreary; and the mud! This wet, especially in the trenches, is sending men sick very rapidly. A large number get quite crippled by 'scalded' feet. Their feet swell out the size of young balloons and they can't get their boots on. We are all topping well fed and can get everything necessary from the Government; field glasses, revolvers, boots, and I hear, even valises. Very glad I didn't bring my sword with me. No one carries one, though a few of the mounted officers still have their swords, now rather rusty, on the saddle.

My Company Headquarters are in a farm house, about half a mile from the little estaminet where I spent my first night, at Battalion Headquarters. We live, sleep, feed and generally have our being, six of us (the officers of two companies mess together), in the farm kitchen, which is also used by two or three females and a farm hand. So it's a little crowded and stuffy.

December 16th

We had a sudden order to parade at 2.30 pm yesterday to replace the Middlesex in the trenches. My own Company was in support fortunately and we fared very well. Of course, no reliefs can take place till dark and from 2.30 pm to 9.30 pm we were marching, halting, swearing and tumbling about in the mud with our heavy packs on our backs and the trenches not four miles away as the crow flies. The Huns are shelling the farm my company are in (The 'Support Barn') and I have just turned them out of the place. Found they were only using shrapnel, so we went inside again. Forty of my men are in immediate support of the trenches, in dug-outs; things so filthy in muck and mud that no farmer, however callous, would sty a pig in any of them. I slept with the remainder of my men in the 'Support Barn'; some of my men in the loft, some in a filthy cellar, the rest divided among half a dozen tiny rooms and cupboards, and in the kitchen and tap-room (for the farm was also an estaminet) where I lay down amongst them on some fairly clean straw. I had no blankets and got but little sleep. My feet, mud up to the knees and my puttees caked as in a plaster cast, just froze and I lay and prayed for the dawn. The fields around are a sea of slimy, clayey mud, smothered with shell holes, some half as big as 'our' pond, full of water, into which, if you are not careful, you slide, and generally stick, till some man lifts you out again.

On our way up to the trenches last night we passed a number of burdened stretchers and wounded men walking back after the attack on the 14th and at one part of our road we had to halt, as a perfect hail of bullets came over us from the German trenches away on our right. They were firing at the trenches opposite them, and must have been pointing their rifles at the sky for the bullets to drop around us. I was proud of my new draft who stood it very well, in spite of a lot of the Middlesex, who had just been relieved, doubling hard over the open, for shelter at the cottage under whose shattered walls we were standing.

The Gordons, on the right, and the Royal Scots, on the left, came into the trenches about 3 am pitch dark, on the 14th, with orders to attack at 7.30 am, Petit Bois their objective. The Royal Scots carried one trench and made forty prisoners, but at very heavy loss to themselves, and they could get no further; some 150 yards from their line. The Gordon attack took the wrong direction went far too far to their right and were mown down from the German trenches on Middlestede Farm. I believe one or two actually got up to these trenches, only to be shot on the parapet. The Gordons lost seven officers and 250 men. The Royal Scots had two officers killed and 110 men killed, wounded and missing. A large number of wounded are still lying out in front of our lines, too badly hit to get back, and it is death to anyone to attempt to reach them by day, and practically impossible to find them during these dark nights. Some of the men brought in this evening had been lying out in front since 8 am on the 14th. I have just visited the 'Dug-outs' and saw a Gordon lying there, hit through the foot. I gave him a tablet of morphia to still the pain. Each Company Commander is issued with a little tube of morphia tablets for such cases.

After this attack the enemy are very nervous, and last night the Germans were doing a lot of funk firing, and both sides, using blue flares freely, were wasting a deal of ammunition. Our windows are fairly rattling with the salvo's of fire our howitzers and the French artillery are directing on the Middlestede and

Wyschaete trenches. This 'funk' firing at night is very catching, as new troops think there is something up, or imagine they see movement in the darkness, and one man firing will set off the whole line. Quite safe as a rule, for those in the front trenches, but most unpleasant for all troops any distant up to a mile behind the lines.

We have now a great preponderance of artillery, and the Germans are doing little in the big gun line just about here. Outside our door is a miscellaneous heap of family property; a bassinette, a red painted wooden thing, prettily curved, on rockers; women's dresses and clothes; boots in all stages of wear; a bowler hat, all the menu articles of a home; Kemmel, the town through which we marched on our way here shows, in its skeletons, shattered windows and pitted roadway, how heavily it has suffered. Just behind the town rises Mount Kemmel, a small eminence on which stands the ruins of a restaurant. This is our artillery observation station. This 'Support Barn' is one of the very few buildings intact in the district, and in order not to attract the Teuton fire, or to tell them we are here, we may not light fires between sunrise and sunset and the little cooking we can do by day, has to be done in the cellars. We cannot walk outside by day, and we do so, at night, only at our peril, as the night air around this farm is full of bullets. Most men agree it's far safer in the trenches than in Support or Reserve, if only one is not fool enough to 'ask for it'. Poor Whelan was killed through his own fault entirely, and Rae in the 4th Battalion lost his life because he would leave his trench during the day instead of waiting till nightfall. A Lincoln officer captured a sniper the other day and would not have him shot. However, when the officer's back was turned, the men cleaned their bayonets in the Hun and finished him off. The shrapnel which burst close to the barn, within 35 yards of us, this morning, all burst on the field across which I and our men had gone half an hour previously to take rum to my men in the dug-outs. Good thing we didn't delay longer. Heard some HAC men going up to the trenches from Kemmel. They took refuge from some shrapnel bursting over them in a ditch beside the road. The second shell killed one man. He was found lying outstreched, and close to his hand his open diary. He had carefully chronicled all his movements and experiences, and his last entry was to the effect that a shrapnel shell had burst over him, the first he had ever experienced. And so the second killed him. I can imagine the hell of advancing under heavy artillery fire. But one gets 'fed up' very quickly out here, because human nature cannot stand it, and the man becomes merely an animal of sorts, and acts, as a horse does in harness, more or less mechanically, driven by long reins of telephone wire from Headquarters three or four miles away.

I saw the Prince of Wales yesterday, as we were parading for the trenches. The first time I didn't notice him as I passed, when I suddenly felt a pretty, serious faced boy looking at me, in his naturally serious, dignified way. I at once recognised him and saluted. He looks a lad of sixteen, but there is that about him which attracts one. He looks a prince where others look merely officers.

This afternoon my sentry reported two or three men in blue uniforms crossing the fields to my left. I ran out and my glasses showed them to be Frenchmen, so I hailed them and had a talk to one. They belong to the French Division on our left. After a few minutes chat we parted, the piou-piou shaking hands heartily. Returning I found the fields strewn with huge unexploded 5 inch shells, fired by the Germans some weeks ago. A dead man, just reported to me lying close by. Went out and found (from his identity disc) he was No. 8863, B West, Suffolk Regiment. Lying with his overcoat tied over his face alongside a ruined farm. Died possibly from wounds. Horrid job, lifting his head to get at his identity disc. I buried him at dusk, and said the Lord's Prayer over him. Couldn't read any prayers as we couldn't have any light, and as it was three bullets came so close to us, they might have been aimed at us.

December 17th

Major Festing was with me. My Company relieved the Company in the trenches (H1 and H2) last night at dark. A perfectly miserable night. Mud everywhere; thick, slimy, deep, stinking, cloying. Rotten job relieving the trenches owing to the stray bullets flying everywhere, and at all times, I slid into Jack Johnstone Holes (hereinafter called JJ's) fell over heaps of greasy mud, grovelled twice for my cap in liquid filth, and returned to my dug-out with my legs, to the knees, in a plaster cast of disgusting filth; several pounds of Belgium, for a foot up, on the skirts of my overcoat. My dug-out in H1 is a place no one would kennel a good dog in. About 2½ feet high at the entrance, and just high enough inside for me to sit upright in, some 7 feet and 5 feet broad. Here my Company Sergeant Major, my servant, the Company Orderly and I have our miserable being. Two feet from the entrance is another dug-out shared by two telephone operators. Night very restless, especially to a newcomer, the French on left repeatedly indulging in terrible fusillades, and our troops, now in single shots, now in bursts of rapid fire, keep one ever on the alert.

About 4 am the French made an attack on the monastery at Wyschaete, from which point they had been held up in the attack on the 14th. There was a terrific attack for about an hour echoed by the French 75's. Stumbling along my line last night in the dark, I came upon three RA Officers who asked for my guidance, and later I met our Divisional Intelligence Officer who wanted to know 'exactly where he was', as he was out to locate eighty dead Germans, somewhere in front of my right, in order to get their shoulder straps and any papers they might have on them. Just about there on the southern side of Middlestede Farm, there are lying the corpses of some hundred or more French and Germans, for across this bit of country, I am told, the French made a tremendous charge last September, suffering very badly.

In front of H1 are the bodies of some thirty or more Gordons, and to my left, many more victims or heroes of the mis-directed charge last Monday.

At dawn this morning, two unwounded Gordons hopped into our trenches. These two men and two others badly wounded had crept into an old French fire trench, some seventy yards in front of our line, and lain there since Monday morning (14th) not daring to come out, as they had lost all sense of direction and did not know where our trenches lay. Starving and drenched the two unwounded men, thinking they heard Irish voices, chanced it and came over. Four of my men very pluckily at once jumped over the parapet and went to the two badly wounded men, taking them some hot tea and food, but the Jocks refused to allow themselves to be brought in then, preferring to wait another day in the cold, until nightfall. Our fellows also brought in two other wounded men who were lying in front of them.

Very heavy cannonading to the north beyond Ypres, whose ruined towers we can just see to our left rear. The Germans have been bursting HE shells some 500 yards behind us, searching for our supports I suppose. They blew in a piece of this trench with a direct hit yesterday, but luckily no men were near at the time. What with the dead men in front of us, and the dead pigs and dead cattle immediately behind us, it's lucky it's not the summer. In our last billet was a refugee from Kemmel, the owner of an hotel there. He and his wife brought their parrot with them. The bird used to be a fine talker, but the bombardment and the noise has so shaken its nerves, it won't say a word now, and sits on its perch thinking an awful lot.

Dogs, cats, pigs and cattle wander the fields behind us, and our trenches, at will, till a stray bullet finds a billet in their stained carcases and adds another victim to the Kaiser's discredit. I do not eat pork killed in that country, my CSM has told me what he has seen pigs feeding on, on the Aisne!

1.45 pm. Just had some food. A moment ago word was given up to me that there was a wounded Gordon in front crying for help. I ran up the line, stripped off my overcoat and had a look, and sure enough saw the poor devil's face about fifty yards in front of us, just beyond our wire entanglements, peering over the top of a shell hole. At my call all the men near volunteered to fetch him in. I took two and went out to him. We found the poor fellow, shot in the groin, lying in the muddy water of a shell hole, and had been there since Monday! My two men picked him up, and wound or no wound, ran him smartly into our trenches, where he stood a moment and stoutly cursed the Gordon Highlanders for leaving him there. He was so grateful to us. I just stayed outside a minute, as I thought I heard another cry, and called out to see if any among the bodies lying thick around were but wounded, but no answer, and I was very glad to skip back again, as the enemy are not averse to firing at men rescuing the wounded. I learnt later that away to our left was a wounded officer. For two days he was heard crying for help. At last two stretcher bearers went out, by day, carrying a stretcher. One man was at once killed. The other put the stretcher down, and had his arms round the officer to lift him on to it, when a bullet hit him through the head. The officer had to be left there and his cries became weaker and weaker and then stopped. But if the Irish Riflemen had been there, I am sure the poor fellow would have been brought in. I was very pleased with my men and am reporting their names to the CO.

Hear we are to be relieved tonight.

December 18th

We were not relieved after all. Festing came up last night and gave us the cheerful news. He sent for two stretchers to come up to take the two wounded Gordons which were lying out in front of us. Festing and I went round to find the man who was to bring in these Gordons, but we discovered he could not induce his pals to volunteer to go out again. The dark frightened them, so Festing telling me to remain in the trench, off with his coat and crawled out. I at once followed and fell over him and nearly yelled with fright; thought I was on top of a huge corpse. After a hideous crawl on hands and knees through a turnip field we found the two men, amid an awful stench; discovered one man was reclining on a very dead German. They were nearly done, and had had no food since Monday, the 14th, except the tea given them yesterday morning. Festing sat down with them and sent me for the stretchers. He remained an hour and then returned to me.*

No word of the stretchers. We dozed all through the night and at dawn I told him we must get them in in ground sheets. So out he and eight men went again, I staying inside to assist them over the parapet and after nearly one hundred and fifteen hours lying wounded and starving out in the winter damp and cold, these poor fellows reached the dressing room station. One man was hit in the groin, and the other in the knee, and it must have hurt awfully bringing them in over the parapet, poor fellows. Most of them were shot between the knee and the waist, as a maxim caught them and mowed them down.

We hold an extraordinary line round here; all indented and

---

* Major Festing died in a charge on April 15th, when 2nd in Command of the 1st Battalion. He was lying wounded in a German trench and refusing to be taken prisoner he blew his brains out. A brave officer and fine soldier.

most irregular and in many cases we can fire into our own trenches, to our right or left, while the Germans can bring long range fire to bear from some directions on our backs. The French just held this line, and it was the line their advance against the Germans reached, and in some parts of course their line advanced further than in others; hence the irregularity. The trenches are merely wide ditches, with very slender and very low breastworks, in many cases the mud thrown out of the trench and no traverses of any kind. On our left some part of our line is so full of water that the Battalion holding them has been withdrawn to trenches in rear. Even if the enemy advance to hold them, they could not remain in them, as they are quite untenable.

At 10 am the French and English artillery brought 500 guns to bear on the Wyschaete – Middlestede line. For exactly thirty minutes it was Hell let loose and most nerve racking. Two of our shells burst short into my rear parapet, knocking over, by the concussion, two of my men who got up laughing; luckily they did not burst. But the ground between me and the enemy some 250 yards was plastered with bursting HE shells from our howitzers of all sizes, while to our left was one continuous deadening roar of the French 75's, as they laid a veritable curtain of fire along the woods to the north of Wyschaete. The whole air rumbled, vibrating from the rush of the shells and the concussion of the bursts.

An unfortunately large percentage of our own shells burst within eighty yards of my front, oft-times smothering us with mud and filth and disturbing the poor dead lying out there. Then suddenly silence and oh! the blessed relief; a relief of short existence as scream after scream of 5.4 shells flung out from the German lines across to us, and for another twenty minutes we experienced what the Huns themselves had just undergone. Fortunately the Germans appeared to be searching for our supports and reserves, thinking, I believe, that like the French, we held our front trenches by day with an odd sentry or so, and that all our men were under cover behind. But their target, to me, appeared to be the ruined farm some fifty yards immediately behind my dug-out, and their shells were bursting now on the near edge of my trenches, then ten to fifteen yards to my immediate front, and at each tearing scream we all crouched close to the inner wall of the trench. Nearer, nearer, we heard the shell; after a time it was possible to tell whether it was coming to right or left of your position, but equally possible to say with certainty 'there's one for us'. And the few seconds terrible wait! Would it burst in front or behind, or would it be *the* one. Somehow curiosity to see what happened, prevented one being afraid, and anyhow it was no use feeling afraid; we had to stick there. For the whole of that hour, what with our own bombardment, and that of the enemy, the din was awful, awe inspiring. The whole of creation was trembling, as does the whole interior of a church when certain low notes on the organ are sounded, and at the end we all got up, stretched ourselves, and shook the mud and filth off our caps, for the heavy shells were bursting so close to us, that columns of liquid filth mixed with stones and bricks were shot 200 feet in the air, to fall back on to our devoted heads.

1.20 pm. Another Hell of a bombardment from our guns and the French, as heavy as that of this morning, and along the line of German trenches hangs a thick cloud of dust and vapour. I hear one man was hit in the Support Dug-outs, by shrapnel, this morning, but in our lines the Hun bombardment appears to have had little effect. This second bombardment went on also for half an hour.

2.45 pm. Food. Today I had breakfast at 9.45, bread and butter, jam, fried bacon and fried biscuit: cooking done in the lid of a mess tin over a charcoal fire held in a perforated bucket. Tea and sugar, no milk; I am getting indigestion from this strong tea. Good thing I like it with sugar as the two are mixed together to save transport, and for better ease in serving it out. Lunch, 3 pm, the same but bully beef in place of bacon. The 1 lb tins of bully are excellent – for a change; anything there may be for tea about 6 pm, and we hope to get relieved at 7 pm when we get

back to our billets with luck about midnight. Another furious bombardment by our artillery; rattling my dug-out and shaking all kinds of things into my tea! It's simply wicked for us; what must it be for the Huns, the target?

December 19th

Got relieved at 8.30 last night by a Battalion of one of our other brigades. As I got out of my trench I could have stuck my fingers into my ears and screamed like a girl. Those bombardments had fairly strung my nerves real tight. However, I was quite myself again half an hour later. Got to our billets in Locre at 12.30 am and eventually to bed at 2 am when we had a good six hours sleep. We all rendezvoused near Kemmel and marched home as a Battalion, took twice as long as if we'd come back by companies independently, but that is the British Infantry all over; can't trust subordinate commanders, an unheard of thing to do in the Infantry. However, doubtless after this war, when all ranks have got accustomed to the four company Battalion system, and Company Commanders really begin to command their companies, instead of looking to the CO or the Battalion

21

Sergeant Major for orders, things will alter, and our Infantry Officers will learn initiative.

I changed my underclothes this morning for the first time since November 30th. Have sent my things to the wash. We hope to get six days' rest now, as, for three Brigades, each Brigade in our sector of trenches for three days at a time, the other two Brigades get six days' rest.

I had four casualties in my Company from odd snipers; but one Company occupying a trench captured on the 14th had fifteen casualties, and two men died from exposure, the trench being very wet and completely devoid of any shelter and of course the weather is wretched. In three days this Battalion had over thirty casualties. Of course the enemy must suffer in the same proportion and during the bombardment yesterday they must have suffered heavily. One of our subalterns saw a coat and a pair of boots shoot up into the air and I only hope the owner, or bits of him, were inside.

Jolly glad to hear the Germans shelled Scarborough. It will wake England up and do more for recruiting than all the posters in the world.

December 20th

Locre. Thomas who had been commanding 'D' Company, went sick (the immediate cause was 'lice', but he later had a bad 'go' of pneumonia on top of this I heard later); and so I took over 'D', leaving 'C' Company to Norman who had been in it from the start. Thomas is, I think, the only officer of the 2nd Battalion who has never been hit; during the early part of the war he had been transport officer. One of my subalterns in 'D', Kearns, late Company Sergeant Major, is 6′ 4″, and my acting Sergeant Major is young Arnott, son of Sir John Arnott, an ex-lieutenant of (I think) the Scottish Borderers.

'D' Company are billetted in a farm, where we officers found a comfortable kitchen, in which we sat, slept, fed, and generally had our being, despite the presence of two refugees from

Kemmel and sundry other women. During the day two or three French Hussar or Staff Officers came in, officiers de liaison between us and the French on our left. Charming fellows, and very smart in their blue and silver laced serges, and blue and silver kepis.

Princess Mary is sending out a plum pudding for each officer and man out here, and strict orders have been issued as to the

23

method in which these puddings are to be distributed, each Company Commander drawing just the quantity of puddings required and issuing one to each man, returning any remaining over. It is really rather touching to think how the people at home think of us. I never thought England loved her soldiers so. I am told 'D' Company is in a positively shocking state of discipline, but the poor fellows had a Hell of a time during their tour in the trenches last week; appalling weather, two killed, one missing, thirteen or fourteen wounded, and one dead of exposure. The man missing and another killed were two Irishmen who had had too much rum. One man was seen getting through a hedge towards the German lines, and was asked where he was going. With a hiccough, he replied he was fetching water to his pal as they were 'drumming up' (ie boiling a can (or drum) of tea). His friends noticed his hand was smeared with blood. 'Sure it's only a thorn I got going through the hedge.' They called him back and as he sat down they saw a growing patch of red on his jacket, opened it, and found an awful wound through his body. He was too drunk to feel it. He died. His pal never returned. Men in another trench said they saw two men walk out and start lighting a fire close to the German lines; so I expect the missing man is lying out there.

This morning I saw a fatigue party marching off, the men all over the place, no discipline, and the corporal in charge, useless. I called out to them, but one man took no notice, so I ran out and gave him two under the jaw. They pulled themselves together then and marched off something more like soldiers. On parade this afternoon I saw another man scrimshanking. Had seen the Company parading but was 'just getting a drop of tea hotted'. I lifted him a couple of the best and kicked him till he ran, and then I spoke a few well-chosen words to the men. Told them that if they did not play the game to me, I'd lead them a dog's life, and if they 'played up well', I'd look after them well; that I knew, and God knew too, how I felt for them, and what they suffered, but that for their own safety I must have, and would have, discipline. This evening I went up into the coach loft where they were all sleeping, and spoke to one man, chaffed another, wished them all 'Goodnight', and I got a real cheery answer back from them in return, 'God blessing me' quite hearty and friendly. I am sure my little show of firmness had its effect. All men like an officer who compels obedience, and it's no use punishing a man on Active Service as one does in peace time; the only thing is to hit him at once and hard, and if the men see their officer takes a real personal interest in them, as I think I do, or at least try to do, well these Irishmen of mine will follow me, I am sure. But I must have a month's rest to wheel them into line. I have about 70 sick in the Company, most of them with swollen feet from standing in icy cold mud and water; and really the whole Company, what with inoculation and general 'done-up' ness is a 'wash-out' for fighting purposes till they have had a week or so's rest. But they get a lot of rum o'nights, and plenty of good food, and I don't worry them with parades.

Kearns is a very fine shot, and has done splendid work in the field. At Ypres, in November, during the attack by the Prussian Guards he bowled over fourteen of them himself. A very cool man, a most trustworthy soldier, and a fine officer*.

No officers are carrying their swords here, only an encumbrance; in a charge I hear the Huns don't often wait, and if they do, well, a big stick, a revolver, or the butt of a rifle are equally useful.

It's bad enough carrying all one's kit on these awful roads without a sword banging at one's legs.

Alston is a charming CO, and Festing all the men love; he's so cheery and hearty, but he can damn 'em too, as they know; but they all understand he'd never leave them in the lurch, and that's the sort of officer men like to follow, and will always follow.

I heard one man coughing his soul out in the loft late this

---

* He was recommended for the DSO for taking up some men and holding a trench out of which the Gordons had bolted, but his name was not forwarded, to save the reputation of the 'Jocks'.

25

evening, and found him with bad bronchitis, so I brought him into the house and got him under a pile of blankets with a hot drink, but as one of our servants said, if I'm too kind all the Company will be getting bronchitis. The farm people are very kind to us; hot coffee (and such splendid coffee too, always freshly ground each day) ever on tap: bread, butter, eggs, etc. We pay for everything, but it does not work out more than 1/6 a day each, and it's cheap at that.

December 21st

We got up at 9 am surrounded by the females of the farm who were in the kitchen. I in my pyjamas. However, I hid behind the table when I dressed. Just read a ridiculous account of the attack here last Monday 14th, in the *Daily Mail*. How the Royal Scots and Gordons took four lines of trenches, that our cavalry were used on the flank, and that the Germans were surrounded by 'a ring of khaki'. Unfortunately it was most the other way on: there are no cavalry within miles, nor could they have been used in this enclosed wire country sodden with water; and we took one trench with awful loss.

Out here, at present, we are holding our own and no more, and we can't get forwarder till K's army comes out. We are for the trenches on Christmas Eve; just our luck! The weather has tried to snow, unsuccessfully, but it's just beastly underfoot.

December 22nd

A rotten day, and snowing, just sufficient to make everything sloppy. My Company is a regular mob, shockingly disreputable. The last man fairly let 'em go, in every way. Their clothing is in rags and they don't care how they turn out. It's heartbreaking. Quite the worst Company in the Battalion. However, all the more interest to make it the best. I've only one officer, and my NCOs, well, I have three of any use. Luckily my Company has a fighting strength of only 140, the remainder sick. At present the

Battalion only does 24 hours in the fire trenches, 24 hours in the Support, and 24 hours in the Reserve, and then six days rest; not so bad for us officers, but the men get wet, and those who do the first 24 hours in the fire trenches never get properly dry, till their return to billets, and so the men do suffer a good deal, poor devils.

December 23rd

We return to our trenches (H2 & 3 & G4) tomorrow for Xmas. It was trying to snow this morning and now it is sleeting. We don't get our plum puddings till we return for them. Some Battalions had theirs issued already, and my Sergeant Major tells me the place is littered with lumps of plum pudding simply chucked away. It's pearls before swine to try to treat some men as human beings; they don't appreciate anything that is done for them.

December 24th

The Battalion marched into the trenches, my Company going into the Reserve in a big derelict farm just out of Kemmel. All

27

the living rooms full of hay, on which we sleep, and we found a few plates, soup tureen, cups, etc, and there's an odd cane chair or so; but not so much in the way of firing, and as all the windows are broken, it's cold and draughty.

Our Yule Log is an old paraffin tin, perforated and filled with live coals: not a bad substitute as it's freezing now.

Xmas Day

Hard frost last night. Captain Becher (who has just rejoined from hospital where he'd been for some 8 or 10 weeks recovering from a wound) and I shared the old bed, only a frame filled with hay and a blanket to cover us. There was a bright moon last night and a lot of musketry fire, and as we are within rifle shot of the German lines we were kept rather on the Qui Vive.

At midnight our guns fired 21 rounds and the French cannonaded up to daybreak when a thick fog came down, and all firing ceased, with the exception of an occasional shot.

During that bombardment 10 days ago we had 45 batteries in action and the French nearly as many, and I am told that altogether there were some 500 guns firing.

Found the graves of two French officers in the Chateau park in Kemmel this morning. On one lay the owner's walking stick and gloves; on the cross of the other hung a soft cap, at the foot the Kepi; all rime-encrusted and almost obliterated.

The 7th Fusiliers (I think) lost an officer in the trenches yesterday, but the Battalion we relieved didn't seem to have half such a bad time as we did last week, only 7 or 8 casualties in all. I rather funk relieving the fire trenches as the moon is now so bright.

A Merry Xmas! A slowly dying fire (and no fuel to replenish it) in a big room, the windows broken, a frozen midden pond outside and a heavy fog. Inside a litter of hay and newspapers, a big deal table, and on the mantel the usual glass covered statue of the Virgin and Child; dinner is laid, bully beef, stew and potatoes, ration biscuits, a few sweets and tea minus even tinned

milk. The food was so poor that Becher refused to wash before dinner and so came to the festive board, as he said, 'dirty'. We drank to 'Absent friends' in rum and water, but out of the four of us, no one could give the toast. So we all stood up and stared very fiercely out of the windows and gulped it down. Our Christmas Dinner was very much a frost, as I fear we were all contrasting our present with the past, or what we hope will be the future.

At 9 pm I took my Company into the Support farm, and Sergeant Arnott, who had a piece of plum pudding (which had been sent out to him) left, gave me a tiny piece, as I said I must have one bit of plum pudding on this day.

December 26th

We all, as usual, stood to arms at 5.30 am. A veritable Star of Bethlehem shone down on us from the East, and made the picture with the bright blue sky and frosted hedges and ground a regular Christmas Card.

All the country white, and a topping sunny day. Arnott and I walked up to our dug-outs some 500 yards away, a few 'singing birds' whistling over our heads, as we are not half a mile from the Huns here. All very nice and pretty and beautiful, but I wish I were going into a nice warm room to a nice warm breakfast, and afterwards to read about the theatre of war, instead of being one of its very frozen actors.

We can't leave this house during daylight, we can't have any fires, and so we just have to lie about in the more or less clean straw on the floor, smoke, throw our matches about (highly dangerous and so very usual) and feel our feet slowly lose their sensibility. Shaved, had a 'lick and a promise' and cleaned my teeth, in a tiny basin of hot water, and then told my orderly, Boyd, he could throw the water away. 'Ah, Sir,' says Mr Boyd, 'I think I'll have a bit of a clean in it myself.' 'But I've cleaned my teeth in it, why on earth didn't you tell me sooner?' says I. 'Indeed Sir, that's no matter', warm water, after all, is scarce.

Two or three mornings ago the French on our left, charged some trenches and found them full of . . . water. Discovered the Germans lying out in the open and took them all prisoners. So the Huns are suffering as badly as we are.

We are at present engaged in digging a new line of trenches in front of our present line, and our regimental 'prisoners' are made to do this (were always a goodly number, and naturally they hate the job); also they have to bury the dead lying about in front near our wire.

Becher heard from Mrs Spedding. She has not much hope or faith in that report which was only that some rifleman (name unknown) saw Major Spedding in hospital in Lille (in German hands) and she cannot imagine how he came to be there. During the battle of the Aisne (or the Marne, I forget which) he went back with a party to fetch rations up; that was the last the Battalion saw of him. But he had to cross a bridge of boats which was continually under hostile shell fire. Someone saw him urging his men across one by one, and shells bursting about, and all fear he was most probably knocked into the river and killed or drowned.

Colonel Ballard, who lately commanded the Norfolks, commands our Brigade.

Talking of the necessity for the censoring of letters, Becher told me he did a good deal of it when he was in hospital and one day he came across a letter in which the writer said '45000 wounded had just passed through Rouen!' Imagine the result such ridiculous news would have had at home. Becher made enquiries as to the author, and found he was an officer with a bad wound in the head, so not entirely responsible.

A man in the RAMC who had never been out of Rouen wrote home saying 'We are getting quite clever dodging Jack Johnstone's'; but I find quite a number of men writing absolute lies about the danger they go through; and their extraordinary courage and all that sort of thing; the more illiterate the writer, the greater the lie as a rule, and not one letter in ten, printed in the papers, received from men in the ranks, gives anything like an accurate description of any action which they attempt to describe.

Extraordinary rumours always floating about. A few days ago we heard the Guards had all been cut up but next morning we, most gratefully, heard the rumour was quite unfounded.

Becher told me the following curious story about poor Captain Carbery (Irish Fusiliers) who was killed a couple of months ago. On his way out to South Africa (during the SA war), he passed through London, and went to his mother's house in town, to bid her goodbye. A maid, who had never seen him before, opened the door to him. Some weeks later, this maid ran up to her mistress and said 'Ma'am, Mr Jack has come back'. His mother, who had received no telegram from him, and knew him to be in South Africa, told her not to talk nonsense. 'But he is back, Ma'am, I've just seen him walk in through the hall door and he has gone into the library. He is dressed in the same uniform he had on when he came before he went out, but it looks very dirty,' she added in reply to a question from her mistress. Somewhat startled, though not crediting the story, Mrs Carbery went down to the library, and of course, found it empty; but a few days later she received a telegram from the War Office to say her son had been severely wounded. She kept a note of the maid's story and of the time it occurred, and on the return of her son from the war, the two of them compared notes, and it appears that at the time her son was seen to enter the house, he was lying insensible and almost dead on the veldt. He told his mother he was practically dead, but a heavy rain storm broke over him and the water, for which he had been longing was sufficient to pull him round. He was lying out unattended for some 36 hours. I firmly believe that in certain states of life, the soul can leave the body, returning sometimes to it again, and I believe the maid did see Carbery's other self.

I have been out digging rifle pits in front of my trench, a preliminary to making a new trench by connecting these pits, but we got down to water after digging a couple of feet. No fun either, digging in the dark, out in the open, within 200 yards of the Huns. We buried five Gordons whom we found lying there. Three of them we just rolled into water-filled shell holes which we afterwards filled up. Seemed very sacrilegious, but we had no time for more, and out here, after all, the dead are but carrion. We did our best to mark their graves by sticking their rifle muzzles down into them. No means of identifying them though, as we cannot get at their identity discs, poor fellows.

Becher has been telling me something of the hardships of that retreat from Mons. With so many regiments it was a rout, not a retirement.

Along the column rode one hussar; he had evidently seen a picture of the sole survivor of the expedition to Kabul; a regimental doctor, just hanging on to the saddle riding into our lines; and it is entitled (I think) 'All that was left of them'. This confounded fellow put himself into a similar attitude and rode along crying 'All that was left of them'. The rest of his regiment were scattered. The Battalion interpreter, a smart Frenchman, was somewhat amusing quite innocently; he was discoursing of some of his holidays and the wretched weather he generally experienced during their course and he turned to Becher, who very wet, and very cross, was trudging along at the head of a very disgruntled Company, and said in his quaint English, 'In my hol-i-days it ees like theese all-ways', as if every year or so he did a retreat from Mons.

December 27th

Early about 5.30 am I woke up my Sergeant, who shared my dug-out and told him to go out and serve each man with a tot of rum, before it got too light, as during the day we cannot move along the lines at all. He went off, the Company Orderly Boyd, carrying the Rum Jar; and returned about three-quarters of an hour later smelling strong of the stuff, having done one half of the Company.

He was very talkative and chatted on to me till about 6.30, when the sky was getting quite pink and everything shewed clear; I told him to hurry up and serve out a tot to the other half of the Company, and to be careful. Off the two of them went; an hour later Boyd burst in on me 'Sergeant X has been hit Sir'. Apparently, the two of them were crossing an open bit of ground, hidden from the Huns immediately in front, but in full view of a sniper's post to our right. A bullet hit the Sergeant in the calf of the leg, another drilled a neat hole through the welt of Boyd's boot, never even reddened the skin of his foot. Boyd dropped the demijohn and dragged X into the trench, to be at once abused by the frozen men for letting go the rum. However, X was not badly hit. He went home wounded, and later received a commission in the 3rd RI Rifles.

I am sick of this issuing of rum in the fire trenches. It's impossible to trust the men to issue it themselves, and a Sergeant or an officer must do it personally, and when in such trenches as ours it has to be done in the dark, well, it's impossible to do it properly.

Just before I joined, Kearns visited a section of a trench held by this Company, and found the four men in it dead drunk, and they had been in this condition for 24 hours. Last time in the trenches this Company lost a Sergeant, shot because he was too drunk to be careful, and my servant tells me that Sergeant X lay asleep in the trench for two whole days, having drunk nearly half a jar of rum and ten days ago while in billets, a pig of a man took a jar of rum to bed with him, and was found dead next morning and buried in the field outside the barn in which the men slept. These brutes, a lot of them would rather have rum than food and don't care what happens to their officers or their pals, so long as they get their rum. It's a regular curse and my Company can jolly well perish of cold before I issue any more to them while we are in the trenches. Makes me sick! How can one be proud of such hogs, or feel any confidence in them. I reported all this to the CO and asked his permission to distribute no more rum in the trenches. Afterwards it was given out as a battalion order, and a few weeks later the GOC in divisional orders forbade the issue of rum in the fire trenches.

Just overheard my two orderlies talking together over the apparently usual system of marching a Company up to the trenches. The Company officer goes off in front, never looks back and expects everyone else to follow him; never stopping to collect men together, and I heard Dixon say my men 'very well liked' the way I marched them up, as I used to halt the men every few minutes and collect the platoons together and generally look after them. But that's my training in the 3rd DG's. From the little I have seen of the infantry, I confess the officers seem to have very little consideration for their men, but then I've always said our infantry, in infantry drill, as in everything else, is existing in the days of 'Good Queen Anne'. But my little lot are appreciably improving in discipline. I've kicked a few old loafers, and they all know I'd not hesitate to knock a man down if necessary. Kearns nearly killed one beauty the other day. Coming out of a trench not 80 yards from the enemy, an idiot started yelling for 'Mikey'. Kearns simply hit him once under the ear. It's the sort of discipline they're used to in civil life, and which they understand; any appeal to their better feelings they regard as weakness. On the whole, I like all my men and I think they like me, but I want to get quit of my old rum-swillers who should never have been enlisted.

Just returned from the trenches, and got back to our billets at West Outre. Most unexciting time the Battalion had.

Only some 4 or 5 casualties in the three days, and the last time we were in we had 5 killed, and some 25 wounded, but oh, the weary trudge back, the awful roads. Going into a farmhouse to ask my way, I saw a solitary young gunner. Looked at him; where had I met him? At last it came to me. He is young Hext of Tredethy in Cornwall, and I last saw him when he rode in to leave his card on me at the Kennels.

December 28th

We get the Daily papers, *Chronicle, Express, Mirror* and *Mail* sent out by the proprietors as a gift to the troops, every morning,

only a day old; it seems very wonderful, but after all the fighting is far closer to London than Dundalk is to Dublin.

In beastly dirty billets in the village school, and we are crowded into the Schoolmistress's house; the door of our living room won't latch, a little detail intensely annoying; we have to wedge it with paper each time anyone leaves the room.

A steady drizzle, mud over the ankles just outside the door, and stinking. We are a holy mob. Half my fellows' rifles won't work properly; simply too lazy to trouble to clean them or even to take the mud off them. But the weather just feeds them up. A very large number of our rag-tag are no use to us or to anyone else. I'd like to get hold of the recruiting officers who enlisted this riff-raff for the SR.

Two more of our fellows went on 8 days leave today: only takes some 16 hours to reach London. Hope to get my leave in a month's time.

A man tells me he found among the Gordons dead in front of the H's, one man sitting up in a most lifelike attitude in the act of bandaging a wounded comrade. Both men were dead, and I suppose occasionally a bullet strikes some vital spot which destroys life and does not relax the muscles.

Met Treffry the other day, our Unionist Candidate for Launceston. He is commanding the HAC Battalion in our Brigade.

December 29th

We all received our Princess Mary's gift today, a neat gilt box containing tobacco and cigarettes, and a jolly good pipe.

Now I hear that each Battalion is to be 4 days in the trenches and 8 days out, but it doesn't make very much difference to us, except that we get eight days instead of 6 days in billet.

I am getting very fat and out of condition. In billets we don't walk a mile a day, it is so unpleasant walking along these greasy heavy roads unless one is obliged to; we can't do much route marching, and, besides, my Company is being inoculated again, and when we are in the trenches we get no exercise at all.

A tremendous conversation with Mames'elle, the schoolmaster's lovely daughter, all on her side, as I could not get a word in edgeways; subject (1) coal, (2) a servant of ours sleeping in their kitchen. She is the first woman I've met in Flanders who talks decent French, but she had a voice that would rasp a nutmeg. Managed to send her away content; by promising her all I could perform and many things I could not.

My bedroom is very small, about 10' square, up a very steep flight of steps. Next door is the big schoolroom filled now with men, who shout at each other by day, and snore all night. Kearns, who is very 'dotty' on his legs, poor chap, has the bed; and I sleep in my 'fleabag' on the floor.

December 30th

Thank goodness, a fine frosty day; I bought for 2/6 each, two of Princess Mary's boxes, one for my father and the other for my brother Cuthbert, and am sending them both home to them. The one I sent to you, dear, I really rather value, as it was issued to me.

I got three letters posted in Ireland on the 26th, and in England on the 28th, this afternoon, so letters are reaching us as quickly as if there were no war. It's really rather wonderful. Our mails all come to Bailleul, and thence to us by motor transport.

Treffry just called on me. Tells me a German crept out of a trench, opposite their lines, to throw a hand grenade; the grenade exploded in the man's hand, and blew his hand off. Some of the HAC very pluckily jumped out of their trench and dragged the man in: when an officer bandaged him up, the German shouted 'Hurrah! now I'm soon in London again'.

Some fools in the HAC stood on the parapet on Xmas morning, I hear, and sang 'Auld Lang Syne' and the Hun let a volley rip into them; and a little later in the day, some of the officers were out of their lines talking to the Germans. But there are very strict orders against this sort of thing. We leave here tomorrow and go to Locre for a rest for four days.

December 31st

We moved from West Outre, into Locre, and I am back again in my farm. The old woman delighted to see us again: 'Ah, c'est Monsieur le Capitaine, et le gros Monsieur' referring to 'Long' Kearns. We hear with some considerable spiteful pleasure that all the staff who are in nice comfortable billets at the base are to be booted up to the front, and some of our weather-worn warriors are to replace them. Must say, I'd make no great difficulty about exchanging my job with some Rouen transport officer: though after a time that would become a very miserable existence.

One of my beauties had the following conversation with Kearns, 'Sure, Sir, I'm over 50, haven't I done over 30 years service Sir, and sure Sir I don't know how to fix the sights of this rifle, I who haven't seen a gun for 15 years!!!' And we found another man who didn't know how to work his rifle. Useful sort to send out to us! I've one man who hasn't a tooth in his head! On the understanding the War Office would give him a complete set, he had all his old stumps drawn some years ago. Then the War Office refused to give him a free set, and as he refused to pay for one, he was invalided out of the 2nd Battalion. He told Kearns that on the last day he would be 'done in'. 'What d'ye mean?' 'Well Sorr, don't they say at the day of Judgement there'll be weeping and wailing and gnashing of teeth; I'll have to gum it!!!' The trench or fighting strength of my Company is now only 123. They will sink lower in the 3 or 4 days and now we are to do 4 days in the trenches.

Twenty five sick or other useless men per company are to be left behind, to dig trenches, repair roads, etc, under the supervision of a Royal Engineer officer, and the rest of us will do 48 hours in the forward trenches, two companies at a time, and 24 hours in Support and Reserve. We're so weak, one Company isn't strong enough to hold one line. I'd rather stay 3 days in the fire trenches with sufficient men, than 24 hours with too few. The nervous strain when you know you are holding a line very weakly, is quite considerable, and especially when the Companies are of such stuff as we have. Luckily it wouldn't be of any advantage to the enemy to break through just here, and they'd get awfully hotted if they did, but at the same time it would be fairly rotten for the men in the trenches, and my old cripples would, I fancy, do a bit of hopping. However, the enemy just in front of us are as good or as bad, as we are, and some of the prisoners we've taken are bald-headed old gentlemen of aldermanic proportions.

I have yet to meet the man who does not either know Kitchener, or who doesn't know someone who knows him, and who had heard him make some ridiculous prophecy about the duration of the War. It's too silly, the opinions which are foisted on to Kitchener. But Kitchener doesn't say silly things. He doesn't know any better than I do when this War will end, though he can possibly give a better guess; but I do know he is likely to say something rude to anyone fool enough to ask his opinion on the subject.

We see some funny things when we are censoring our men's letters. One hero wrote home 'We are fighting every day', and one of the men who fetched in a wounded Gordon, wrote an account of it in the three local papers near his home, saying he hoped they'd print 'his brave act' and that 'if he did any more brave acts' he'd tell them of it. One man was pathetically quaint: 'Christmas Day we spent in the trenches; I didn't get any food'. (His own damned fault if he did not, but I think he was just piling on the agony. A man can't starve out here.) *'We had a very quiet Christmas.'*

Rarely do the men write of their life out here; too illiterate; most of the letters are confined to remarks on their own health; questions as to the welfare of those at home, and prayers, so very often, prayers to God to take care of those they have left behind them. From 90% of the letters you would never discover the men were on active service. A very strong religious strain runs through most of the letters, and I rather admire my old shell-backs for it.

Looked over the Church in West Outre before I left; it is sad to enter and see the men lying about the place with their caps on, smoking, spitting, laughing and swearing, all under the shadow of the Cross. Over one party hangs a really rather fine statue of the Christ; over another a huge be-jewelled Madonna; behind a pile of chairs some NCO's have formed a Mess. Only the Chancel is kept free for religious purposes. There is quite a difference between these Flemish churches and those I have seen in France. The decorations here are stolid, heavy, less tawdry, and there is a wealth of beautiful wood-carving round organ-lofts and pulpits.

The War news seems rather more hopeful, to judge by the papers; but, of course, there will be heavy fighting yet before the War is over. I confess that with my Company I sincerely hope I shall see little of it. So many of them are far too old and stiff to move quickly; they can't run, much less make a charge. A number of them really haven't the heart to go on, and I suppose if 20% of the Battalion advanced to the attack, it's as many as we could expect. We all loud and strong curse the War Office, the recruiting officers and the Commanding Officers for sending out drafts of such 'miserable things'. Why, a number of them ain't even fit for the lines of communication; simply too lazy and spiritless to do anything; a proper lot of curs; just old age and intemperance – Belfast and Dublin corner boys. A whole crowd of them, ex-regulars who were chased out of the First and Second Battalions 10 or 15 years ago, as useless. But the majority of our regular Battalions now, are almost as bad, as they are all more than half S Reservists.

1915

January 1st

New Year. A simply beastly day; bitter cold wind and rain. New Year's Eve appears to have been very quiet in the lines, as we heard no shooting during the night; but about 2 am my Sergeant Major told me there was a tremendous cannonade and heavy rifle and machine gun fire, from, probably, the French lines to the North of us. A rumour that two platoons of the Middlesex Regiment got into some German trenches and were blown up as the trenches were mined; however, probably as true as the rumour that Italy had declared War on Germany.

Horrid shock; here no one is allowed to go on leave till they've been out here for three months. Our Battalion is the 'bad boy' of the Division, and tomorrow the Divisional General (Haldane) is to inspect us, and I suppose, give us Hell. We are a lot of rapscallions, I confess; that's the fault of our GOC's precious brother who ruined the SR to build up his 'Terriers'. All of us are deploring the state of the Battalion, and we trust we may not be asked to attack, before we have had an opportunity of weeding out the men and instructing those that are left. It's disgraceful that we out here should have to do the work which should have been done by those at home.

January 2nd

Haldane made us a short speech, quite a nice one; said

nothing unpleasant. Don't think half the Battalion heard a word he said, and I am sure not a fifth of those who heard understood. Extraordinarily religious, these scamps of mine. Nothing like the Roman Catholic religion for catching hold of a man. In one letter I censored a man thanked 'Maggie for having Mass said for me', and several write 'Tell so and so not to send me any more tobacco or cigarettes as we get all we want out here and often more than we can carry'.

At Ypres last November, where this Battalion suffered so heavily, the South Lancs also found themselves down to 130 men. Their CO and Adjutant had a bit of an argument with the CO of this Battalion over a dug-out, and carried it to the Brigadier, who allotted it to the South Lancs. During the afternoon those two officers went into it and a shell dropped on it, and blew it and its occupants up.

This Battalion left Neuve Chapelle 280 strong, marched to Ypres, and in 16 days lost 150 men or some 60%. Heavy losses; makes one proud to fight with such a Battalion, doesn't it?

The CO is sending into Head Quarters the names of those men who rescued the wounded Gordons. I don't suppose they'll go further, but he seemed to think it rather a fine thing getting them back to our lines by day.

January 3rd

All day and all last night our guns were going about every five minutes, and every now and then a low thundering vibration from the North signals the rafales of the French 75's.

Did I mention about the Christmas puddings we each got on the 27th? They weren't very nice. Some horrid flavouring in them; these were the *Daily Mail* puddings, and, I suppose, are paid for by their Advertising Department.

A man in another Company, coming off parade, deliberately, it is said, put a bullet through his instep, in order to get sent home wounded. There's a good deal of self-mutilation out here; but it's after all, a very old military crime, and a very despicable one. However, this man will probably be court-martialled. Sentences are heavy here. I read out on parade today a sentence of 10 years PS on a private in a Scottish regiment for 'striking a superior officer' (a Lance Corporal), and several others; three years hard labour for drunkenness, assaulting a gendarme, etc. Gives our men something to think about. If only I could get rid of about 25 useless old wasters, get two or three real good NCO's, and have a month in which to train my Company I'd get them quite all right.

We go to the trenches tomorrow afternoon and return on Friday to our billets in West Outre.

January 4th

Rain and an attempt at snowing. Alston just back from the Brigade officer to tell us that as one of the Brigades of this Division (the 8th I think) is taking over part of the French lines on our left there will only be two Brigades left in the Division, and so we shall only get four days rest in billets, instead of eight days. I hear 500,000 troops arrive from England on January 15th, and that we shall then take over all the line now held by the French to the North of Ypres, the French troops being sent to the South of the line. General Foch commands all this part of the line down to about La Bassée, the Belgians, English and French troops within that area being under him.

Impossible to do anything at present. The country is simply impassable except actually in the roads, and then only for very small bodies of troops.

My Company is 149 strong today, and I have exactly 94 men in the firing line, whereas out of a Company at full strength (264) I should have 197 in the trenches.

Censoring letters, I came on the following passage in a letter from, presumably, a very young and devoted husband, 'I do often laugh over the time you threw the jug at me', so in the best families they quarrel at times, apparently.

A wounded man on his railway journey across England saw a

Battalion of new troops passing the train as it was drawn up at a siding. 'Are you downhearted?', he yelled. A stentorian 'Noa' answered him. 'Well, you jolly soon will be, when you get to them blessed trenches.' But it's wonderful how the younger fellows keep up despite the miseries of trench life.

A long hospital train passed our last draft, as they were slowing down into Southampton, and some of them asked a ganger what the train was. 'Wounded, mate; train you will be coming back in when you return.' Cheery fellow!

Had my hair cut by an old Belgian peasant this morning, and jolly well cut too.

January 5th

The Battalion went into the trenches yesterday evening and I with half my Company are in Reserve in Kemmel. I go up to the trenches tomorrow, again, Thursday night, doing our 48 hours altogether in the fire trenches but the men get a day's rest in between and have some chance of drying their clothes.

The Farm of Kemmel 5.1.15

The Reserve are in a fine farm, the buildings run three sides of a square, in the centre of which is the usual stinking midden and pond. The roof has been blown in over the living rooms, but we occupy the kitchen and the big room in which we passed Xmas Day. We've now installed the Flemish stove taken from the ruined sitting room, and it keeps the room a little warm, and we are not so uncomfortable. The men are in a huge loft, and in the barn on the west side of the square where there is plenty of hay and flax to lie on.

Our artillery and the Germans' have been playing at long bowls all day, and just now the Huns put a few big shells into the Chateau gardens about 300 yards from here, wounding a sapper. Our artillery are making this room fairly rattle, and the enemy guns, from some positions behind Wyschaete, are shelling the Chateau and all their shells pass in a direct line over this farm and make such a whistling.

My orderly has just returned from Brigade Headquarters in the Chateau and tells me one shell burst at the front door, just in front, pleasant for them. Horrid sound they make, you hear the whistle and hiss for some 40 seconds, coming nearer and nearer and wonder when it will stop. Then a nerve shattering window-breaking explosion. Our guns are replying hard. One gets into a sort of Kismet mood. It's no use cowering down unless there is good cover; if a shell does burst in the right place you don't know anything about it, as a rule. In the trenches there is a certain amount of cover, and if one is buried, there is always the chance of being dug out safely.

Met Corporal Howell yesterday, one of the Military police. He used to be in my old squadron in the 3rd DG's.

9 pm in the trenches. With some 148 men I had to bring rations for 1½ Companies up from Kemmel to the trenches, perhaps 1½ miles. We took over 1½ hours to do it. Pitch dark, men in heavy marching order, of wretched physique and poor courage, heavy unwieldy boxes of biscuits and jam to carry; 4 jars of rum and a bag of coke. We smashed one rum jar. Men dropping their burdens and trying to scrimshank off carrying

47

anything. The road very bad, full of shell holes. Off the road across the fields a sea of liquid mud and slippery as ice. Had to plough our way through clay over our boot tops. Luckily I've a new pair of boots and they kept the wet out well. Splendid boots, these ordnance store boots. A fair old job getting my slovenly beauties into the trenches. They would *not* hurry, and I do not like standing outside a trench, right in the field of fire, and waiting.

My subaltern Kearns sick, drinking bad water, and so I have to place a young Sergeant in charge of the ½ Company holding the left, my worst trench; where this morning, one poor fellow was shot dead by a sniper. It's rotten this trench work. Tedious, uninteresting, and ever death waits behind the curtain, thrusting out a hand to clutch some poor careless lad. Little of honour or glory apparent to us here, yet of course it's all in the day's work, and we are really jolly well paid for it, to put our duty on its very lowest level. We have slightly improved our trenches by putting boards and fascines along the bottom of them, and in the worst places are half tubs, with a bit of plank as a seat, nailed across. A man can sit in this and keep his feet fairly dry, or rather, out of the freezing mud and water.

We have a lot of old French trip wire along our front, coils about 3′ in diameter, and roughly pegged down by large stones, sods, etc, get your feet caught in it, and it pulls tight and there's no more unpleasant feeling than being caught by the cables on a dark night, with flares going up pretty frequently, as I know well from experience. Eerie work around here in the dark. The continual pop-popping from both sides; an odd bullet overhead now and then, and at frequent intervals, a blue star sails skywards, to burst and light up the country, throwing parapet, hedges, trees into bolder relief.

Very pretty if it was at the Crystal Palace.

January 6th

A rotten night; managed about an hour's sleep – never

thought I should get off. Putties had tightened with the thick layers of mud on them, my feet would not get warm. In my dug-out my Sergeant-Major* sheltered as much as possible in the doorway with my Company orderly, my own servant and the servant of another officer on leave. A decent lot of fellows, but all night long they kept up a whispered conversation, and my Sergeant-Major would snore: never heard anything like it. Could not wake him up, poor chap, as he's only a youngster and has all the hardest work in the Company.

About 11 pm walked all along my line. A bright moon, and not a pleasant walk though the snipers did not bother us, my Sergeant-Major and myself, for I never allow a man to leave cover without a companion, and of course, I never go out without either my Sergeant-Major or my orderly. A man could get hit and might lie for hours quite close at hand and yet never get assistance.

On my left the trench is nothing more than a water course, very little head cover, and only some 80 to 100 yards from the Germans in Petit Bois. Parts of my trenches (H2) we cannot even man; a spring runs through it, and the bottom in places is a sort of quicksand into which I have sunk to my knees, and the suction is so great a man cannot get out without help. Sent down some planks to build up the parapet where the man was killed yesterday. A peaceful night on the whole; little shooting, though the French started their artillery 'frightfulness' between 3 and 4 am.

Letters arrived at 7 am just before dawn, brought up from Battalion Headquarters by an orderly who distributed them to the various officers. The ration carts under the Quarter Master bring out all the officers' letters. As it is impossible to distribute the men's letters in the trenches, they have to be left till our return to billets. I was standing by a machine gun just now,

---

* He was killed at a charge at Hooge, June 1915, leading the Company; he got well behind the 3rd line of German trenches before he fell. A fine soldier and a gallant man.

looking through my glasses at the German parapet 350 yards away, when 'plop' and a gunner said 'They are sniping you, Sir'. It had gone into the sandbag just in front of me. A quite good shot. I moved back to my dug-out, and climbing on to the roof, put in a clip full of beautiful shots at the spot where I thought the bullet came from; my SM 'spotting' for me through my glasses. Unfortunately they don't signal the shots.

There are now 3 crosses behind my trenches. One of them a Gordon Highlander. I counted 22 dead Highlanders still lying along a hedge 100 yards in front of us, and within a length of perhaps 80 yards lying in small groups of 3's and 4's.

About 15 yards in front of us are some old French rifle pits full of dead, and I can see the red breeches of one poor fellow; yesterday, when the sun came out for an hour, the men opposite them said they commenced to smell.

Watched our guns and the French, shelling the German lines on our left, very prettily. Huge volumes of smoke when the heavy lyddite shells burst in the ground, and then little dainty feather balls bursting in the air, shewing our field guns, sending shrapnel all over to catch such of the Huns the lyddite sent running from their trenches. Very pretty against the dark background of the woods which extend to the N of Wyschaete.

One of our MG Section was telling me of the charge the Gordons made on December 14th (all our machine guns were brought up with those of the other Battalions in the Brigade that day). An officer drew his claymore, yelled 'Advance' and they were up and out over the poor parapets, and went real well. One young NCO he noticed, galloped ahead, his rifle in the air, yelling 'Come on, boys, at the .... '. He pointed out to me what he thought was the poor boy's body, not 50 yards from the German lines. A number of the Jocks found cover some half way across, in an old shelter trench, but could not get out in the dark, and the charge was made just before 8 am. Our guns were pouring a heavy shrapnel fire into the German lines and many poor Highlanders were knocked over by our own shrapnel. This is always unavoidable, as it is always impossible to ensure telephonic communication with batteries in rear, and any other kind of signalling is out of the question.

The Royal Scots and Gordons were brought up to the fire trenches, from which they had to advance, at 3 am in the morning when it was pitch dark. Neither officers nor men knew the positions of their objective, and the Gordons, instead of charging the trench lining Petit Bois, to their left front, went for the parapet right in front of them, and the half right of the Gordons, made a big swing round the right and were caught by enfilade machine gun fire. The whole affair was apparently very badly organised; never thought out at all. But then the whole time I have been out I never once saw any of our Brigade or Divisional staff come up to the trenches, and the ground around is to all the staff a terra incognita. I have heard so many other troops in other divisions say the same thing. In the whole five months I was in the trenches, I only once saw one of our Brigade Staff visit us, and not once did any of the Divisional Staff come near us. After a time we dreaded the idea of making attacks knowing it would mean heavy casualties and a failure.

I hear that this morning the Huns put a shell into Kemmel which landed in an outhouse, killing a Corporal and six sappers.

My dug-out in H1 is some 8′ long, 5′ broad, and 2½′ high. I can just sit upright in it. Roofed with planks, on which are a few very old ground sheets and a rough thatch of stinking rotten straw; a brazier with charcoal is our stove for all purposes.

Everywhere, outside, slippery slimy clay; put out a hand to steady yourself and in it sinks, up to the wrist. The bottom of the trenches are floored (sometimes) with planks, fascines, off which the foot slips into ankle deep mud.

5.45 pm. My poor careless boys! One lad, one of Kitchener's (a number of K's army have been transferred from the service Battalions to the SR) only 19, killed at 8 am. He was right on the left of H2, a very bad trench; in a spot I would not have left by daylight for any money. He rushes out to get water and gets a bullet through the heart, and now my servant whom I had sent back on a message has just tumbled into my dug-out, shot

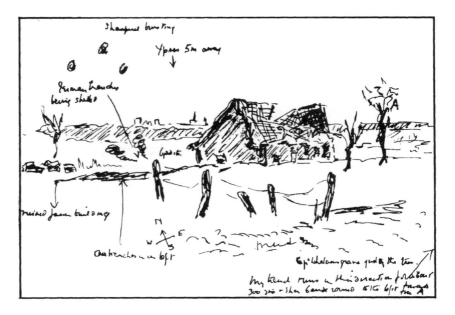

through the forearm and bleeding like a pig. It's quite dark, he was carrying his rifle at full cock, with the safety catch forward. Falls into a shell hole, and blows a hole through his arm. But a brave lad, for instead of stopping at the 'dug-outs' to get his arm bound up, he comes on another 200 or 300 yards (and 300 yards in the dark out here is as bad as $\frac{1}{2}$ a mile by day) to tell me he had failed to deliver his message. Bandaged him up, but he bled all over my boots and putties and is in some pain. But Boyd is a lucky man; only this afternoon he showed me with pride the photograph of his wife and child, and now he'll get home to them both.

January 7th

I wonder if it will bore you to have an account of my last 36 hours. We paraded on the 5th at Kemmel (the farmhouse) at 5.45 pm in the pitch dark. The men in their khaki coats quite invisible, and one ran into them, and was lucky to escape a rifle muzzle in the eye. We stumbled out of the farmhouse across a slushy field, clattering over a causeway of old jam and meat tins, and into Kemmel where we, almost literally, bumped into our own ration carts. Then we had to collect rations for two complete Companies, our own and one other. Wooden cases 18″ by 18″ by 12″, each containing 2 jars of rum; square unwieldy weighty tins of Army biscuits; cases of jam, sacks of charcoal (1 per Company, for cooking purposes), bags of tea and sugar mixed with a good deal of dirt, and failing spare sacks, the cheese and bacon carried in the same sack as the tea.

The Quarter Master Sergeant with an electric torch divides the rations into two Companies, and the CQMS sub-divides these as best he can into platoons. Pitch dark, only the tiny circle of the flash lamp and with all, a most persistent damnable drizzle. And the mud, the heavy greasy filthy mud underfoot. The rations are served out to the platoons of my Company for further sub-division, by daylight in the trenches, and the rations for the other Company are apportioned out, in their huge cases to men most unwilling to add to their already heavy kit of 150 rounds, pack, entrenching tools; full waterbottle; rifle, and rain sodden, clay caked overcoat. Then commences a veritable 'March of the Damned', which I lead. At first a mile of road, 'mind the hole'. I slip and slither and save myself, and the rest, in single file, a line of scarcely visible shadows, curve round the big 'JJ' hole, whose waters had caught, just in time, the reflection of the Star lights which are bursting dimly in the haze a thousand yards away.

'Bang.' Who the Hell has dropped that tin? I go back: fall over a tin of biscuits no one owns to carrying. 'Here, you', and I touch a bent shadow with my stick, 'pick it up and carry it'. And so we shuffle on at about a mile an hour, halting every 100 yards or so to readjust our burdens. And ever round us and over us, sing those blessed bullets, now striking sparks from some flint in the mud alongside, now whistling overhead, sometimes with a wicked 'phit' burying themselves viciously at our very feet. For our track lies right along that zone of fire, where unaimed bullets from the German fire trenches to our right, hit the ground.

'Come on, follow me, boys, and for God's sake keep up and buck up.' We turned off the road, and sank in over our boot tops, sliding and slipping forward across a field, over a long greasy bank (heavy casualties here to jam and biscuit tins) on to a plough. Heavy 'Funk' firing breaks out on our right; bullets come our way more frequently; a pyrotechnic display in the distance gives form to my shadow line, and silhouettes the trees on which I am directing my march. How we curse the men in the trenches for firing and irritating the Germans to fire back; neither hurts each other, it is we poor devils 1000 yards behind who get it all. We slosh on our way, my men, sullen, patient, spiritless, I cursing, urging, imploring, threatening, exhorting, in every endeavour to get my poor sheep safely and quickly across 300 yards of high open, shell pitted, slippery, waterlogged clay plough into which 'strays' are thudding, most unpleasantly and frequently. I fall full length over a telephone wire, and my leading men, missing me, at once go astray. Get them right once more; the dug-outs at last, mud deeper than ever. 'Sergeant Byrne.' 'Here Sir' answered a voice (from nowhere as far as I could see). 'And Mr Kearns is in his dug-out Sir, very sick, and my platoon is all ready.' Damn! No officer at all now, to help me. Kearn's fool of a servant had made him tea from some foul water and given him bread on which some paraffin had soaked. Told him to go to Kemmel and report sick.

My Push straggle up and fling down their burdens. We leave the other Company's rations at the dug-outs; distribute rations to each of my four platoons, but no torch to aid us here. All done by touch, the dainty touch of clay-fouled fingers.

'Go on Byrne, you take two platoons to H2 and you will be in command. It's nasty, but you can do it, can't you?' 'Oh yes, Sir.' 'All right, clear off then, and I'll come round and see you later. Numbers 13 and 14 follow me.' Another 200 yards, greasy clay heaps catch one's feet, water-filled shell holes; alongside a communication trench; perfectly useless, as it has two feet of water in it, over loose wire, the ruins of a farmhouse, heaps of bricks, timbers, and a dirty midden; over, or into all the horrors of a dark night close to the trenches. I find myself alone: 'Number 13, Number 13? where... is Sergeant X? Pass the word for Sergeant X, and bring your platoon on close behind me. See that high tree there? (a flare silhouettes it just then)... *there*, you fool; well, that's on your right. See that light there? In the ground; well, that's the brazier in my dug-out. You hold the trench between that tree and my dug-out; get on and put your men into it; No 14, follow me; Dillon, Corporal Dillon.' 'Here, Sir,' and a form cannons into me. 'All right, come on.' We stumble forward, Dillon, No 14, and me. 'That you, Burgoyne?' I am challenged out of the darkness. 'Hullo, McLaughlin, awful sorry I'm so late, but I've been since 6 pm getting here (it is now 7.45 pm and less than two miles), any news?' 'No, very quiet, got a man killed on our left this morning, sniped in his trench.' 'Poor chap.' 'Goodnight.' 'Good luck to you.' 'Thank 'ee, 'night, 'night.' McLaughlin draws off his men as mine take places. I lead No 14 to the entrance to their trench. 'Come on, d--mn you: *move*, will you, and *stand up*: they'll hit you whether you crouch down or whether you stand up; for... come on and don't keep me standing here; I don't want to get shot and I don't want any of you hit'. At last they're all in; I enter my dug-out, take off my equipment, and then sally forth again to walk round my trenches and see how many of my sheep are missing and how many have been unpenned. With difficulty, I find Sergeant X (I shall 'break him', he is very useless). He seems to have only half his men with him. Get them all out of the trench and lined up. Find among them three men of No 14 platoon. The sodden fools, too careless, too stupid to think – straft them out of it and back to their platoons.

'Please Sir,' from another bit of trench, 'It's all water here.' I promise to send 'em some tubs to stand in, and back I go again through the stinking quagmire, my stick is dragged out of my hand by the heavy clay, and I fall on my knees over a half filled drain, and get clay up to my waist. I find the tubs and have to get men to carry them, not easy; the men hate work naturally, most of 'em born tired, and work under a slight, very slight shower of bullets is anathema to them. Have to practically haul a couple out by the scruff of the neck and I can't trust the men to do a single thing. I return with them to see the tubs properly delivered. Sounds so simple, but it's raining, it's pitch dark, and the ground is a morass with drains, shell holes, branches of trees, ladders, planks, picks and shovels, old tins, iron hoops, every imaginable impediment to walking, every imaginable trap to the unwary footstep.

Hopelessly unreliable, not so much 'fed up' as naturally useless; my men, most of 'em, would rather chuck a tin of biscuits away, if they can do so in the dark without being caught, sooner than carry it, even though they know it contains all the rations their pals have to live on for the next twenty-four hours. But they're so selfish; don't understand the meaning of 'pal'. These fellows are always doing this, and that is what makes the carrying of rations up to the trenches such a labour of pain.

I regain my dug-out; regain my breath, and on along to the other end of my line; tell Corporal Dillon to get planks and shore up the parapet which is sliding in, and then on to the Kemmel-Wyschaete Road; cross it. 'Halt, who's that?' 'Burgoyne, Irish Rifles,' and I bump into a heap of sandbags and three men. The sandbags form a parapet across the road.

'Sergeant Byrne, take me down to your trench, I don't know it.' 'Right, Sir, this way, Sir. Look out, Sir', as 'plop' I go, up to my knees in a regular lake. 'Better get out of the trench, Sir, and come along the back. Just here, the man was killed this morning Sir. All the parapet has slid down into the bottom of the trench.' I literally clamber, hands and knees, out of the quagmire of clay and water, over a clayey heap into which my hands plunge to the wrists, in and out, round about, for fifty yards which seem like 500 yards, through some ruined cottages, past a smelly evil looking pond, and a slither down into the bottom of the ditch in front of which is a straggly hedge. 'Here's my left, Sir, one man here.' I peer into the gloom and discover an object huddled up half kneeling in the mud, half crouching against the rain soddened bank, with no head cover and little cover from view.

Rifle on the bank, his bleared eyes straining out into the dark, from where I saw two tiny spurts of flame come, as a couple of bullets sung overhead. On our left again, are some empty trenches, water to the brim, and some 80 yards to the front are the German lines. Our line here bends back at a right angle. I'd be sorry to be one of the four men who occupy this small section of trench, for during daylight, there can be no movement of any sort without risk of life; and the ditch isn't more than 3½ feet deep at the outside.

Wishing them 'Goodnight' I make my way back to my dug-out fast as I can paddle, only halting when a blue flare, in my near neighbourhood, makes cardboard models of parapet, trees, hedgerows; then the order is 'bend down'. A battalion order forbids our men 'Funk' firing, and any outbreak of rifle fire with us, is at once stopped, but sentries fire a shot every five minutes, just to put the fear of God into any Teuton who may be scouting round in front. All round our lines are lying little bits of mortality; the blue coats have been there since September, most of the khaki date from December 14th; unburied, they remain until they desiccate or dissolve, I suppose, and nothing is left but a few whisps of scarlet, or blue, or brown, and scattered among them all, is all the paraphernalia of a soldier's equipment; web belts, and packs; black leather belts, horsehide knapsacks; bayonets and rifles, like sea-wreck; half engulfed in the furrows of the turnip fields.

Throwing myself on straw which happens to be fairly clean, I doze more or less; my Sergeant Major snores; my feet freeze until 5.30 am and it's 'Stand to', and everyone all along the line wakes up, and stands to arms. To keep them on the alert, I pass the word down 'Look out on the right (or left).' The men think I know something and are extra alert.

As another tedious, miserable day dawns, and all is seen quiet in front, swords are unfixed, one man in every four watches, the rest begin to 'drum up', frying their bacon, opening their jam, and generally preparing breakfast. I can stand upright at the door of my dug-out; my head is well above what sandbag parapet there is, but H1 runs alongside a thin hedge and that gives some cover from view. Yet I don't do even this oftener than necessary, and so spend most of my day full length in the dug-out. I can walk for 50 yards, bent double, through a running stream, but further no one can go, as the parapet has all slid into the bottom of the trench, and for 20 yards or more, H2 is only a mere depression in the ground. The day is just one prayer for night and the Reliefs to come. 6 pm. Thank goodness, we'll be relieved in another hour.

7.30 pm. Collect my kit together. 'Reliefs should be here soon, Sergeant-Major, our candle will just about last out.'

8.15 pm. In the dark, candle gone. Ring up Head Quarters and enquire where our relief is. 9 pm. 'I hear 'em Sir!' (to the darkness). 'Who are you?' 'Captain McLaughlin and his Company.' 'Damned late, McLaughlin!' 'I know, old chap, awfully sorry, but I had an awful job with these rations.' My trenches are relieved, and with a 'Goodnight, good luck', I and my staff step out of the dug-out to find it beginning to rain again. Collecting my men I go along the trenches to the road down which I go back. A halt every half mile to enable my poor old cripples to close up. A section is reported absent. 'Oh! damn Y and his men, can't keep all the men out in the rain for a Lance Corporal; they can jolly well lose themselves, and get shot.'

The road is like a veil, all holes. I lose my cap over one JJ hole and recover it by a miracle.

About 10.30 I reach Kemmel, and our billets. Two jars of rum for three platoons! (one platoon at Battalion Head Quarters). A jolly good tot all round, and my Thermos full. Found Kearns here with boiled red cabbage and bacon. How I ate! and drank rum and water! And we talked till our half inch of candle gave out. Then in the red glow from the top of our stove, we snuggle down under our blankets on the straw; taking off our wet boots, putties, and as I settle myself, I see it is 12.30 am.

Thank God, another 18 hours of peace and quietness and then...oh! well, another 26 or 28 hours in those blessed trenches; after which, a four days' rest in billets, and our parcels from home. Anyway, the weather can't be worse, and we might be worse off, easily.

I hope you won't be horrified by my language, dear, but it's 'drive, drive, drive' with these overburdened men of mine. We have to get them there somehow, and it is no use saying 'please' to a tired man. And so many of them you can't lead; you have to shove them. It's up to the officer to get them there, and they know, or should do, that there is no resource whatsoever, he may find it necessary to employ, that would not be forgiven him, so long as he can satisfactorily explain the necessity. And this is War, not Peace, and instinctively all recognise it, and a blow, or a word in time of stress is forgotten and forgiven when the light comes, and the strain has eased. I know my Irishmen, and they know me, and I don't think they think the worse for me for methods which in Peace time would strike me as, well, German.

I've so many old humbugs who should never have been enlisted, and it's these who require driving. Luckily the wastage among this class is some three or four per day, and now we should be getting back drafts of the 2nd Battalion, who returned home wounded earlier.

I've written you a perfectly accurate account of one day in the trenches; it is not in the least exaggerated, and each tour is very much like it. A course of this life soon makes one sort of hopeless, sort of 'don't care what happens, things can't be worse or more uncomfortable'.

January 8th

It rained all day yesterday, practically, up to 11 pm last night. We left the farm with the rations at 6.45 pm and I arrived here at my old trenches at 7.55 pm. And wet! Luckily I had a ground sheet I fastened over my shoulders. Some 50 yards of the road was under water, it seemed to silver-plate the whole country-side. Found the straw in dug-out afloat. The ditch t'other side of the hedge was full of water, and this had leaked through some roots of the hedge in the dug-out. That lazy devil, McLaughlin, had never taken the trouble to locate the flow, or even to trench the floor of the dug-out; luckily my servant had brought up some dry, clean straw covered in a ground sheet. Soon found my breeches soaked through. Found I had been lying on my overcoat tails. An awful night, and my feet slowly froze: no coke or charcoal, and only a miserable fire. However, there isn't a man in the Company who is not worse off; none of them can lie down. H1 is flooded a foot deep, the poor men were standing precariously on planks or tins; and the water was rushing through the telephone dug-out till I diverted it. Was ordered to put a listening post 50 yards out to my front. Called up two men and found one of them had no ammunition 'and Sir, me rifle don't work very well'. I'd had a rifle inspection only yesterday and he'd never reported this; also all men are issued with ammunition before coming up to the trenches. This man is the Company's curse; a grouser, a cur, and a coward. Well, I just made one leap at him, I kicked him as far as I could and then hammered him over the back with my stick, till I got him running back for another rifle and some ammunition; and then the other man and I had to stand waiting for this brute, out in front of our line in the open! Of course the thing was afraid and didn't want the job and thought he'd get off it. I think I'd have shot him had I had my revolver on me at the time. I thank God I hadn't it. He's one of those brutes who would imperil, and willingly, a whole Company to save himself a ha'porth of labour and risk.

Hear the French on our left did fine work yesterday. Their artillery shelled the Germans out of their trenches and what were not killed, were taken prisoner. Also about midnight of the 6th and 7th, the Berkshires caught the Germans, relieving guard, and got off about 800 or 900 rounds of maxim into a mob of 'em. Discovered B Company had buried my dead man – under a dung heap. Horrid idea and rather insanitary, but it was quick, and it doesn't matter to the poor fellow. All bodies, man's and animal's are the same, it is only the soul which makes the difference and when that goes, what does it matter, really? Some

20' of parapet tumbled into my bad trench on the left about 10 pm. Went across to them, and they eventually repaired it with sandbags. But if the rain goes on, all our parapets will be sliding in, even without the weight of sandbags on top of them. After watching the hands of my watch all night, the dawn at last; no rain, *very* cold; and no fire to boast of. Snipers firing at our dugout. Spotted some smoke arising from their parapet and put 5 rounds into it, to show them we were alive. About 9 am cussed Rifleman McIlhare for wandering about outside his trench; all men strictly forbidden to do so by daylight. Saw him return to his trench. About 10 am 'Man badly wounded in right trench, Sir', was shouted down to me. 'Who is he, and where's he hit?' 'Rifleman McIlhare, Sir, hit in the kidneys.' In response to my enquiries, heard he was in great pain, so sent up ½ grain of Morphia to be put in his mouth. Every Company Commander is supplied with a tube of ¼ grain tablets of Morphia; 1 to ease pain; 2 (or ½ grain) to cause semi-insensibility, and 3 to give complete insensibility till death comes. Five minutes later, 'Have you rum, Sir, he's very bad!' 'I haven't. Order up a stretcher.' Stretcher bearer sent off to him. Another five minutes and a message comes, 'He's going to walk to the dressing station himself, Sir'. These idiots, half of them would walk into the German lines for a tot of rum. I saw the man later, hopping it like a young 'un, across the open ground towards the rear, so he can only have got a very mild graze, I fancy. All his own damned fault, and had he not gone down, he'd have imperilled the life of a stretcher bearer to reach him. He got a slight flesh wound on the hip, I heard afterwards. 2 pm. Another man wounded on my left; he died at 3 pm, hit just above the heart by a bullet which enfiladed the trench; very little head cover here. Sent him down ½ grain of Morphia but I think it arrived too late. A married man, too, and he had just written a letter to his wife.*

* This was Rifleman Burn. Oddly enough, by a curious coincidence, only yesterday his wife called to see me about her late husband's pay book, etc, which had not been sent back to her. A very respectable woman. August 1915.

January 9th

Our reliefs, a Company of the Northumberland Fusiliers arrived at 7 pm last night. A prize fool in command, very nervous, delayed me half an hour. Then some of my own prize fools delayed me another half an hour by saying their Sergeant was behind in the trenches, which kept me waiting for him. At last in despair I gave him up and went on to find him with the rest of his men waiting for me half a mile further on. And oh, that punishing march of five miles, it seemed 15 to West Outre. And my poor men who had been for the last 24 hours standing in water, their feet swollen and bursting from cold.

Just written a French letter to 'Madam Mère' at the Convent at Locre asking if I can have a bath there this afternoon, I want it. Kearns and I are billeted in a tiny attic in one house but we mess and wash, etc, in another house with the rest of our officers. We have beds and sheets, and each a stuffed straw mattress. I slept till 8 and never got up till 10 am and didn't want to do so then.

January 10th

In billets at West Outre.

The Worcesters, on the right, last week rushed an advanced German trench and bayoneted the 20 men in it, and clubbed the officer to death; then they returned to their own lines. A pretty piece of work as they only had one casualty. There must have been some reason why they killed them all instead of taking 'em prisoners. The Northumberland Fusiliers last week caught two spies in the church tower at Kemmel, manipulating the clock hands. They were shot. A new Division, the 27th, passed thro' here on the 8th. They were shelled along the Dichebusche Road, and their advance delayed 5 hours. The Worcesters captured the trenches, as mentioned above, on the night of January 3rd.

January 11th

In billets at West Outre.

January 12th

Left West Outre at 4 pm and after our usual terrible march arrived at the trenches some 2½ hours late. D Company in support tonight. Two platoons in Support Barn which is simply stinking. I fancy a dead cow or two, which I know are buried just behind the house, have been floated to the top by the rain. Anyway, the place stinks. It's the only word. Have left my last joined Subaltern, one Mr Leask from Canada, there. Then up to the 'Dug-outs', left a platoon there with an also lately joined youngster, one Tuckett. The officer's dug-out has been blown in by a shell lately. I hear two men killed at the same time and two wounded in it. However, I found him a fairly dry dug-out with a bit of dirty straw in it. Flashed my lamp in a neighbouring dug-out and the light glistened on a slimy oozy floor of dirty mackintosh sheets and old sacks, filthy. I wouldn't kennel a farm dog in it. However, there are still worse dug-outs and men have to go into them, poor devils. Came back to Battalion Head Quarters where I have my 4th platoon and which is fairly respectable. A decent, clean farmhouse. Festing, the Adjutant and I dined (?) together quite decently. Bully beef, bread, butter and jam, cake and tea. A nice bale of straw to sleep on. The country is merely quagmire, impossible for any work. On our way out we saw a few German shells bursting above Kemmel and they have been shelling our trenches, luckily a trench on my right, but they have so far made no direct hit in it.

A wire just came in from Brigade Head Quarters to say that '2nd Army reports Germans in front of 1st Corps wearing British uniforms'. We are in the 2nd Army and I suppose our Intelligence Officer had discerned this. What perfect swine the German Head Quarters must be to so clothe their men, that, should any be captured, they might be shot, not as a matter of fact we should be likely to shoot the poor devils who could scarcely help the clothing they are put into.

I am sending a postcard to Aroon with some of Festing's nonsense rhymes on it. He is always making up rhymes on all and every kind of thing.

NONSENSE RHYMES for Aroon

To me it is a dreadful wrench,
When I am told to leave my trench;
For up to date I've always found
It very pleasant underground.
Although I must admit as yet
I've found that same a trifle wet.
Still notwithstanding cold and stenches
I like my sojourn in the trenches.

A well-directed German shell
May very likely give you Hell,
The only thing that we must say
You hear him coming all the way.
So if you're spry, with any luck,
You may avoid him if you duck.

Should you go out to shoot the Hun
You must not take your scatter gun,
And if you wish to down a partridge
You must not use an SA cartridge.

(Re order:–'Officers must not shoot
game in front of the trenches!!!' SA
small arms ammunition, i.e. rifle.)

By Major Festing,
RI Rifles.

Midnight. Festing and the Adjutant just gone out to go round the lines and so I am going to bed. I have to be up at 5.30 am to see my supports all standing to arms. A regular rattle of musketry is going on; a newcomer might imagine that it is an attack, but it is dying down now, only 'funk' firing.

More than ever I aver those men who, when they are sent

home wounded, say they are anxious to return to the front, are liars, and bombastic liars too. Of course, every man at home wants to come out here, lest he be the only man left at home, but no man who has ever seen any fighting can jump for joy at the idea of coming out here. It is a stern duty, not a cheery picnic.*

January 13th

'Stood to Arms' at 5.30 am and just before that hour I got off my hay couch after a perfectly sleepless night. The other two came in at 2.30 and we talked till 4.30, so sleep was impossible. Visited the farm and the dug-outs and got the men on to parade from the half hour till dawn. Touch of frost during the night but it began spitting with rain about 7 am. At 8 am a telephone message came down to say that Pigot-Moodie (a Lieutenant of the Rifle Brigade SR and attached to us) was badly wounded and half an hour later another message told us he was dead. He was in H3, our dangerous trench, and the bullet entered his neck and came down through his nose and he only lived about 7 minutes after he was hit. Poor fellow, a real good sort – brother in the Scots Greys. He was over the day before yesterday to see his brother. He was probably supervising the repairs of his trench. So silly, poor fellow, to expose himself in open day. It is said that 90% of our casualties in this trench work arise solely from want of taking the ordinary precautions.

A message from the dug-outs to say my Subaltern has just buried the two men he found in the shelled dug-out. I suppose they were killed yesterday.

We have only three Companies here. Two doing each two tours of 24 hours in the trenches and one in reserve for the whole four days. The Reserve Company brings up our rations, etc, and also provided a platoon to strengthen our Company so that each platoon in that Company does one tour of duty in the trenches.

* I altered my opinion later. There is an extraordinary fascination about the life in spite of all the discomforts.

The 4th Company, with ten men from each Company who have been longest out here and really require a rest, is having fourteen days' rest at Bailleul, and my Subaltern Kearns is with them as his feet were giving him trouble. This fourteen days' rest may be impossible again so there is no immediate hope of my getting it – it all depends. All leave in this 3rd Division has been stopped. However, this is probably only temporary, and by the time I am entitled to my leave I shall probably get it all right, so I am not worrying.

There is a very general impression that our lines are full of spies who report all movements of our troops to the Germans who are thus able to get their guns on to them. Our interpreter, a French NCO one Bertrand, suspected an interpreter (also a French NCO attached to some artillery); he reported this man, who was tried by Court Martial, Bertrand himself giving evidence, and evidence was provided which convicted the fellow of being a traitor, and he was shot. This happened in this district and within the last 5 days.

Our artillery examined an unexploded German shell the other day and found it contained a very few bullets and a lot of old nails! Their ammunition must be giving out for their manufacturers to put such stuff inside a shrapnel. 4.30 pm. Our guns have been, and still are shelling hard and the Germans have replied. A few shells flying overhead, evidently on their way to Kemmel, a mile behind us. But they don't do much in that line, and it is more than evident that we have a great superiority in ammunition.

Re leave: Major Festing says that stopping of all leave probably means nothing but to save the Staff trouble and that we shall doubtless all get leave in due course.

January 14th

In the trenches. Got into the trenches and settled down by 9.30 pm last night, and about 11 pm I was able myself to settle down and I slept well till 5 am. I had had no sleep for over 24 hours and I wanted a bit. At 5.30 am went round and saw all were standing to arms, and had a look at such improvements as had been made during the night, putting up fresh head cover, repairing breast works, draining trenches, etc. A very quiet night, though the French guns were going hard all the time, and all very quiet up to midday. Saw my first Germans in the opposite trenches. Two stupid looking faces peering over the yellow clay about 400 yards away. Shot at them five rounds and they disappeared. Don't suppose I hit them, as it was impossible to see them except through glasses.

At midday the Germans started to shell our trenches and burst about 2 dozen shells between me and the maxim gun 100 yards away. Some burst quite close, 20 yards, and flung up mud 100 feet in the air which fell all over us in the trenches. We lay jolly close under our front parapet, I can tell you. In three shells they got the range, and began landing shells into G4, one of my trenches (I have G3, G4, H1, 2 & 3), just on my right and Gray at once moved his machine gunners up to me. A couple within a very few feet of the right of H1 (where my dug-out is) and I called in the platoon on my right and cleared that portion of the trench. Owing to the water and the beams stretching across the trenches to hold up the front parapet of sandbags, beams in many cases only 2½' above the bottom of the ditch, progress for my men was very slow and wet. I remained where I was by the telephone, and as our men began to move the Germans started shooting. I telephoned our guns to bombard their trenches; also gave them a rough indication of where their artillery was firing from and they shelled or tried to shell that. Anyway, after some 2 dozen shells the enemy ceased firing and now all is quiet. But I have three men killed and two wounded; one very slightly by a piece of shell, I think, thrown back possibly from our own shrapnel. A German shell hit Gray's dug-out and blew it in just after he had left, burying two telephonists and another man. The two telephonists, one completely buried and the other only his head and hand showing, were dead. Another man we dug out, hurt about the face and legs, but he will, I hope, prove not dangerously hurt. Another man who left his trench to run across the road was killed in the open. I haven't been to see them but sent my Sergeant-Major who had a pair of gum boots on (I don't wear mine in the trenches, could never get about in them quick enough, so likely to stick) to wade through the trench up to where the casualties were, with three other men to help dig. He found a Lance Corporal and five men in a dug-out, within 15 yards of the buried men, not stirring a hand to aid them. They might otherwise have been got out alive. I am running the NCO in for cowardice, and hope he will be tried and shot, the cur. The men with him, barring the recruit, are equally culpable. The recruit was the only man who stirred when the Sergeant-Major called to them.* He had to kick the others out. Of course it *is* nerve racking, but you'd think the men would go to the assistance of a wounded man lying so close to them. But they are of that type who bravely watch a human being drown rather than risk getting wet. Oh, curs, curs, curs. I'll get their Lance Corporal shot if I can, to encourage the others.

We must make the trenches better by digging support trenches in the rear, and good and easy approach trenches, so that directly we are shelled, we can, under cover, get into comparative safety and wait while the Huns shell empty trenches. It is the way they construct their own trenches.

3.30 pm. All quiet in the German lines opposite us, as yet, our guns still putting in occasional perfect shrapnel right over their parapet, and on our left the French are bursting salvoes, 4 shots at a time, over the German trenches. Blowing up for another wet night. All around grey and God forsaken. Little villages attract the eye, but on examining them through glasses they are only gaunt blackened skeletons of houses; wherever we point our glasses, and look, nothing but the most complete ruins can be seen; even Ypres standing out so fair against the grey horizon, on inspection, holds out roofless buildings and broken spires. I

* I was unable to bring this man to trial, as I could get no evidence; every man there lying stoutly.

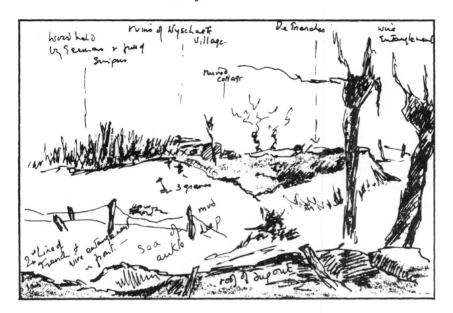

noticed, near that town, what I took to be the smoke of a factory; an hour later, huge flames betrayed its mystery. The wood, and trees, and even fences have suffered, and hold out to High Heaven blasted limbs, showing white where the shells have shattered them, the tops a mass of interlaced broken boughs. Huge stumps stand out prominently, their upper part slivered into firewood. A blasted country, damned and cursed in every meaning of these words. One wonders can it ever recover; not, I fear, in our lifetime. My glasses bring out dead cattle, with here and there, other dead things: little sodden wisps of cloth, some blue, and red, others khaki, who still lie along our front, and, I fear, have disinterred, some of them; and everywhere glistening clay fields waterlogged, and over tracks to and along the trenches, a sea of heavy glutinous mud. I have re-roofed my dug-out, throwing off the manure which existed under the name of thatch. But what odds! We sleep on manure covered with dryer straw. I want my successor tonight to clear out all the inside of the dug-out and put in all clean bedding. Our telephone dug-out next door is being re-roofed and re-floored;

a mass of putrescent filth around and on it. Men of three or four different Battalions use it. They chuck their waste food anywhere, half empty jam and beef tins, rotting biscuits, etc, 'never mind, the next lot can clear it up' and the next lot are quite content to live their four days in filth, and leave it, and so these unholy insanitary conditions continue. Thank goodness, it is not hot. I managed a shave and a wash this morning in ½″ of hot water in my canteen. Good thing I got over it before the shelling commenced. But Gray and I both remarked what a terrible moral effect (as well as real effect) shell fire has, and yet how very quickly (an hour's quiet is sufficient) one's nerves recover and one's heart beats normally, and one can think clearly. Of course, I've not been under bad shell fire yet. I pray Heaven I may be fortunate enough to escape that experience, but so far, it has not bothered me much, just because somehow I can never forget that Promise (for I feel it is a Promise); still, my pulses do go quicker; every man's does, must do: I am thinking all the time so hard how to protect my men, what to do with them, and that takes my mind off the actual danger. But that blessed relief, when our guns start and the enemy's cease.

It is 4.15 pm. The Germans haven't shelled us this afternoon, and only just a few shells in Kemmel, and it's rather late for them to start again this afternoon, though the other day they put three shells into a field as one of our officers was crossing it, about 8 or 9 pm. He couldn't run, ground too heavy, but he didn't loiter. Of course they were only chance shots.

Our guns (4.20 pm) still bursting over the Germans on our right, in salvoes. Well, now they know what artillery means, just as they, on the Marne, and at the Aisne, taught us.

We buried Pigot-Moodie in the military cemetery, set apart at Kemmel. There are already several graves there. Found a French Cross to put on him; oak with top cut out as a convenient handle, about 30″ long, the French made; possibly still have them, for the soldiers' graves. We should do the same, and the War Office ought to have some sent out. It is difficult in the dark to make a cross which will last, and many officers' graves must, by this time, be quite nameless.

Shape of French military Field Cross . . . oak, plain and solid and easily handled. Ours are only two bits of wood, perhaps only tied together; of course, they can't last, and they get knocked over and trampled in the mud, and you never guess a grave was there until you dig into it, or go through it, or it is washed out.

My Subaltern buried, or rather threw earth over (he couldn't bury it) a body lacking head and arms, one of the poor fellows blown bodily out of the dug-out three nights ago, a Northumberland Fusilier. I do think the Battalion might have buried their own dead. They had all next day to do it.

January 15th

I was eventually relieved at 9.30 pm last night. Thought the reliefs were never coming; delayed, because Festing wanted some breastwork built up in H3 by my men there before they were relieved. A nasty bit of work as the German snipers saw it by day, and were sniping at it in the dark, and the blue flares they sent up lighted it up well. Young Tuckett had the very greatest difficulty in getting his men to work, or even fill sandbags, on this account, and at last he got six of 'em outside the trench, drew his pistol and swore he'd shoot the first man who entered the trench without orders. He thus managed to get sandbags filled, and did his job excellently, though owing to the ground the parapet is not yet completed.

Left our trenches in pitch darkness and I promptly stepped into a Jack Johnson hole; thought I'd never stop falling; luckily it wasn't full of water, only of mud. They measured one JJ hole in the roadway near Ypres; 15' deep and 28' across! These 4.5s they fire at us make tidy holes though, as they are very powerful. A Sergeant of mine is missing since the shelling started; we fear he is buried somewhere about the trench by a shell; the wounded man died yesterday afternoon; might have lived could a doctor have got to him, but that is impossible until dusk in most of our trenches, and anyway – even if he did make a dash for it – the stretcher-bearers could never carry away a wounded man in daylight. I didn't go across to see the state of the blown-in trench; the MG officer did, and he said it made him just sick. My Company had one man hit the night before in the Support Farmhouse. A stray bullet came through the roof, and that evening my orderly got a bullet through the back folds of his overcoat when he was following me. Told me afterwards he 'felt the bullet grazing along his back'. But we in the Supports are only some 900 yards from the German trenches, in a hollow, and their bullets come over us, as a rule, fairly high up, though this morning, as the platoon here (at Battalion Headquarters) 'was standing to arms' in the roadway at 6.30 am, 2 or 3 bullets zipped past; I thought it time to move them under cover, also myself too. I hope we have accounted for the snipers who have been annoying us on my left, as Captain Mayne has just telephoned down that the men in his left trench (H2) spotted two Germans returning at dawn to their trenches from the sniping positions, and they 'downed' both of them. Had the greatest difficulty in turning two of my platoons out early this morning. They would not move. I know they're tired, poor fellows, but they're also curs, and they'd not hurry if they knew the whole of the Royal Irish Rifles were being cut up; in fact, they'd be slower than ever.

As a whole, of course, the same as in everything else, there are exceptions. Had to use my stick to wake them up, and I stirred them up to some purpose.

Had all the farm awake and moving, and at the end I spotted a loft; not 7' above, and in the first room I entered, there found a lot of men who made no attempt to move; the fools below hadn't even taken the trouble to arouse them. I went up the ladder with my electric torch in one hand and my stick in another and jolly soon got them moving. Spiritless, heartless, soulless sheep, very willing to be driven, but hopeless to lead. Rather heartbreaking: they'll do, or try to do anything you tell them, but you must stand over 'em and make 'em do it, or they just 'cut it'.

January 16th

Had a rotten night – raining and blowing hard and black as pitch. I fell into two communication trenches and into most of the old shell holes and I am sure into all the new ones, also into the drains, in one of which my legs were glued so fast another man had to help me out. However, by 10 pm I got all my men in the trenches. Tuckett told me that, in the light of a flare sent up, his men had seen a number of Germans crossing his front towards the wood where their trenches are. Frightened me, of course, as our line is so weak, though at that part the ground is very bad for attacking on. Expect they were only German reliefs going to their trenches. If my men were not such fools . . . they'd have opened a rapid fire on them.

Some wire entanglements and other pioneering equipment sent up and I had to get them distributed. Sounds easy, but it was very black, raining and blowing, a sea of mud underfoot and drains and shell holes galore! At 2 am Festing turned up and took me with him to place the wire entanglements in front of H3. Such a job, awkward unwieldy things 12′ long and 3′ high. The men wouldn't work, funking like blazes. I had to drive them over the parapet. Admit it was no pleasant job and I'm sure Festing hated sitting and standing some 20 yards in front of our trenches, and walking about, as much as I and the men did. There were German trenches certainly within 150 yards, if not very much closer, and we crouched like hares when their confounded flares lit up the country. Lot of corpses about too, relics of the fight over a month ago; all added to the gruesomeness. Luckily we could only see something lying there, a dark outline and details were mercifully spared us. German scouts lie out within 60 or 80 yards of our line, they have been seen going back at dawn, and I thought I saw a German walking about not 20 yards from us, but didn't say anything. Found afterwards Tuckett had also seen him, and didn't say anything for fear of frightening his men.

Got back to my dug-out about 3.15 am and thereafter a quiet night, with rain and wind, and so far (1.30 pm) we have had a quiet day, though our artillery have been doing their usual bombardment, and of course there is always a certain amount of intermittent rifle shooting at the Germans which our shells forced out of their trenches this morning; and one of our men got hit in the temple, but Tuckett tells me he is still alive and hopes to save his life; poor chap, he has to remain here till dusk before the stretcher party can come up to carry him away. A bitter cold day with piercing wind, and rain, or snow, or something beastly, blowing up, I fancy.

The way we are all fed here is wonderful, packets of pea soup and cubes of Oxo are issued as rations. Machonocie tinned meat and vegetables. 'Home & Colonial' margarine and very good too, and so much jam, cheese, bacon and bully beef that any amount is wasted. Tea and sugar is of course issued, but I can't understand why they don't issue compressed tea. We had an excellent dinner in our dug-out: pea soup, hot stew, bread, butter and jam, which all things considered is not too rough out here. I have heard any number of complaints of the hospital orderlies stealing wounded men's kits.*

Captain Bowen Colthurst overheard two orderlies chatting together outside his bunk on a hospital train; they were congratulating each other on the number of field glasses and revolvers they would 'make' that trip. Becher lost *all* his kit, revolver, glasses, etc his first night in hospital, and when they took his clothes away to be disinfected, the disinfectant took ⅔rds of his buttons off his uniform, all his regimental badges, and his cap badge. It is an awful shame that the doctors can't look after wounded men's kits better. Nothing can be traced. A man doesn't know who attended him; probably not even the hospital he was in.

10.15 pm. Thank God, out of those accursed trenches for some ninety two hours, and I am billeted in a charming little villa, the property of two old servants of the Chateau de Locre,

---

* The nickname for the RAMC is 'Rob all my comrades'.

who are worn out and are spending the evening of their days here. The old lady showed me a ripping little bedroom and topping bed, 'Nous sommes que des ouvriers, monsieur, mais tout est tout propre', and it was indeed.

The old man with the withered wrist, sunk in, toothless mouth was the picture of a very fine old age. She very proudly showed me the pictured plate presented to him by some Society or other to show that he was 'decoré'. Poor Sergeant Neile! We have now found out he was one of the poor fellows buried by the shell, so we had only four killed then, in all; but to-day, I had two wounded; one man in H3 shot slap through the top of his head from side to side, he may recover; we got him to hospital; and another shot, I hear, in the shoulder, in G4 trench, but I don't know any details. H3 is a nasty trench. It is always under snipers' fire, and as the Northumberland Fusiliers were relieving my platoon in that trench, a bullet grazed the nose of one of my fellows, and went through one of their men's eyes. He just said 'I'm done,' and went out, poor chap.

However, Tuckett hit, and badly, two snipers on their return to their trenches this morning at dawn, and they fairly pasted the twenty or thirty Germans who were shelled out of their advanced trench about mid-day: and they said they saw several drop. A Wiltshire officer (the Wilts are on our left) came across to Tuckett and warned him that the Germans were massing troops opposite and to look out for an attack. I am doubly glad to be in Locre. If the Germans do push home an attack they'll go through our line like knife through butter, and 'pon my word, I don't know what to do; we can't hold them, a number of my men could never get out of their trenches in time and they'd certainly never fight in them, they're so especially and particularly slow, don't know how to use a bayonet and I certainly could do no good by hanging on till I'm captured. However, with good luck I shall not have to bother about such things, yet it is a thought that is present with every officer in this line and causes a bit of a strain.

A yarn or two to brighten things up.

As Tuckett was taking his men in last night to relieve the men of A Company, he saw a fool in A Company strike a vesta light to his pipe (and this is a trench where every day, at least one man is hit, and probably five a week are killed by snipers). Tuckett with great presence of mind went 'woosch' with his hand, hit match, pipe and face flying. In G4 – during the shelling a man was making soup, when a shell came within 10 feet of him on one side, and in a few minutes, the same distance away on the other. He took off his cap and put it carefully over his canteen, for, as he said, 'he couldn't let the dirt into it'.

The Northumberland Fusiliers were relieving the Middlesex: 'Any casualties to-day?' 'Yus,' replied the Cockney, pulling his questioner's leg, 'by the hundred.' 'Thought you was called the Die-hards,' remarked the Fusilier. 'Well, so we are, wot of it?' 'Well, I'd say you was the Die Jolly Easy's.'

A friend of mine overheard the following:

Two NF's in a trench full of water up to their knees 'Bill! you 'ere? where you bin to all the time?' 'Just come out of orspital, ad the bronchitis.' 'Ho! well you've come to a blooming sanaterium, I must say.' Tuckett and his servant were having their soup when one of our shrapnel burst a bit short, day before yesterday, and a bit flew between them knocking the canteen of soup some 4 yards away out of the man's hand. 'Well, I'm glad it's fallen the right way up,' said TA who then noticed his hand bleeding, and began to feel it very sore. The fragment of shell had caught him. A young German, 18 to 19 years of age came across to the Wilts line the other day, by day, quite unharmed. He asked for bread, and wanted to give himself up. The men let him come within 20 yards and then riddled him with bullets. I call this nothing less than murder. No necessity to take a leaf out of the Germans' book; the same regiment marching out to the trenches notices a lot of provisions and a sack by a hedge. As they approached they noticed the sack start rolling. Two officers went up and emptied their revolvers into the sack, in which was lying hid, a German sniper. Some time ago the French, digging trenches by night, were much annoyed by a sniper at close range. At the finish the party were paraded and were numbered 'off', previous to marching away, and it was found there was one more soldier than had come out with them. Hun-nature not being so fertile and in much speedy time, all the men were narrowly inspected and a German spy in French uniform was found. He was led to the hedge and shot.

That jolly old farm, a sketch of which I sent you, and where our reserve slept, when in Kemmel, was completely burnt out to-day. One of our prize idiots in B Company flung his cigarette end among the hay. As we passed to-night, we saw it guttering and flaming, and heard the loose cartridges popping off. Last night the sentry over this farm was walking up and down with his rifle slung over his back. A bullet hit his rifle which saved him from a perforated lung, and stripped all the wood-work off, down to the magazine, and this is quite a mile from the German trenches; but errant 'song birds' whistle round there at all times, though I can't say I have heard any; the road through is about the limit of them; they hit there and ricochet away.

Rae's Father has been bothering the Commanding Officer about his son's burial and kit, etc. So silly, all was done that could be done, all sent home that could be sent home, but there is no one here to actually pack up a dead officer's valise, and his servant or any other man probably takes his breeches, handkerchiefs, etc; things of use to them here; of no use at home.*

We have told Rae his son has, as far as we know, been buried in the Chateau at Neuve Chapelle; but as a matter of fact the Battalion lost very heavily that day, and on the lawn of the Chateau were laid several officers and many men awaiting burial when the Germans started to shell the Chateau and the Battalion had to clear off, leaving the dead lying there. It is

---

* This state of things was altered: but the Battalion had such a knocking about at Neuve Chapelle, and later, at Ypres, that kits, correspondence records, etc, were all lost. It was not the fault of the system but of the extraordinary circumstances.

regrettable that this War should be so unlike other Wars that there is no armistice for burial purposes; so officers' and men's graves cannot be marked, they are just buried: 'dig a hole back of that parapet' or 'over there by that tree'. With officers some note is taken of the position of the grave, and relatives generally know within a few yards of where they lie, but the actual crosses on the grave are soon obliterated; perhaps even the farm where they lie, levelled. However, it makes no difference to the poor fellows themselves. It's only those left, and they should only remember and think, not of where their friends died, but why they died. Delighted to hear from G's letter that we shot some 20 of those Nationalist traitors who sowed Lough Swilly with mines last October, but I think it should have come out in the papers to 'encourage others'.

January 17th

Never woke up till 10.30 am when I told my servant to bring me some hot water, a minute hand basin, *not* a thing to bathe in; however, did the best I could and after all I was not as dirty as my subalterns, one of whom had not washed for the whole four days, and he was simply black. Topping bed with clean sheets and everything nice. Arrival of several parcels and letters most welcome. Never got up to breakfast until 11 am and couldn't rouse Leask up at all till I sent him word he was to inspect the Company's billets at 3 pm. The only thing that got him out of bed.

Three servants and my orderly making a deuce of a row downstairs talking to the old couple; on the principle that the louder you talk the better they understand. They talk very slowly, using mostly, only nouns, repeating the words 'butter' 'coffee' etc, etc, and no doubt, gesticulating with fingers and hands; and as much of Flemish is similar in sound to English, our men manage to procure us what we want better than one would think. Am so sick of this all; everyone has only the one topic of conversation; those blessed trenches and what each had seen and done in them.

January 18th

Several inches of snow on the ground this morning when we awoke, and still snowing (9.30 am) and looks like continuing. I pity those poor devils in the trenches; their feet will 'go' like broken sticks, for all the boots get worn very quickly, at any rate, TA is very careless with his boots, and it's impossible to give any but the very worst cases new boots. I know a number of my own men have boots 'by courtesy' only; toes worn away, or broken at the sides, and standing in such boots in sodden trenches simply ruins the feet, brings on frost bite, etc. I must warn my men to grease their feet with any grease they can find, but I know they won't do it, far too lazy.

Three scoundrels were sentenced last week to Field imprisonment No 1, 28 days, which means tying them up an hour at a time, for two hours a day and giving them, of course, every dirty unpleasant job you can think of. So far, they've done nothing, but I'm tying them up to-day, hands behind their back, and then tied on to a loop or ring or anything to prevent movement. In SA we used to tie 'em up to the seat rail of a waggon; this pulled their arms (tied behind the back) up and forced them to bend their bodies forward. An hour of this was perfect torture, but there are many natures to which this is the only appeal, and really flogging would be quite a good thing with some men, as there are natures so low that nothing but actual physical pain can appeal to them.

Talked to a useless Sergeant who came out with a draft from the 3rd Battalion. Told him he'd better revert to Corporal before I had him reduced, as he was of no use to me. The spiritless one asked if he might not become a 'Private'. I jumped at it, 'Rather' I said, and 'Rifleman' he is. No use for men of that stamp as NCOs, but it's easy to make a rifleman out of an NCO.

Can't find the Lance-Corporal and men who displayed such craven spirits. The NCO, whom Sergeant Major Courtney is prepared to swear was there, is now able to bring evidence he was elsewhere in the trench. Such a lot of miserable lying.

At Battalion Head Quarters, 'The Six Brothers and Sisters',

an hotel, I fancy, is a big dolls house in the garden. I went to see what was inside and found a pair of love-birds; one lying dead on the ground, the other hopping about. I at once went off for food and found the owner who told me they could get no more seed, and had tried bread, etc. I told them just to try again. It is so sad how everything living suffers in War time, even pet birds.

Have just been down to see about my weekly bath at the convent, immensely flattered the Mother Superior by asking if I might take her photograph. If it comes out, I want you to get it copied and send it to her.

> The Revd. Mother Superior,
> The Convent,
> Locre,
> Belgium.

as I promised she should have one.

Our guns are still shelling – Our Intelligence warns all ranks against giving any information whatever to any officer or anyone else asking questions as two men in British uniform, riding, stopped a peasant and asked if he knew where the big guns were. He reported this. These men were evidently Germans, as, of course, no English officer would ask any information respecting the troops from a peasant. Our lines are undoubtedly kept under good observation by the enemy.

A newly joined subaltern, my Canadian hero, tells me he has to go to Hospital now for the 'Itch'. He thinks he got it coming over in the transport. Have told him not to come near me or any of my kit.

Another two casualties this morning. A fool on guard goes to sleep with his rifle at full cock. On being awakened to go on sentry he shoots himself through the foot, the bullet going on into another man's legs. What can one do with fools of this kind?

I had a listening post; one Lance Corporal and two men out 59 yds in front of G3 in a ditch alongside a hedge. Quite safe at night, as they can't be seen and they come in directly it gets light. Their duty is to listen and give warning in case of an advance by night. As they were relieved by the Lincolns, I hear a Lincoln got three bullets through the head, but though he was probably shot, I doubt the three bullets, it's impossible for any sniper to aim in the dark, and it is only un-aimed fire.

My sergeant Major tells me when I went out there last week, a bullet struck the ground at my feet just between me and Sergeant McCabe. I don't remember it myself, but the German trenches in view are some 400 or more yards away. That poor fellow who was hit through the head, was buried last night at the Hospital. We had 21 casualties last week: 4 killed, 2 wounded and all the rest sick; and we got three back from Hospital and a draft of 25 out from home, so we are just seven better off than last week and we are about 207 strong now, or some 148 rifles for the actual firing line. With such wastage, and we are doing no fighting, it is easy to understand how men are used up. After dinner this evening, we went up to Battalion Head Quarters and played one rubber of auction. Saw the flares from the trenches some 3-4 miles away on the black horizon; our guns bombarded somewhat heavily for 20 minutes or so about 9 pm and returning home shortly after we heard a heavy crackle of musketry, probably only the usual 'funk firing', but it's almost worse listening to it here than being in the trenches; you don't know what is really happening and imagination has, unhappily, full play: and during our all too short four days rest, Oh! my God, if only we could get right away from talk and sound of trenches and war. But the papers are full of it, and of course, there is no other hope of conversation.

The snow ceased about 10 am and we have had intermittent rain, and things are slushier than ever.

January 19th

Went for a short route march, close day and thawing; country more slushy than ever, but sky looks like more snow. Some of my men's boots very bad, but fear no chance of getting them new ones. General Haldane sent round to-day a memo, re men of the Division turning out, when in billets, so untidy. That is a hit at us, as our fellows are *beastly* slovenly, but I fear we can't make 'em better until we can get 'em right away and refit them and knock some discipline into them. The staff out here, are, quite rightly, very strict on discipline; men saluting, shaving and being clean etc. The only way to keep an Army on active service together, and to prevent it becoming a mob.

January 20th

Played Auction last night at Battalion Head Quarters with Alston and our Jesuit Padre, a jolly good parson, probably, but a shocking bad Bridge player.

A quiet day and night, as far as we could hear, and there seemed little signs of activity on the Germans' side.

A memo came round this morning from General Head Quarters, with some good advice as to rubbing feet with whale oil, before going into the trenches; (This oil is being issued) and men are to take a dry pair of socks with them to change into; boots not to be tightly laced nor putties tightly wound, and Battalions to make arrangements on return of the men from the trenches for supplies of towels and *cold* water etc., in order that the men might wash their feet and put on dry socks. Unfortunately, this is all very well, but it's difficult when the men's boots are mostly uppers and lace-holes. Also a note, to say that No. . . . Private X and No. . . . Private Y, of the Middlesex Regiment, were tried by court martial for desertion; found guilty and sentenced to death, and they were shot at 7.30 am on the 12th inst – So silly of 'em to attempt it. But in the South African War, several men deserted. We caught and shot one at Ventersdorp, and in the Peninsular a number of men went over to the French lines, and even when our troops were besieging those lines, for instance, at Badajos, a few men deserted from us and were caught in that town when it was taken. However none of our fellows are likely to try to desert *to* the Germans: too much afraid of getting shot; but they clear off with a vague idea of getting out of the country.

January 21st

We paraded yesterday at 4.30 pm and being the first Company for the trenches we led the column and had quite a comfortable march. Went straight on into our usual trenches. Three Platoons went one way. I led the remaining Platoon another and shorter way. Returning, I tripped over a plank, when crossing a gutter and fell, over my wrists into slime and clay. I grovelled in it; all over my arms and body; stick and gloves a sludgy mass. You know how I just loathe anything of that kind, and this was the loathliest kind of oily slippery day. My orderly said he thought I was hit, as I fell 'with a kind of squeak'. If it was a squeak, it's a great compliment to my self control. I think it was much more likely a swear word of the strongest and worst description. The Huns have been shelling these trenches the last four days, badly. Put 51 and 38 shells respectively, on two different occasions, into the field where the dug outs are. Luckily there wasn't a man within 300 yards of them. They also hit our trenches, and I hear killed 10 or 12 men of the N Fusiliers, and they made real good practice at a neighbouring trench, causing heavy casualties. Rained all night and still raining (10 am). My dug out is beyond description. There are two tiny streams percolating under the straw, which is all rotten. I've many a time seen men sitting on a cart full of manure, and not envied them. I never dreamt I'd be sleeping on manure, but it's about what this dug-out is floored with. I'm clearing it out to-day, the smell is so bad.

About mid-day the Germans sent us 30 shells in 35 minutes over our heads. I counted 10, and then dropped off to sleep I suppose, as my Sergeant-Major counted them and timed them. They were all put in the same old place at our dug-outs, but we don't keep any man there by day and only some 12 men by night; but I don't mean to do even that if I can help it as the dug-outs are not really fit to put men in.

My Sergeant-Major, putting on a pair of new socks, found a packet of cigarettes in the toe with the following note enclosed:

> Dear Soldier,
>   Soon these socks will be worn out. When you want another pair, write to
>   Miss Meta Kerr,
>   Mullagh,
>   Islandmagee,
>   Ireland.
> A Merry Christmas and a safe return,
>   MK

Some of the socks have tins of Vaseline in 'em. Bit of difference between where the note was written and where it was read!

A soaking day, our trench wetter than ever. We saw the Germans baling out their trenches this morning, and flinging the water out. Their lines are surrounded by a lot of high wire entanglements, and there are a lot of dead all about in front of their lines. Through my glasses I could see the face of one Frenchman. It was almost black. I fear most of those lying out there are all labelled 'missing', and some poor woman is hoping against hope that the close of the War will bring them back.

January 22nd

A very peaceful day in the Battalion Head-Quarters Farm; decent meals, even though one had to eat jam off the same plate on which one had eaten tinned salmon and Bully Beef.

Topping day, frost in the morning from 4 am, cloudless sky, and aeroplanes of both sides were up. We witnessed some pretty shooting by our guns at an enemy plane; 31 shells fired at it. Very pretty to see the little tiny balls of fluff break out and expand to drift along like feathers, but no luck for us, the beggar got away. The Hun shelled a bit too, but fortunately none of our trenches. Few casualties in our trenches. Last night, just before relief, a cur blew his right fore-finger off; must have done it purposely; men don't pull the trigger with their left hand! I had several men with bad feet, and three or four cases with frost bite. Relieved the trenches this evening, and got a Lance-Corporal hit in the chest as he was going into his trench. Plucky fellow! Said he could walk alright. But I ordered a stretcher to come up and meet him. Think, and hope, it was only a graze on the ribs just over the heart. Had it penetrated he could never have walked or spoken.

The Company we relieved had a couple of casualties, but they were only slight. Cleaning out a drain we came on what looked like a bit of the brain and face of a man, I didn't stay to investigate it – I fled. Good frost coming, very glad as my dug-out stinks, must get some chloride of lime. Have cleaned it out as much as I dare and put a door in it and a floor and a lot of clean straw, but 'pon my word I'd not be surprised if a Frenchman were underneath. Hope not!

January 23rd

At about 2.30 this morning I heard a poor devil moaning and crying outside my dug-out. Bitter frost and I *knew* and felt with 'em all. I was cold *in* my dug-out *with* a fire. He was crying, 'Oh, God, take me out of this; oh! God, take me out of this.' Got him to the fire, but as he said his feet were frost bitten, I sent him over at once to the dressing station. I believe he was a decent young fellow, but of course a lot of these fellows would scrimshank like a shot, if they thought I'd be kind to them. The chances of an attack on the newly-frozen ground got on my mind and I woke about 5 am with cheers and screams ringing in my ears and could have sworn an attack was going on about half a mile to our right, and I was awake with a start. However, a false alarm. 'C' Company in H3 said they'd shot a German sniper and his body was lying only nine yards from the trench. I sent out to

85

fetch it in as we want shoulder badges, papers, etc, from their bodies, but it was gone, *if* it has ever been there. It is reported that Germans in our uniform have been seen about Wyschaete.

Breakfast at 8.30. Thick frost and all our front very still, but on our left a Maxim is rattling. There are a lot of blind German shells, about 45, lying about in the fields around here, and, last evening a gunner officer came up and screwed off the top and found one filled with dust and bits – nothing that could explode.

11.30 am. The Germans sent 18 shells, 'howitzer, HE', (high explosive) over my Head Quarters, bursting 50 to 100 yards in the rear. Fancy they were trying to reach the support trenches held by the Wilts. Their shells were exploding about 80 to 100 yards from me, and I took some snapshots. Should have got two or three good photographs. They then turned off and shelled further back, either again to the trenches on our left, or endeavouring to find our guns. Hope they have finished with us to-day. They do not, as a rule, fire an unlimited number, and, after firing about 30, generally stop. Some heavy firing NE of us, about Ypres, and our guns are fairly busy. We are vibrating under the whistle of distant, and the scream of nearer shells, and the explosions.

A good deal of pretty but unsuccessful aeroplane shooting this morning. Watched the Germans send about 25 shells after our aeroplanes. I know nothing prettier than to see these small shells burst, the white puffs enlarging and floating away against the clear sky like air bubbles. I wonder where the shell and the bullets go to! Must drop somewhere, but though I've watched these burst over-head, I've never heard anything strike the ground around me.

The bright sunny day has appreciably cheered the men up. The trenches are not so horribly wet under foot as they were. Hear the Lance Corporal shot in the chest reached the dressing station alright, so it must have been only a graze.

Tuckett in H3 told my orderly he'd got a bullet through his cap last night; possible, as snipers have his trench well under observation, and doubtless, have rifles fixed on it. But his yarns of the sniping there are hair raising. Personally, whenever I am there, twice or so during the 24 hours, and sometimes twice or three times a night, I have experienced nothing of the sniping, and they seem to do very little. Tuckett is very young, and also, I think the trench has got on his nerves. Don't blame him a bit, most of our bad casualties have been there, though it's fairly safe now, and, as a trench, is more comfortable than any of the others.

4 pm. A 4.5 exploded and blew up a cartload of mud not 10 yards from my dug-out; Nos 2 and 3 fell further away. No 4 fell 10 yards the other side. We shifted, and they put in shells every few minutes, every one of them all too close to our H1 trench. We sat out in the mud in H2 for half an hour till we thought it was over; disgraceful of the Germans to shell us so late. Their last two shots I fancied, must have blown to the right of H1 and I was going down to see the damage when I met Sergeant Byrne coming up, and he reported the trench was so far alright and no casualties, Thank God.

A heavy cannonade and musketry fire between us and Ypres, as though the French and Germans were making an attack.

Thawing since mid-day and everything soft again, but it will freeze tonight and it looks as if winter were here at last – Well, we can stick it better than the Germans.

January 24th

Sunday. After our relief yesterday the enemy displayed unusual activity along the line, and there was a continual fire from their trenches all night, as if they had manned their front trenches in expectation of an attack. However, nothing was done. If the Kaiser wants Calais for a birthday present, he has only three days to get some 5 miles and he'll have to start on his march within the next hour or two. I spent a rotten night at Head Quarters getting no sleep as my feet were so cold, and the continual firing kept me on the Qui Vive. Five bullets came through the house at various times during the evening, clattering the tiles into the loft. We are in the line of fire from one portion of the German trenches, and just far enough from them to be at 'the point of impact', and it's quite risky going outside the door between dusk and dawn as bullets are always 'sipping' into the ground around.

Festing went out last night about 10 pm and came back shaking with laughter. He'd heard a man crying in a barn, where a platoon of my fellows were sleeping, and, asking the sentry what it was, all he got was 'Ah, it's the m-a-a-n what's wounded' and, being told there was no wounded man there, 'Ah, he's buried under the straw.' As there seemed a good deal of turmoil, Festing sent me out, and luckily he did so. I took my electric torch and found my men had been under-mining a small hay-stack in the barn to get straw for themselves, and three men slept under the actual rick. A chance sneeze, probably, brought the lot down on them, and we eventually rescued them, when they'd just had about enough of it – the Germans got the Wilts trenches yesterday alright with their shells. I heard that dead and wounded were lying 'all over the road', but – I believe they had five killed and four wounded.

Our guns and the enemy's making the day hideous again. All the frost seems to have gone, and it's soft, mild and horribly muddy once more. When I went round to the farm where the other three platoons of my Company are sleeping, at 5.45 am this morning, I was not challenged by the sentry, whom I found asleep – made a prisoner of him.

January 25th

Back to billets in West Outre; the man I ran in for sleeping at his post has just been remanded for a Field General court martial. I fear he will be shot. He is, I hear, a useless rotter; and, yesterday, had the enemy broken through our line, it is not by any means an impossibility; our men here sleep so soundly the noise might never have awakened them 800 yards from the firing line, and half a dozen Germans coming into the farm could have captured the whole of the 100 men and two officers sleeping there, with ease. And there is no excuse for the man; he'd not had a trying day and anyway, in the face of the enemy as we were, men *must* keep awake; I fear this fellow will have to be made an example of.

A damp muggy beastly cold day – no signs of frost. In one part of our lines, about E or F trenches, the South Lancashires who were there, tell me salients of their trenches are within 25 yards of the Germans; but there is no sniping as both sides are far too afraid of each other to put their heads up, and neither side can rush the other's trenches, as if they did take aim they'd only find themselves enfiladed by their own trenches on either flank, etc. so that unless an advance of the whole line is made, matters at any particular point, (just in this district) are stalemate for both Germans and ourselves.

January 26th

I hear that the heavy bombardment all last Saturday, and the musketry and the machine gun fire in the evening, which was heard on our left was due to an attack made by the French SE of Ypres. They pierced the German lines, but a counter attack forced them back. However, I have no confirmation of this.

I have my billet in the Curé's house. His Mamma is dying of Gall-stones, and they sent to me for peppermint: so despatched them all Tuckett's peppermint creams. Can't do the old lady any harm. I feed just across the road, in the half-shop and half-inn we were at before.

D Coy. 2nd ROYAL IRISH RIFLES   27th January 1915

Distribution	Officers	Rankd & File	Total
On Parade	3*	141	144
Transport		12	12
Stretcher Bearers		2	2
Orderly Room		2	2

Bailleul	1	9	10
Kemmel		4	4
Signallers		2	2
Sanitary squad		3	3
Police		1	1
Pioneers		7	7
Cooks		3	3
Coy. GMS & QMS Stores		4	4
Supply Column		1	1
Reported Sick		9†	9
Off. Servants		2	2
Company Orderly		1	1
Guard Room		6†	6
Total strength of Coy	4	209	213

* 1 of these attached.
† These men will all be in the trenches unless being ill.
Rifles in the firing line – 158 less sick unable to march.

Stood to arms at 7 am. I was 20 minutes late as my servant never called me till 7.10 am. I dressed and walked 400 yards in 10 minutes, so I didn't wash much. Hard frost early this morning, but it is thawing again now (10 am).

January 27th

The Kaiser's Birthday. He was to have been given Calais as a birthday present. Haven't heard it has been handed over to him yet.

As a punishment for being late in 'Standing to Arms' yesterday, I was out this morning quite unnecessarily. Told my CSM to tell the guard to call met at 6 am *if* we stood to arms at 7 am. He gave the order. Before I went to bed I heard we had not to stand to arms unless other orders arrived during the night. At 5.50 am down comes a man from the guard to tell my servant the

Company was standing to arms at 6.30 am. Got up hastily, cup of coffee, and on parade at 6.20 am to find everyone still snoring in the straw. Then I found out my SM had forgotten to cancel his order to the sentry. Found a covering of snow on the ground, only a little dusting but I suppose we'll get it soon.

One of my ruffians stole two eggs from the farmer whose farm buildings the Company is using. Instead of making a crime of it, my Sergeant Major told off a Corporal and one man to give the fellow a good hammering; not to mark him, but just to punish him well in the body.

My Company, all told, is just 209 strong, with three officers, or, in other words, I can put some 155 men in the firing line. During the last month I have had over 100 men, new drafts sent to me; but still the Company keeps the same strength, so it shows the tremendous wastage of war, even without an action.

Since December 24th, doing merely outpost work, we have lost six killed, and five wounded in action and three wounded accidently, and the remainder going sick; bad feet mostly. Now we have to make the men rub their feet with fish oil before they go into the trenches.

I have just heard that somewhere on the Dickebusche line, a mile or so N of us, the Germans made a heavy attack on the Guards Brigade and drove them out of the fire trenches; and 500 wounded were sent down to Neuve Chapelle.

The French and our guns shelled the enemy out of their trenches and our men re-took them; some 900 killed and wounded Germans were found, and some 500 were taken prisoners. I state this with some reserve, and the figures are given in round numbers, but there was such an attack and successful counter-attack, as I have stated.

The Germans also shelled the line of trenches we usually hold, yesterday (I believe), and killed sixteen men, one officer of the Liverpool Scottish being killed by a sniper. The farm we used as our Battalion Head Quarters has been successfully shelled, but I hear it is not destroyed. However, I suppose as it was the Kaiser's Birthday to-day, the enemy felt they had to do something yesterday in an attempt, very vain, luckily, to give him a birthday present.

I enclose a Company's Parade Statement I'd like to keep as a matter of interest.

January 28th

We are billeted here in Reserve, the first time 'D' Company has had a rest. On arrival, we sent up to the trenches a platoon with a certain amount of pioneer equipment, and I went with it to show Gilliland (the new Capt) who has just brought us a draft, round the line of trenches. A most pleasant walk along the back of the trenches, quite untroubled by bullets, but on our way both there and back, when some 2,000 yards from the German lines, a certain number of 'singing birds' fell really all too near, and 'A' Company on its way to the trenches had a man punctured through the liver this evening, at about that range. Last night all the Locre Garrison were turned out at 10 pm to come into the second line of trenches round this town, as that Brigade were ordered to 'take all precautions': presumably an attack was feared. Yesterday two spies were caught in West Outre, one in a sort of khaki uniform, and six spies were caught in Kemmel last week.

One of the few shells that reached Kemmel last week struck an estaminet, and killed a woman and a baby, and wounded another baby – I fancy they have a big howitzer here now; I mean in the German lines, as they fired four huge shells, to judge by the holes, three round H3, H2 and H4 and one just outside the Battalion Head Quarters. Luckily they were fired yesterday.

January 29th

Woke up with my throat very painful. I am sure it's the result of my 'stinking' dug-out last week, and the dead Frenchmen under it, or at any rate, the rotting straw. Shewed it to our

Doctor last night, but he had nothing out here to make a gargle.

We three officers are in a little cottage containing a fat old Flemish woman and her cross-eyed daughter, and I think the husband and son live somewhere about the place too. The old lady paid a quite unmerited compliment to her daughter's beauty and fascination by refusing to go to bed until we had all gone off to our own room. Gilliland and I shared one big mattress together, very uncomfortable, but I must have eventually fallen asleep. I brought a blanket up this time on the back of my saddle. Freezing hard all day yesterday, and it is still freezing and the fields last night were more painful to cross than when they were muddy, as all the mud is now frozen hard into lumps and ridges.

Our guns, not far behind Kemmel are busy this morning and the Germans are trying to find them, unfortunately for us, as their shells are whistling over the roofs. Aeroplanes very busy, don't know where they come from or who is firing at them, but we had a pretty little exhibition of anti-aircraft artillery work just now. Some 18 or 20 shells flecking the perfectly cloudless winter sky with dainty little puff balls of smoke – which did not seem to trouble the aeroplane much.

Met General Haldane in Kemmel this morning; he had evidently just come from the Chateau (our Brigade Head Quarters). On his staff is Maurice, son of the late General Sir F Maurice. He recalled the time when we met at Woolwich 19 years ago in 1896. Also met Hilliard, General Hilliard's son, with whom I was on a course of signalling at Aldershot in 1899.

Went to bed this afternoon after lunch, to get warm and to pass away the time. Heard guns rattling the windows. Tuckett came in to tell me it was the German shells bursting in Kemmel. However, I couldn't stop them, so went to sleep. Later on awaking, I heard the Germans had shelled the town very successfully, as they put some shells into some houses occupied by the South Lancashires and killed five men and wounded some 10 or 12 more; and their new Commanding Officer only joined them during the shelling. Cheery reception for him. All put down to the fault of the Royal Scots: on the night of the 27th, four men in khaki coats and German trousers and boots stopped a Royal Scots sentry and asked him a number of questions, and then made off. The fool never attempted to stop them. Now the Germans know we are again occupying Kemmel, of course, they'll shell it. Tuckett got up as the last shell had fallen; found two men lying about without heads, and men rushing about the place like ants. Said it was most laughable. Saw one young officer running down and playing catch-ball with a huge piece of shell he'd picked up, and, apparently perfectly certain of where he went so he held on to his 'souvenir'.

January 30th

Took some photographs of the tiny military cemetery here: only some 25 graves there yet. Lt Pigot-Moodie's grave is the one with the palings round it, just to the left of the tree; and behind it, is the grave of an officer of the Middlesex Regiment. I see 9 fresh graves dug last night, where the South Lancashires were buried, so with killed, and three or four wounded who died during the evening, they lost 9 dead, and there are some 13 or 14 wounded. A man told me that as the dead and wounded were being carried through the town yesterday, he saw two or three women laughing about the matter and sneering at the groans of the wounded men – scarcely credible, find these sort of things always appear to happen when there is no officer about to arrest people of this kind.

A sprinkling of snow over the country, but a fine bright morning. The Germans started early, about 8 am to send shells over the town (Kemmel) searching for our artillery. One almost wonders when these shells are going to be dropped into us, except that it's no use wondering; time enough to think what to do, when they do start. The shells they sent us last night are larger than 4.5, but not as large as the Jack Johnston. I fancy somewhere about a 9″ shell.

Slept well last night as I kept my feet warm by pulling two

sand-bags over each foot and leg; as they are some 30′ deep, they come well over the knee and keep the feet very warm.

Tuckett and the servant thought themselves very clever last night. They had marked down a solitary fowl, and, at dead of night, they murdered it, plucked it, cut it up and had all the feathers and bones buried within an hour of the crime. The cross-eyed one arose early, however, this morning, troubled by both suspicion and hiccoughs; (the latter could only be assuaged by much peppermint, and even then the wretch made the windows rattle) found a couple of feathers and raised Cain. She got into such a temper she broke a chair. Eventually, they paid her 5 francs for the bird and she calmed down, and after all the bird was uneatable.

As we marched out here, I found one of my newly made Lance Corporals drunk. Made him a prisoner of course, and he is having now a wretched time, as far as my orders are concerned (5 biscuits and a piece of Bully a day and only cold water to drink) but I suppose the other men feed him. He'll be tried by court martial on his return all right.

One of the new draft, a huge burly man, who had been a curse to his Company in Dublin and was generally in durance vile, came to my Company. On arrival, I asked him where he came from. He tried to be funny, by saying, 'Ireland'. Cursed him, and told him I was not the sort of man to try that kind of thing on; and that with his record I'd make or break him, as I had plenty of dirty jobs for things like him to do. He said he only wanted to soldier! Ye Gods. I know the waster who boasts he only 'wants to soldier'. Sent him up with a ration party last night, and, to my relief, heard a stray bullet got him in the thigh, soon after leaving Kemmel. Delighted, save me much further trouble. This frost has frozen the fields and the bullets seem to ricochet more than I think they used to do; anyway, the last three or four nights, several men have been hit by stray bullets when they were 1,500 yards to 2,000 yards away from the German lines.

Walking back from Battalion Head Quarters last night 2 or 3

'sipped' into the plough quite close to my orderly and myself. But their range is always bad anyway, as men are invariably inclined to fire high at night, and the ground 2,000 yards behind our line is more dangerous than the actual firing line at present.

We bought two dozen eggs yesterday for eight francs, or about 2½d each; we also managed to get some rice in the town, and there is any amount of bread; huge round flat loaves they sell for 75 centimes. The bread is nicer than our ration bread, but the men spend their pay on it as a rule (when they can't buy brandy) as so many of our miserable old things have no teeth. The wastage in rations is terrible. Going round the place this morning, I saw enough good tins of Bully thrown away, or simply left in their boxes, to feed a Battalion. The men really get too much, far more than they can eat, and extra rations like tinned salmon are counted extra and the same amount of Bully is issued to the men. The same with the biscuits. Men prefer to buy bread, and tins after tins of biscuits are lying about everywhere, while the wastage in ammunition is remarkable. Every man is supposed to have 150 rounds in his pouches, and, going up to the trenches he carries an extra 100 rounds in two bandoliers. These bandoliers he has to leave behind him, either in the trenches or in the Support Farm, etc, and so since, so far, few of our men fire more than a few rounds a day, the trenches are full of cartridges and clips of cartridges; broken bandoliers, etc, half stuck in the mud or frozen on the parapets – and every farm used for supports is almost paved with them. However, I suppose the country can afford such waste.*

We are most uncomfortable in this billet, the women have awful strident voices, and are *so* dirty. There is only one decent member of the family at all; a little black Schipperke with a long tail, called 'Miss'. She bit me the first day when I took her on my

---

* Waste was one of the many points no Staff Officer ever gave a thought to, until there was an outcry in the Daily Press, and then we at once got orders for every conceivable Staff Officer with regard to issue of food and ammunition wastage, etc.

lap, but now she jumps on it – when I sit near the fire. She is a regular Schip and is all 'tummy', and so one can only get at her love by means of food, but I have always found this in 'Schips', they're little pigs. Maria, Miss's mistress is ill now, I fancy, and sincerely hope. Her awful outburst of temper this morning brought on the hiccoughs, and now she is wearing a wet cloth round her untidy head, and sitting in the kitchen like a sick hen, her face tied up in a huge shawl and her clogs in a portable brazier, which the old mother lit with a tiny bit of charcoal and the vigorous use of a huge iron blow pipe some 3½ feet long, kept in the kitchen chimney on purpose.

I'm ever so much better than I was last night. I had a touch of fever on returning from my walk to Head Quarters, and sent up to the Doctor for some quinine, which quickly warmed me up and I slept it off, and my throat is better, too, but still whenever one has anything wrong with one, no matter how slight, one always feels a bit below par and that's what I feel; and I hope I do get my leave, just that little change would do me a lot of good; and one gets *so* stale here; always the same dreary work, and one can't pick up a book or paper without reading some story or other written about the War. We don't want to read about War out here; we are all 'Captain Kettles' who only like to think of peaceful farms, and lowing kine and all that sort of thing.

Just returned from a bâk with Treffry, who commands the HAC. He is my Unionist Candidate for Launceston. A wire had just come to him to say the Germans had concentrated three Army Corps between Menin and Courtrai, and ordering us to strengthen all our lines. Any real determined attack, however, is I fancy, likely to take place somewhere to the South of us; Messines way, and, as far as our particular line of trenches go, the Germans would hardly be able to make an attack on us at all, as their own parapets are so surrounded with wire, they can scarcely get out but they may make an attack to the North of us from Petit Bois towards Vierstraat for instance. Petit Bois is the smaller of the two woods (the Western one) on the West of Wyschaete. Can't think what they can hope for from any attack,

97

however, unless it is delivered in great force, and even then it is bound to be swept away by our immensely superior artillery power.

I am trying to find out about that Rifleman Masterson, I can get no news of him in my Company, but I may, by referring to some old casualty lists, now with my baggage behind us, be able to let you know whether he was killed or wounded. I fear though, he is but one of the many wounded (or killed) at Neuve Chapelle, where the Battalion lost so heavily. Most of the wounded had to be left where they fell, and could not be brought in, and the wounded were slaughtered by the advancing Germans. There will be, not hundreds, but thousands of men 'missing' after the War, of whom nothing will ever be known. They fall, and the man next to them, who saw them fall, is killed too, and there is no one to say whether Private X was killed or wounded, and the inhumanity of the German prevents any armistice for the purpose of collecting the wounded.

I hear the shells fired into this place last evening were 6″ shells; some of the HAC found a bit of one and reconstructed the circle.

It has been a perfect day; the sun thawing the ground a bit has made it slippery and greasy, but it's likely to freeze hard again tonight.

General Wing (Freddy Wing whom I used to know as a Captain when I was a 2nd Lieutenant in 1896), commanding the Divisional Artillery here, had a narrow escape this morning. As his motor came over the rise of the hill near Mount Kemmel, a German shrapnel burst just over him; breaking the glass in his car and sending a bullet through his chauffeur's arm. This bullet made a tiny little hole, like a rifle bullet.

January 31st

Owing to the concentration of three German corps on the Menin–Courtrai road, all our front lines were ordered to be reinforced 25%, so I had to send one platoon to the trenches and one to the dug-outs which have been rebuilt – Gilliland and Tuckett; they will relieve each other tonight. The Huns apparently have a big (11 inch) howitzer (the Jack Johnson) here now, as they put one slap into H3, making such a hole (22 inches wide and 9–10 feet deep) that we were most of last night building fresh trenches and parapet round it. The enemy also scared the life out of the men in the dug-outs by placing a dozen or so shells round them, but only one went really close, and we suggest turning the hole it has made into a dug-out; it would hold comfortably fifteen men. Our guns will have to destroy this monster. Two men were killed yesterday when the shell burst in H3. They were blown out of the trench, and, if not killed outright, possibly got up and ran, half stunned, into the open, where they were shot down and the Germans opened rapid fire on them. My remaining two platoons I had to take up to Head Quarters as a guard and reserve, bringing them back here at daybreak. My throat is making me feel below par, and after walking all round the trenches posting Gilliland's platoon in H3, I returned to Head Quarters. As I was dozing, feeling really awfully tired, down came a message from Festing, who was superintending the rebuilding of H3, telling me to come up to relieve him, and I was there from 9 pm to midnight, very cold; little sniping though, but there was a considerable amount of musketry fire on our flanks; mostly, I believe on our side. Told my Sergeant-Major to wake me at 5.30 am. At ten to five he came in and woke me up. Told him to call me again at 5.15 am but no use, couldn't go to sleep again. So up I got and put on my belt, etc, and hung about in the bleak, bleak dawn till a party of B Company came down to relieve me, and I could return to Kemmel. Directly I arrived, back to bed at once, and I never got up till 10 am, when I found it snowing fast. After breakfast and my 'Service', bed again, from just after midday to 2.30 pm, to awake and find the guns thundering and the sky cloudless. The girl has just come in to say a big shell burst close to the school not a minute from here. Told her I trusted they wouldn't come any nearer, but she smiled and agreed; perfectly calm and collected.

They were here when the Germans passed through on their way to Paris! They only outraged one woman in the place and she was enceinte; and before her seven children too, and the louder the children yelled the more the brutes tortured her!

The Prussian and Bavarian officers were very much at daggers drawn one with the other, and there were continual private quarrels among them in the hotel here. For several weeks before the war the (and presumably others) district was overrun by German 'travellers', who with two or three articles on which they placed an impossible price (safety pins ½ each, towels one franc each), used to gain entrance to all the houses around and collect information. A man went up to a farm and asked for some ham. They had none. 'What, you have none; why you killed a pig only fifteen days ago?' For such little details were noticed. The place was packed with troops, and the horses were, apparently, never un-harnessed or un-saddled all the time.

I believe the Church here is quite an interesting old place, but it is locked up and no one can get into it now. First, the British authorities locked the belfry as they would not allow the clock to be wound up (it would naturally tell the enemy that people were living here), and then some rotten Tommies were found dancing in the Church, so the authorities quite rightly locked up the whole place. It's different when troops have to be billeted in a Church, as at West Outre, but even that I believe is unnecessary. Our RC Chaplain had to stop men billeted there smoking during Mass, which he says in the Chancel. But upon my word, it's surprising how just ignorant the lower classes are towards all things religious. They don't mean to be irreligious I am sure, but they are simply thoughtless, and have been taught in our Board Schools.

We dug into several corpses yesterday filling sandbags; took the hand off one, came on the feet of another, and the body I believe of another, while cutting a trench. But, thank God, night was merciful and hid such horrors from me. I don't mind them, one is callous out here, but I think it's my sense of fastidiousness makes me hate all that sort of thing. We covered over one poor unburied Gordon: he was so soft we couldn't move him to a grave. But we couldn't do more, there are so many about here and the only thing is quick lime. Impossible to ask a man to search for their identity discs now.

February 1st

A quiet night as far as our trenches were concerned, though on our right there were some heavy outbursts of musketry.

I stood to arms at 5.15 am and during the half hour we were waiting for B Company to take our place there was a heavy rattle of musketry and a number of flares sent up about J and K trenches, on our left, and the guns were firing too.

It was like a display of summer lightning. A momentary glow in the skies on my left, followed many seconds later by the sound of the gun, before which I could see the equally evanescent glow to my front where the shell had burst. I think the Germans must have made an attack of some sort. But it was not very severe apparently.

A topping spring day. It was a white frost about midnight, but could not have lasted long, as all the place is mud once more. But the air is soft and mild. Just the very day for a hunt – and scent would have been grand.

The women here tell me a lot of the people in Kemmel sell cognac and braut wein sub rosa, and they put peppercorns into it to make it 'bite' more. This concoction makes men simply *mad*, crazy. I have reported it to the Head Quarters staff and told them where they sell the stuff. They've been waiting to lay hold of some of these sweeps who make our men drunk.

My report of a big fight south of Ypres on the Kaiser's birthday, is, I see, confirmed by the papers, there being also heavy fighting at La Bassée.

February 2nd

My 41st birthday, oh lor! In these last four days my two

platoons which I had to send up to reinforce the two companies in the front line had one killed, four wounded, and three men crushed by being blown up by a shell in the dug-outs, or getting mud etc, blown on to them. They are not bad, only complaining of their backs. The Battalion lost in all four killed and some dozen men wounded, quite a heavy casualty list for four days outpost work. One shell falling behind H3 blew up an engineer officer we buried there the first week in December. A Sergeant took off his spurs and taking off one spur he felt the knee give way! Horrid, offered the spurs to me, I fear I am superstitious, I couldn't use anything belonging to a dead man.

A parcel of a hundred Tinder Lighters arrived, addressed to me, sent by 'some friends at Clandeboye'. So have just written a note of thanks to Lady Dufferin. Two pounds of 'My Mixture' arrived this morning enclosing a little note of birthday wishes, and I think you know dear, how pleased I was, and I know how pleased you will be to know the present arrived so à propos.

The very worst billets we have ever had. The officers' is an estaminet where the owners are poor and badly equipped with table utensils, and also very averse to putting themselves out for us (which, I foretell, is going to be unpleasant for them) and our men in barns and lofts, with practically no straw. Am trying to get some straw for them to lie on. It was raining this morning and the mud is as bad as ever, but it's not quite so cold.

A large number of troops have passed through here the last two days, going northwards, several batteries of all kinds, and some brigades of infantry; some of the artillery are from India, as their transport is drawn by mules driven by natives, who, poor wretches, look the picture of misery huddled up in their wraps in the damp and rain.

February 4th

Yesterday I met a gunner Captain who asked me what sort of a time we were having in the trenches. I told him we all wished he and his blessed guns would knock out the German guns who were bombarding us. He replied that he quite felt for us, but that some people thought the proper target was the enemy's trenches, to which I replied that those people ought to put in a day in our trenches when they were being shelled. He said they had not as much ammunition as they'd like, as there were strict orders to build up big reserves against our advance in the near future, and that when they once got the position of an enemy trench properly marked, they could place their shells into it accurately every time. They had only a few days ago a direct hit on one of the German guns.

This morning the Germans were wasting a lot of ammunition over Kemmel, apparently trying to find our guns, and by the volumes of smoke and dust they were searching for them with their big howitzers.

Got granted eight days leave and left Locre at 7.30 pm in the tool limber with one of our CQMS's and a Lance Corporal, also going on leave. Got a chair put in the limber for me to sit on, but even going at a walking pace, I got jolly well shaken up over the pavé, and can faintly imagine what gunners feel when riding on the gun carriage. Our train leaves Bailleul at 10.35 pm and arrives at Boulogne shortly after 3 am and we don't get a boat before 10 am I hear.

February 5th

Arrived at Boulogne about 4.30 am. I went straight to the hotel. Got three hours sleep, a jolly good bath, breakfast and on to the boat about 10 am where, to my surprise and pleasure, I found Munro, also on leave. Boat left at 10.30 and after a topping passage we got to Folkestone and thence to Victoria, arriving 2.30 pm.

Round Armentières way the York and Lancasters had the Saxons opposite them and for some six weeks after Xmas there had been peace. The Saxons said they'd no quarrel with us, and everyday soldiers of both sides were to be seen walking in front of their respective parapets not 100 yards from each other; no shooting or sniping. At first they used to talk to each other, but that was stopped. Erecting wire entanglements one day, a Tommy picked up a roll of wire, 'Hi, hi', shouted the Teuton, 'put it down, that's ours', and Tommy Atkins put it down. There is a listening post between the two lines, and at dusk there was always a rush for this post and whichever side got there first was allowed to hold it. On another occasion Tommy Atkins was hammering in a post when a Saxon came across and offered him the loan of a maul.

However, at last the Colonel of the York and Lancasters said this nonsense must cease and war must start again and told the Captain in the trenches to fire on the Germans. So the Captain sent over two or three high shots and signalled the Saxons to get in under cover. They merely waved their hands at him. However, there is now a 'state of war' between the two lines.

A Subaltern, a few hours previous to the new 'declaration of war' had a rotten time. Had been inspecting a piece of new parapet when he slipped back and fell into a mass of boggy clay, and could not get out or get his feet even out of his boots. It was getting lighter and lighter each minute. His men and the Saxons had agreed to commence war again at daylight. Would he be the first victim? He squirmed and struggled; still the dawn rose higher and higher; at last a man of his came back for him and helped him down into his own trench just in time.

The 'war summary' of two or three days ago contains a funny story. The Turks are jubilant over the capture of an English colour. Now on the perimeter of all camps are certain places marked by yellow flags with, for white troops a white centre, for black troops, a black centre. A party of Arabs crawled up one night and captured a yellow flag with a black centre and went off with it singing songs of Araby. The Quartermaster has forwarded his indent for another flag.

February 13th

Returned off eight days leave tonight. Left Victoria at 8.30 am and arrived at Bailleul, some 5 miles from the firing line, at 7 pm.

A Turkish spy managed to slip through into one of the Havre boats to England a fortnight ago. He was caught in Southampton; had only been some two hours in the harbour, but he had in that time managed to make quite a useful plan of the docks. He was taken back in a troop ship to Havre, tried by court martial and Agnew told me when he left Havre the man was to be shot, so I expect he's dead by now. The Staff Captain at Havre responsible for passengers to England got Hades over it.

On our way across yesterday from Folkestone to Boulogne, we passed two of our submarines on guard close to the lightship. Rained all this morning, but cleared up in the afternoon. The Battalion marched off at 6 pm for the trenches, D Company sending a platoon to each of the two companies in the trenches and in Support; one platoon to the fortified house, and one platoon to Battalion Head Quarters. I am left with eighteen men in Kemmel with A Company which is in Reserve. They shelled Kemmel today in their efforts to find our guns, and one shell burst within 30 yards of the house we are in, shattering the windows – and it's cold tonight, despite the shutters. Once more, bless those Germans.

I was told on authentic authority (which is probably not worth much) that we had sent transports to Japan to bring over Japanese troops, and that there are now several Japanese ambulances already in England.

February 14th

A cold night, no fire, as we had no chance of getting any wood last night, and the shutters did not keep out the cold. However, with two sandbags on each leg I managed to get to sleep on the spring mattress, two of which are on the floor of this room. Awoke at 5.30 am to another wet, miserable, windy day. About 10 am we began to hear the German shells coming over in their unavailing efforts to find our guns. They kept it up, high explosive and shrapnel, till after midday, but the shelling was not heavy.

The week I left for leave I hear two of the Royal Scots Fusiliers were shot in Locre for being absent from parade for the trenches. It took three volleys to kill one of them. The men of the firing party are so stupid, they will not understand that the kindest thing they can do is to shoot straight. Two of the Middlesex were also shot the same week for similar offences. Some time ago two men were shot in Rouen for being absent parading for the draft for the front. Seems severe, but it was becoming almost impossible to collect a draft up to time; not that men were not keen to get to the front, but they got drunk in Rouen and went absent. Each man of a draft is now personally warned of the death penalty for this offence. The man of my Company who was tried for sleeping at his post, got off with three months owing to a technicality. He was very lucky.

February 15th

Last night I was sent up to the trenches where Davey and his platoon were, to tell him what was wanted. Never left the place till 11.30 pm. Very heavy rifle fire about 9 pm on our left, and our guns were going all night. The Germans sent some half dozen field gun shrapnel across to the Wiltshires about 8.30 pm but don't fancy they did much harm. The Germans made an attack on the trenches between the 27th and 28th Divisions during the afternoon. They succeeded in taking the trenches, but these were recaptured this morning at 5.30 am.

It is reported the enemy are to make a general attack along the whole line, either today or tomorrow, and for some reason or other the Staff are very keen on getting hold of a German prisoner. Horrible day: rain and snow and sleet, and even half an hour sunshine: all the district a quagmire. Poor Davey was shot through the head this morning and died in his trench at midday. I had warned him about bullets coming down along the trench from the left. He was a tall lad, some six foot one or so. He got his commission from the HAC.

9.30 pm. Our guns bombarding the Germans on our left, probably the enemy opposite the 27th Division. I had to take some sheets of galvanised iron up to a small post the RE are fortifying, and on my way up I heard a clatter and a yell, and a man dropped, luckily only slightly wounded. He let his sheet of iron fall on another man's toe, and nearly cut his foot off, at least so the other man said.

February 16th

Davey was brought down to our dressing station last night. He was shot bang through the head from front to rear. We buried him at 9 am this morning. All of us here attended, and some dozen men too. I had to read the service, or part of it. A most heart-breaking job as far as I am concerned, and it affected me as much as if it were a relative of mine. I hate funerals, but no one else would take it on, and of course it was my job.

The half dozen shells the Germans threw over the lines the night before last, about 9 pm, went over K trenches where the HAC were, and killed two men, and wounded eighteen, one or two severely.

1 pm. The Germans sent a few shrapnel over us here in Kemmel. They were apparently bursting just beyond the town. They have some aeroplanes up, as it's a bright, cold, sunny day for a change.

6 pm. The enemy sent some more shrapnel over us in their efforts to find our guns. One of their aeroplanes was over us and received a lot of attention from our guns, and our aeroplanes were shelled by the Germans, but, so far as we could see, nothing happened. The effect of the shell bursts was very pretty against the clear blue sky.

February 17th

Shelling intermittently on both sides today; the enemy still anxious to find our guns. I was paddling in the mud behind our trenches last night from 8 to 11.30 pm filling sandbags, building parapets, and clearing drains.

Today rain again, and at 4 pm a telephone message to say the 7th Brigade will not be relieved till further orders, so instead of going back to West Outre or Locre tonight, we have to stop out here.

February 18th

Strolled up to Battalion Head Quarters for orders but they had none for me, so I came back to Kemmel, thanking Fate for it was a simply beastly night. Rain storms at frequent intervals. On the way up a 'fly by night' struck into the hedge quite close to me, and I 'bobbed' so much I nearly fell over my feet which are encased in ammunition boots one and a half sizes too big for me.

Our other Brigade (the 9th, we are the 7th, and the 8th Brigade left us to strengthen the line on our left some weeks ago) marched to Ypres yesterday in all the heavy rain to reinforce the line there. Last night the 27th Division recovered the trenches which were taken from them three days ago by the enemy. The Division, I am told, had a thousand casualties during that attack (when the trenches were taken from them).

This Division and the 28th are somewhere on the line east of Dichebusche, just south of Ypres; about Voormezeele I fancy the trenches run before they turn eastward to encircle Ypres. The Brigadier said we may have to remain here for another three or four days. B Company had a man killed and four wounded yesterday, and so far the Battalion has lost in four days one officer and one man killed, six wounded and three accidentally wounded, as the fool who let his rifle off in the support barn wounded three men, not two.

The HAC in J trenches have been losing rather heavily from shell and rifle fire, and the other night a house, which had been pretty well shelled before, suddenly collapsed, burying 23 men out of 24 who were lying in support in the cellar. They were all dug out, but some of them were badly hurt. Their Colonel, Treffry, told me one man last night was shot through the heart as he was just stepping into his trench, and he gave a most piercing scream, the reflex action of his muscles, as he was killed instantaneously. He also told me the trenches of the 27th Division were very wet and bad, a case of if you put your head above the parapet you got shot, and if you kept it down you got drowned. So, after all, we in our trenches, have no business to grumble.

A lady who was shown over the *Lion*, now being repaired after the Dogger Bank action, somewhere in the north of England, wrote to one of our fellows saying the vessel had fourteen huge holes through her. They are working on her night and day and she will soon be ready for action again. Just been down to the 'Chateau du Lievre', a small estaminet where my men are living in the loft. We had a glass of cognac each (two sous a glass!) Had I not been told, I'd have said it was toast and water which had been kept in a brandy cask. The shrill voiced female who runs the place told me she had the place full of German soldiers last August, and that they all behaved very 'gentil' except that, bar one man, they paid for neither food nor drink.

One man paid and he asked for some civilian clothes (which he did not get) as he said war was a terrible thing and he'd had enough of it. But the woman told me that where the officers were, the Germans paid for everything, and any man not paying got a hiding with fist or whip from his officer. The men seemed terrified of their officers. On the whole the German troops seemed to have behaved fairly (only fairly) decently in Kemmel, and it is surprising therefore, to learn of their behaviour in Bailleul, where the nuns of the convent and the girls sent to the convent for safety were shockingly abused; and of other deeds too horrible to mention which are said to have been committed by the officers personally.

Certainly the German officer has so blackened his reputation that no bravery in the field can ever brighten it again. The world admires brave men, but has no use for savage beasts, and though

109

one gladly records instances of their decent behaviour, the stories of their atrocities are too common and too easily authenticated to in any way whitewash them. Owing to the German 'Blockade' of our coasts, the poor wretches who went on leave last night are all hung up at Boulogne, and the officers and men now in England, waiting to return, have to just wait. However, they at least won't worry, I expect. Quite right though for England to take every precaution and to clear any vagrant submarines out of the Channel first.

One of our servants said to his master the other day, 'Oh, Sir, that there chloride of lime you give me did a lot of good'. It appeared he meant Chloridine.

I hear this, the 3rd Division, is called 'the Morgue of the British Army', because we are having such rotten treatment. Very bad trenches: very little coke or charcoal to burn, rotten billets, no amusements for the men, and lately only two Brigades in the Division instead of three, and now, of course we are the only Brigade in the Division. During the course of the War this Division has suffered very, very heavily, and has had no rest, and this it badly wants. Our Padre (RC) came in to see us this afternoon and told us of some executions at which he had been present.

Two men were shot last Monday for 'absence from the trenches', and the other time one of the men shot was a lad not eighteen years of age; his Battalion are very upset at his execution. It seems his father, an old Reservist in the Gordons, has just been killed, and the lad got very unhappy at hearing this and hooked it one night when his Battalion was for the trenches. Stupidly and inadvisedly he pleaded 'Guilty' and never brought this fact, which might have been considered 'extenuating', forward.

One poor chap required three volleys, as the firing party were very nervous, although the Padre adjured them to shoot straight as the kindest thing to do. The men, on the whole, he said, met their death very pluckily.

February 19th

Last night I took some stores up to a blockhouse behind our line and took Tyndall, a youngster in the Dublin Fusiliers SR who has just joined us, with me. While at the blockhouse a tremendous fusillade broke out in front and we waited till it died down. We then pushed on and I showed him round the trenches, and found all the fusillade came from the East Lancashires. They are everlastingly 'funk firing' which always puts the fear of Heaven into the enemy and starts them off 'funk firing' and any working parties going up to the trenches have a most unpleasant and dangerous trip and a lot of men have been killed and wounded in these fatigue parties from this cause. Got back to Kemmel about 8 pm and, thank God, had not to go up again. It really is rotten work walking up to the trenches and gets on one's nerves.

This morning, no rain for a wonder, I went for a walk and discovered a battery of Howitzers in a farm, perfectly concealed in an enclosed 'walk' made of thatch. Wood and iron platforms, 5 inch guns, a vast supply of 100 lb and 120 lb shells, and although the battery is only 1100 yards from the nearest German trenches, they have so far not been spotted, although they have been there several weeks. Of course, on a clear day, when aeroplanes are about, the battery lie very close, and there is no movement to 'give the show away' to the overhead patrols.

Met an RE officer on my way back, and had a chat with him. The 28th Division (he said, but probably the losses are between the 27th and 28th Divisions) lost a thousand casualties in the three days when the enemy assaulted our trenches at St Eloi, in front of Vierstaate and Vormezeele the beginning of the week.

A friend of his went over to visit a relative, a private, in .... Light Infantry (Canadian) and asked if they'd had any casualties lately. 'Oh! we shot an officer!' I hear the Canadians on Salisbury Plain say they'll shoot all their officers, whose appointments were apparently political. But on all sides I hear the contingent is a very useless mob, so undisciplined.

The late German Ambassador in London, Lichnowsky, has, I hear, enlisted as a private in the German Army, and all the old German diplomatists have gone to 1000 to 3 with the Emperor and his leaders. The Ambassador, sometime before the War was ever thought of, met Walter Long at a private dinner party and asked him about the state of Ireland. Long said he thought there was certain to be civil war there. Lichnowsky repeated this to the Emperor.

My RE friend happened to be in the House and seated close to the Ambassador when Redmond made his famous speech saying we could leave the defence of Ireland to the Irish. He told me the Ambassador turned white, and, leaving immediately, had to be supported into his carriage, the shock of this news had so great a physical effect on him. There are some fine dummy guns behind us which the Germans have been shelling lately. The other day they sent in some forty shells at them.

This from General Haldane: When the Russian Prince . . . came over here the other day to present the order of St George to various people, including HRH, he said that the Russian advance in the north of Pomerania was a feint to draw off the Germans and to permit an advance into Silesia. This has apparently been successful, as the Germans sent four corps north and advanced on the Russians who retired to draw them on. This has permitted a Russian advance in Silesia.

February 20th

The officer commanding the Lincolns brought in several of the Gordons who were killed on December 14th, and he said he found a number of them with the first aid bandage on, others in the act of putting the bandage on, and all of them with a bayonet stab in the throat. The brutes of Germans had evidently gone out at dark and killed as many of the wounded as lay near their own trenches.

Some of the HAC attached to us as probationary officers told me that in their first billet in Kemmel, they found piles of arms

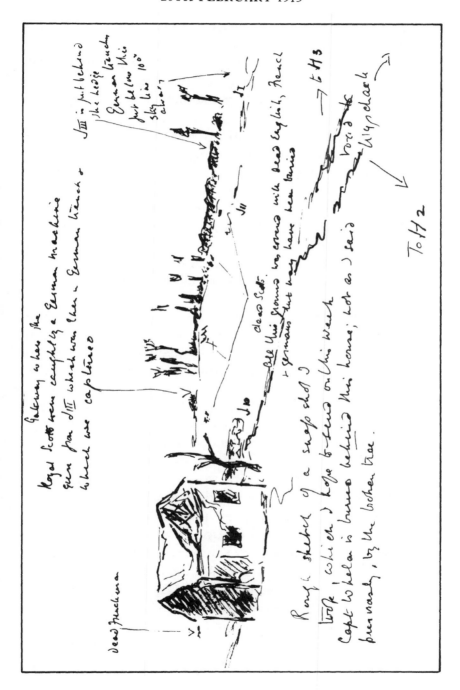

and legs mouldering and stinking. It has evidently been a French dressing station and the slovenly French orderlies had just thrown the amputated legs and arms into a room and left them there instead of burying them. It's almost incredible that men educated as doctors could allow such a thing to be done by orderlies.

Last night sixty of my Company took over J1, a fire trench only some 150 yards from the enemy's lines in Petit Bois, and also a splendidly built support trench J10, eighty yards in rear of it.

I went out in front of J1 to inspect the wire entanglements and found three rows of entanglements there, also a very dead Frenchman, or rather the remains of one. The feet of two poor fellows we buried behind H2 are showing above the ground. The rain of the last few days is washing the earth away from off them.

A fine bright day, and aeroplanes overhead. There was half an hour's heavy bombardment away on our left: apparently from the French lines about Ypres. No mails yesterday, except parcels which had been in the country two or three days; all traffic was held up on the 18th until, I suppose, our Navy certified the Channel safe. This gave those on leave in England an extra twenty four hours, and those going on leave were stopped at Boulogne; but I understood all leave counts from the time they leave Boulgone, so they won't lose any time in England. The Kaiser's attempt to blockade us had therefore made several hundred officers and men happy; bless him.

Took a walk around Kemmel town this morning. I don't think out of a town of some 4,800 inhabitants there is one house quite intact and undamaged by shrapnel, and half the place is in ruins, blown down completely. We passed one building, the front of which is completely wrecked. The wretched occupier has partly blocked up the frameless windows with bricks, above which one can see into a shattered interior. However, outside the door hung a pig; inside we saw portions of the other half, a plate of apples and a few odd things on sale. There are some dozen shops of sorts where bread, butter, candles, chocolates and sweets, the latter three articles mostly from England, can be bought, and milk and eggs can be easily obtained.

We passed a gang of Belgian peasants working at trench digging under the direction of a sapper. They work from about 7.30 am to 12.30 pm at 4 francs a day for the seven days. Most of them live in and around Locre, and some even in Bailleul, eight miles away, so that they all do a bit of walking before they get to their work. Our padre had mass in the church this morning at 7.30. The local curé hasn't been near here since last October, and lives in Bailleul, and had the cheek to ask our padre to hold a service or two here. A number of our men and a crowd of civilians attended. The interior of the church is smothered in masonry dust. A shell has pierced the chancel behind the High Altar and shattered it, and littered the chancel with debris, so the padre officiated at a side altar. I took a couple of photographs of the interior. A lot of the stained glass windows are shattered with shrapnel. It is remarkable that the Christ on the outside wall of the church is quite untouched, though a shell burst at the foot of the cross and the wall all round is pitted with shrapnel.

But similar instances are common and men who have been out here since Mons, have wondered at the way the Sacred Image has so very generally escaped damage. Is it remarkable, I wonder? The Church is very old, possibly 14th century, or earlier, though the oldest date we could decipher on any monument was 1720, but there were monuments some century or more older.

Very heavy thunder about 1.30 and we got the tail end of the thunderstorm – and it's become so cold and damp again. One of my men, attached to B Company, was hit in the chest last night before he'd been in the trench ten minutes. I saw him lying in the mud. I hear he was only grazed though, and could have walked down to the doctor, but he preferred to lie in the mud for an hour till a stretcher came to carry him down.

The other night Captain Becher, returning from the trenches, found two men beside the roadway peering through the dark into the ditch. He joined them and eventually distinguished a head. A question and a quavering voice from the water. 'I belong to the Wilts'; another question as to why he preferred to lie in the stream. 'The bullets is coming so thick.' A few well chosen expressive expletives of a virulent and pungent nature brought the 'thing' out of his retreat, and a kick or two sent the coward on his way to the trenches. The bullets do come over the road nastily, but they can't be helped, and if we all took cover every time one came, we'd never get up the road at all. But I do so pity that miserable wretch, for every moment he lives out here must be filled, for him, with all the terrors of Hell. One of our fellows, while a German flare lit up his trench as it shot over it, saw half a dozen of our raw Irishmen on their knees, praying to the Virgin as if their last hour had come. I don't think it's a bad thing for men to pray at any time, but when they are in the trenches a man should pray standing up; with his rifle ready. I think too, such a man's prayers are more efficient. The people here say the weather we are having is quite unusual at this time of the year, and that they never expect any dry weather before the end of April. Jolly climate! Flanders.

February 21st

I was sent up to the trenches last night in place of a subaltern who was sick, and I had not done any duty in the trenches before this time, so it was only fair I should go up. Took over J1 and J10, a subaltern and thirty men in J1 and myself and thirty-five men supporting him in J10. A nice moonlight night and we buried a couple of dead Frenchmen and one of our own who was blown out of our trench about three weeks ago. We found him, his face smashed in and both legs gone. I came across one of his legs, in the boot and puttee, this morning, and buried it. A heavy fire round St Eloi about 10 pm last night, as if the Germans were attacking, but it died down in half an hour. A flare fell into the thatch of a small farm to our left front and the house was burnt to the ground this morning. A bright day but the country clothed in a dense mist and we were able to walk about. We found two Germans of, by the lions on the buttons, a Bavarian regiment I believe (uniform – grey with red pipings and red facings), and two or three more Frenchmen. We buried all of them. Horrible sights, they'd been there at least five months. Some of my men went through their pockets! and got some tiny souvenirs for their disagreeable job. I collared a little cheap locket, found in a German's pocket, containing evidently the photographs of his children, a little girl and a little boy. Poor fellow, sad he should lose his life in such a rotten cause. We discovered another corpse in the gutter, alongside the road, from which all the drinking water is, and has been, drawn for months; the man had been there also since last September. I had him covered up and diverted the stream round his bones, instead of over them. Callous as one does become, I'll never get used to it, it so disgusts me, and I've still rather a childish dread of dead people in the dark, and always dislike the little bit of our way up here which passes through our Military cemetery at Kemmel, into a newly dug grave in which I nearly fell last night. I have a telephone in my trench in direct communication with our artillery, and if we are being badly shelled I send an SOS signal down the line. Their operators *at once* attend to my message, and the guns are switched on. Yesterday the Huns put sixteen shells round this trench; some of them fortunately blind ones. Kearns switched on the artillery to the place he thought the Germans were shelling us from, and after three shots from us the Germans stopped shooting.

I'm told, with how much truth I know not, that our artillery put the German 8.5 howitzer out of action day before yesterday. Hope it will not recover.

A yarn – probably untrue, though it's quite possible with our Special Reservists:

After a burst of rapid fire an East Lancashire officer asked one of his men if he had any cartridges left. 'Yus, Sir, five in the box and one up the funnel!' For your feminine intelligence, dear, he meant five in the magazine and one in the chamber of his rifle.

Captain Whelan's grave was destroyed and trodden down, so I had it made up and surrounded with wire, and a new cross over it.

Had a walk round H2 and H3. In front of H3 I saw five of the Gordons and they were smelling most unpleasantly. Got the subaltern in H3 to bury two of them. On the parapet of H2 noticed the left leg, from the top of the hip to the foot, of a Frenchman. It was covered by a bit of red trouser, probably blown up by a shell. Had that buried too. In a Jack Johnstone hole full of water within 30 yards of my trench, and on the road, I noticed a body, the face above water, a bearded German. He had been there for months. Could do nothing but fill the hole in with stones and rocks. One never sees these terrible things on ordinary days, as by day it's impossible to walk about outside your trench, and by night one sees nothing. And men have been getting drinking water from streams fouled in this manner; ignorance, laziness and I am sure carelessness too. A most fortunate opportunity to bury all these poor fragments, as it will help to prevent unpleasantness later on.

February 23rd

We returned to our billets at West Outre last night, I got home about 10 pm, but my Company did not all get back till after 2 am, as some of our Companies, to which platoons of my men were attached, were very late in being relieved. During the nine days we had four killed and twenty-three wounded, my Company losing one killed and five wounded, while it also has nineteen men admitted sick to hospital with bad feet etc.

Some Germans surrendered to the Wiltshires last night; two men walked into their lines in the fog, whether purposely or not I can't say. One was a very old man for a soldier, over fifty, and in a dreadful state.

During the reliefs one man of the Middlesex got a 'fly by night' through his leg, and a man of the Buffs got one through the heart.

A Company lost a Sergeant killed and one man wounded the day before yesterday. In the mist they went out to bury two Gordons just in front of their wire. The mist lifted and the Germans shot them. The three or four other men of the party had a run for it. One of my youngsters tells me that he watched a man in his trench. This fellow had, during the day, seventeen cans (canteens) of tea, and for his tea finished off one tin of Machonochie, one tin of bully beef, and one tin of jam with, of course, biscuits. And yet he is a miserable emaciated looking man.

Another of my youngsters heard three men squabbling in his trench. He crept along to them, and the Lance Corporal immediately explained, 'Please Sir, these two men won't do a thing I tell them', on which both men together replied, 'Please Sir, he's a Welshman, Sir, and speaks to us in Welsh, and we can't understand him'.

But the 3rd Battalion enlisted a number of Welshmen. A few days ago among the letters of the Company, which were sent into me for censoring, I found one written in Welsh. I returned it to the writer and said he must re-write it in English.

I got on my ex-hurdle racer and rode into Bailleul this afternoon to send off a cable. Found I could only send it off through the courtesy of the Signalling officer there, and he has to send a cyclist messenger to the French Post Office at Hazebrouck, there being no direct communication for private messages to England from Bailleul. On my way back I passed a gang of Belgian soldiers, with spades, returning from work on the roads. I didn't take much notice of them except that among the two dozen or so I saw a criminal looking face or two. But there were none of them fine looking men, rather on the small side than anything else.

I didn't remain longer in the place than to send my cable. The town has plenty of 'va et vient' about it, and is crowded with khaki, but I saw no civilians of even a decent bourgeois class; all peasantry and little shop-keepers, and the place did not interest me.

119

From a German prisoner we hear that the War is to be over by the end of June – unfortunately for the prophecy the Hun foretold that we should lose! He's an optimist though, must be.

February 24th

Hard frost last night and snow showers this morning. The French Summary states that from information collected all along the line, from the sea to Switzerland, the enemy seem short of ammunition. In our Summary it is stated the enemy are using dum-dum bullets, and reverse the bullets in the cartridges, firing them base foremost. Several clips of cartridges with bullets reversed in the cartridges were found on a dead German. This accounts for the bad wounds sometimes made. All leave is to stop after March. What a good thing I get my leave in time! But I expect this is only a temporary order, and that leave will be opened again when the present tension is relaxed. Head Quarters of my Company are in the same corner estaminet we've been in several times before. We have a decent comfortable sitting room (in which two officers sleep) and I have a bedroom and nice bed off the sitting room, *with* washstand etc. Quite a treat. My other officers sleep across the way. Our servants share the family living room and store where they cook for us. The place has the drawback of being rather noisy. The Belgian inhabitants scream instead of talk, and there are several screaming children to add to the general row. One of our fellows passed a trench carrying a huge jar of water. A dirty ruffian yelled out to him, 'Hi Murphy, give us a mouthful of that water'. 'I will not, but I'll give ye a canteenful if ye like!!!' Another of my subalterns was bothered by a miserable man who came up to him in the trench with a, 'Please Sir, I've got dysentery'. 'Oh! have you? Sergeant, what's the matter with this man?' 'Nothing Sir, that I know of, but he's eaten two tins of jam today!' One result of the fight on December 14th was the capture, by the Royal Scots, of one of the enemy's forward trenches, and this Battalion had to hold this particular trench for three or four days. The way to it led through a gateway about which there were many casualties, and which is now known as Hell Gate. It is watched by a German maxim, and the German trenches are not eighty yards away. The gate is filled with barbed wire obstacles, and is awkward to pass through in the dark.

Kearns gave me an amusing account of his platoon going into this trench. They got tangled up in the wire and it was, 'Mick me trousers is ripped', or 'Murphy mind the wire will ye', 'Jock me coat's cot, lift the tails for me', all within a few yards of that – maxim, and Kearns knew it was there.

He simply stood and shivered. Daren't call his men what he'd have liked; and the row they made; dropping their rifles, jangling the wire, tripping up, cursing, laughing. Fortunately I think the Germans had been so terrified by the attack of the two days previous, that probably they had left this trench. However, they are, I believe, back there now, but luckily we do not hold the vis a vis trench.

The Second Battalion has had 25 reinforcements up to date. They came out 1,100 strong. Average each reinforcement at only 80 men, 25 x 80 = 2,000 – 3,100 men in all, and our present strength is roughly 900. 2,200 men killed, wounded, missing and sick. Of course the majority sick seems very heavy wastage for 6½ months. I suppose the Battalion has lost about 1,000 in killed, wounded and missing. They went up to Neuve Chapelle about 800 strong, and after some eight days fighting they came out only 130 strong! The other day a youngster in Kemmel picked up a German shell which had fallen blind; he started to carry it away when it exploded. I believe there was nothing to bury. Near West Outre a kiddie was playing with a hand grenade which went off. He was buried today. I was told he was lying in his people's farm all yesterday, just covered with a sheet, and none of them seemed to mind, they all went about their usual daily duties quite peacefully.

February 25th

Found my little gold safety pin with the little tiny ruby in it. It fell out of my knapsack; don't know how it got there. Must have got caught in my woolley I was wearing when I lost it, and thence dropped into the sack when I put the woolley into it sometime. I feel quite happy at finding it, and look on it as a real good omen.

We are ordered to train 30% of our men in the use and throwing of hand grenades. When the 28th Division were so cut up ten days ago, I hear the enemy sapped close up to their trenches and then blew up the trenches with mines, and though our fellows had plenty of grenades in their trenches, they didn't know how to use them. Had they done so they could have cleared the enemy's sap. I don't know how to use the beastly dangerous things, but I mean to learn how.

A Summary issued today tells us that we still have only Bavarians opposite us, but they are their indifferent troops, ersatz reserve etc, round Wyschaete. It is reported in the German Press that a census is being taken of men of the 1883-1885 classes, that is of men between 49 and 51. It is believed that this census portends the raising of the age limit of liability to military service to 51.

A Bavarian, who walked into the Wiltshire lines last Monday, said a number of his men would surrender, but that they heard our fellows shot single men coming in. He stated their trenches were very bad and constantly required baling, that they were well fed and well shod, and that the war would soon be over as Russia had been defeated. But – if he believed all this, why on earth did he surrender?

Woke up this morning to find snow falling; the country all white and the roads simply tracks of liquid mud.

Paid my Company yesterday, and a large proportion of my NCO's took the opportunity of getting drunk. All of them SR NCO's. Had them all down to my billet and talked to them. Blighters, they've so little self-respect. No use running them up before the CO; they'd be tried by court martial, and I couldn't

122

get other men to take their places. The next Company to me in billets was just as bad, and a Company being paid out today will, doubtless, follow suit.

A rifleman came up to Kearns the other day and reported he had 'crumps'. 'What?' 'Crumps Sir, crumps in the stomach.' Kearns discovered he had just eaten two tins of Machonochie Ration for his dinner, which accounted for the 'cramp'. Kearns gave him no sympathy. Poor ignorant devils, they're just like a lot of children. They are animals lacking animal instict. Animals don't gorge till they are sick.

February 26th

Hard frost last night. The men in the trenches, after all the snow and rain of the last few days and then the frosts of the last two nights, must have suffered pretty badly. We have three men in the Guard Room who will, on trial by court-martial, probably be shot. They have been wasters all the time and have all deserted, or rather, scrimshanked from the trenches and gone 'absent' for weeks at a time, and now they are certain to be sentenced to death. My Company is tonight in Reserve in Kemmel, taking on the billets of the Liverpool Scottish who left us a topping fire in the room we use as a mess. Tommy Atkins, or at any rate our fellows, have a quaint expression: verb 'To drum-up'. Apparently it means to cook, or more particularly to boil, a canteen full of tea. My hero who boasted of having drunk seventeen canteens full of tea, said he'd 'had a record day, seventeen drums up'.

A force I have heard of today for the first time is 'Kitchener's labourers'. I hear they've been going for many months at Rouen and Havre. They were dockers from London, Liverpool etc, brought out for unloading work, not enlisted at all, paid 4/- a day; a lot of hardy ruffians who used to be escorted to and from their work by a military escort to prevent them running amok in the town. I wonder if this force will get a medal. They'll have seen as much of the war as a good many staff officers and staff clerks have seen, or are ever likely to see, who will add ribbons to their coats.

February 27th

The 85th Brigade, who arrived from India only some three weeks or so ago, and who were badly cut up at Ypres a fortnight ago, and came to us to replace the 9th Brigade which took their place near Ypres, seem to have undoubtedly 'the wind up' as the expression here goes. The last four days they have been in the trenches they 'panic fired' so much that the Liverpool Scottish sent a message to their Brigadier to request that 'the panic-firing on their left might be stopped as it interfered with their working parties'. The 85th filled up a whole message book of telegraph forms sending messages to Brigade Head Quarters about 'Heavy firing' on one part or other of the line, and how they 'stood to arms twice one night' etc, etc.

Our Brigadier says that their losses at Ypres were largely their own fault. They never took the trouble to put any wire entanglements in front of their trenches, and the men removed the sandbags from their parapets and put them in the bottom of the trenches to keep their feet out of the wet. On taking over H2 the CO of the 7th Royal Fusiliers disagreed with my high parapet of sandbags I had erected after poor Davey was shot, and he had them all removed although he was warned of the sniping. Yesterday he had an officer killed in this trench at the same spot Davey was killed, and last night our fellows had to spend several hours replacing the parapet as it was.

These Belgian peasantry are about the limit. Going round Kemmel we came to a house where the smell was pretty bad; and we traced it to a heap of slack near the stove. The woman told us she mixed this with human excreta, and certainly it burnt very well and made an excellent stove fuel for those whose senses are not too fastidious.

This morning the Hun has been shelling Kemmel ridge quite heavily; firing salvoes of three or four shots over the town, bursting them about 1½ miles beyond us. But one or two have burst much closer, and a few odd shrapnel having hit the billets of the 4th South Lancashires (T), they were moved out of them.

5 pm. All the afternoon the Germans have been intermittently shelling Kemmel I hear, and during a very pleasant sleep they dropped one close to the church, within 100 yards of us; one into the chateau precincts, and one into the crossroads just beyond the chateau. The civilian inhabitants were busy packing up and ready to fly at the approach of further shells, but it seems rather like leaving it too late, should any shells elect to pay them a visit.

February 28th

Into the trenches last night; very cold and very muddy, and constant showers of sleet. One of our Brigadiers reports having read a German lamp message to the effect a general attack was to be made on our line at or after midnight. So we were all very much on the qui vive.

A rotten night as the dug-out was most uncomfortable and very cold. Intermittent firing, varied in the few silences by the earth shaking report of one of our own big guns, or the deep hollow bark of the German trench mortar somewhere on our right. The dawn broke to a fine sunny day with a freezing wind. After a biscuit and a bit of fried bacon we started on to build another dug-out and made a most successful one, but it wants straw and a bit of living in to make it really comfortable. At present it simply smells of chloride of lime which we had to put down freely, owing to this end of the trench having been dug through a cottage manure heap. I had settled on another spot, until I was told that one of my proposed walls also served to wall in a corpse. The Huns threw a few shells over Kemmel this morning, and have been sniping my corner very hot. Some dozen bullets have hit the sandbags over my dug-out and threw earth into it, and they've been splitting sandbags all along the parapet.

Well, two officers have been killed in the trench during the last fortnight, and 'forewarned is forearmed', and I am taking no risks. During my little church service two bullets flopped into the wall of my dug-out, one of them sending dirt into it. We have periscopes in the trench. Saves men putting their heads up. But all day they have been splitting our top row of sandbags, and 'plop-plopping' into our parapet and on the few occasions I have gone outside my dug-out I have had to walk bent down; not easy for me to do; so I spent all the time I possibly could in my dug-out, lying on unmitigated corrugated iron.

March 1st

Came into the Supports last night. Just before we were relieved (8.30 pm), one of my men was knocked down by a bullet which hit him in the head. I examined his head in my dug-out, and all I could find was a real big knob, size of a sparrow's egg. A bullet had either just grazed his nut, or thrown up a stone which had hit him.

One of my men in H3 got a bullet across his head, laying bare his brains. He was breathing easily, and pulse normal, so I hope he may get all right. A man in H1 was cooking his tea, and had made up his fire with a cartridge as it went off, and hit him in the finger. No serious damage done. Heavy wind and rain last night, and bitterly cold today. Errant rays of sunshine, but the sky is mostly covered with snow or rain clouds. Very cold. Intermittent showers until 6 pm when we had a very heavy thunderstorm with huge hail stones. After that it cleared up and a full moon came out. Rations were very late in arriving and we never relieved the trenches till 9 pm. In Kemmel today a man of the South Lancashires blew half his head off carrying, and presumably dropping, a hand grenade. The Huns shrapnelled Kemmel today and put one shell into the moat of the chateau where our Brigade Head Quarters are. My Company took over one forward trench and the supports and the two fortified positions this evening.

I and two officers were just outside our advanced trench, considering a piece of work to be done. As it was very bright moonlight we were all sitting down on our heels. There was a certain amount of fire from the Germans about 120 yards in front, and they seemed a bit 'on the hop', also I fancy they could see us: anyway I felt a slight blow on my arm. I thought a bit of dirt had hit me. On returning to the trench we found a bullet had gone through the outside seam of my left coat sleeve, making two holes about three inches apart, and ripped a hole one and a half inches long in the back of my coat just below the shoulder blade. Three holes in all and in neither case had it cut the lining of the coat. A wonderful escape.

March 2nd

At 12.30 am a 60 lb gun battery, if not two, firing from somewhere behind Kemmel, commenced a heavy bombardment of the German lines some mile of so north of us. I timed them and counted twenty-four shots fired in one minute and the average rate of fire for a minute was about sixteen, and the bombardment went on for an hour exactly. The rate of firing was rather low towards the end, but I estimate that battery sent over to the enemy 900 sixty pound shells. The ordinary field gun shell is 18 lbs, but 'Mother', a big 15 inch gun which has just arrived in these parts under charge of some marines, throws a shell of, I hear, 2,000 lbs, almost a ton, and it has a back-blast (i.e. on exploding the effects are felt behind it) of 800 yards (and the concrete base splits up) and is liable to injure anyone half a mile behind where the shell lands, and I am told it has a devastating effect of twelve acres.

At 4.30 am a young gunner officer arrived at my dug-out! I sent him on to H2 where he can observe better, as he was sent up to observe artillery fire today. He'd only been out a fortnight. They all sleep in 'piggies' (I eventually gleaned what he meant): in fleabags, and he'd never seen trenches before and asked me, with wonder stealing in his be-pince-nez'd eyes, whether 'I stayed here all day!' Took him to H2 myself, and left him after an earnest prayer that he'd confine himself to the periscope and not try to put his nut over the parapet.

Just as I had settled myself to sleep again, my Canadian Leask in J1 sent down a message to suggest our guns should shrapnel Petit Bois at once, before its night garrison left for their day dugout. Did so, and half an hour later, too late I fear, some eight or ten shrapnel burst perfectly on their trenches. The Hun has a trench mortar somewhere in Petit Bois, for he sent three or four bombs into the Wilts trenches somewhere about J2 about 150 yards away.

About 6 am Corporal Mills ran across to me from J1 saying he was shot through the lungs. I sent him down with another man to the dressing station, and think it can only have been a graze as otherwise he could never have walked. Mills is under arrest and awaiting a court-martial, but this wound may 'wash out this now'.

This morning about 4.30 the Germans started to shell the trenches near us with a field gun, and favoured us with half a dozen within ten yards of our trench. Was glad when they stopped. Nasty vicious sound, the field guns. You only hear a 'woosh' and a bang, no warning beforehand. One seemed to clear my head by inches and I bowed politely and very hastily.

March 3rd

Following yesterday morning's bombardment the 27th Division captured a German trench, but now I hear we only held the trench for half an hour.

Lieutenant Tyndall, Dublin Fusiliers, SR attached to us was killed yesterday morning early. He stood up and fired some say two, others four, flares from the same spot and one after another. Either he was spotted by a sharpshooter or it was a stray bullet, but he was hit in the face, the bullet shattering his spinal cord in the neck. A very nice fellow, he only joined us a week ago. We buried him last night on our return from the trenches, together with an officer's servant, who had been sent into Kemmel to buy bread. He was killed by a stray bullet in the wood.

With regard to the incident of a bullet making three holes in my coat the other night without hurting me; within an hour of this occurrence and at the same trench, two men each got bullets in their clothes without actually wounding them.

Yesterday the Germans shelled a farmhouse about a mile from Kemmel, setting it on fire (I took a snap-shot of it burning) and injuring an officer and one or two men of artillery who were there. The injured men were taken to the Wilts' dressing station. While the Wilts' medical officer was bending down dressing a man's wound, a shrapnel burst outside in the street, and a piece, entering the room, killed the doctor at once. The room was crowded at the time, but he was the only person hit. To my relief I met an RC padre (chaplain) who buried Tyndall and the other man of ours for me, and he also buried the doctor. We have now another man awaiting burial tonight. The man who was badly wounded in the head two days ago, died without regaining consciousness.

It is dreadful how this little cemetery is growing. Last night I saw three buried, and there were seven empty graves awaiting men of the Wilts, I believe.

Much interested to hear of the German floating petrol station off the Isle of Wight, and the bottling of the two submarines. We've heard they were captured, but we are all remarking how strange it is that there is nothing about them in the newspapers, either with us or with the French. We never got to bed before midnight, and we didn't breakfast till about 11 am but as it's a steady drizzle, we are just as well sleeping while in Reserve.

March 4th

Yesterday afternoon while I was writing letters in 'Erin House' at Kemmel I heard a shot and then the most awful yells.

Thought at first a man had got shot in the street, so rushed out, and just outside the door of the room, I found my orderly Dixon writhing on the ground in the kitchen with a bullet wound in his knee. My servant (McKeown, late Mess-Sergeant to the 4th Battalion) was about to clean my pistol (Colt automatic), when Dixon took it up to show him how to take it to pieces. The stupid idiot fingering it, managed to load it, unknown to himself, and after flourishing it around, saying it was 'all right', he lowered the muzzle and the thing went off and put a bullet through the top of his knee, coming out in the pit of the knee. I expect he'll have a stiff leg all his life. But he was in awful agony and screaming and it turned me quite sick.*

We came up to the G4 and H trenches last night, and had a fairly quiet night. The Germans in a trench on S side of Petit Bois were annoying the garrison in J1, so the subaltern there fired three rifle grenades, bang, very fortunately, into their trench, and they shut up very quickly.

This morning there is intermittent shelling on both sides on our trenches.

The Germans have been using a horrid little field gun to plunk in some dozen shells in the corner formed by the H and the J trenches, bursting them 40 or 50 yards from us and considerably closer to J1 and J10.

There is a rumour that General French is coming up to Locre to see 'Grandmother' (our 15 inch howitzer) fired. 'Mother' is the name for the 9 inch gun, I understand.

Rumour also says 'Grandmama' is to be fired today and we are all very keen on seeing this and the result, but I don't fancy she will be used about here; our trenches are too close to the German trenches, and if she is fired at all, it will be at some target well behind the German lines.

Lt Grounds in H3 was just drinking a cup of tea when a bullet ripped up a sandbag and a bit of the casing flicked a piece of skin off his thumb.

* He recovered and on my return to my Battalion in July I found him on Sentry Duty as fit as ever.

About 4.30 the Germans started in again, with, I think, 4 field guns and for 20 minutes fired very viciously just at the piece of roadway between my dug-out and H3 down to J10, some 60 yards behind. They rather annoyed J10 but the nearest shell to my dug-out burst some 30 yards away. I kept in my dug-out all the time as I thought it just as likely they'd put all the sandbags and roof down on top of me, as they'd damage me if I got out. Of course, if they'd been using their HE shells we'd have all shifted further up the trench and allowed the shells a fair field, but the afternoon they seemed just to fire anyhow, like a spiteful child throwing stones in temper. They didn't do any harm to any of the trenches round us.

March 5th

We were never relieved till 10.15 pm last night. The Buffs relieved my right trench and the Royal Fusiliers my other trenches. As a consequence I got back to West Outre at 1 am exactly with my Company. The last three miles over pavé, over which one scuffles and stumbles and slips; the round greasy sets seem to bruise the soles of one's feet every step one takes; and these miles are a veritable task of Sisyphus, and towards the end of them we almost begin to think that we too, are being punished by the gods. It's pain for me, what it must be for the poor devils with bad feet I cannot think.

However, we had sent our servants on at 7 pm and they had eggs and bacon ready for us in our old billet in the corner estaminet, and hot tea *and* our rum ration. And a drop of rum in our tea worked wonders. Just what we wanted, for when we came in we would willingly have paid half a guinea for a whiskey and soda. Sir Victor Horsley and all the drink cranks can say what they like about the issue of rum to the troops, and drink generally, but if instead of writing from the comforts of a nice cosy room, they'd put in a few days in the trenches I am sure they'd change their mind. We don't want rum in the cold, or for the cold; but we want it just as a 'pick me up' when we are 'done to the wide'.

The last six days haven't been so severe as usual; weather a little less inclement, but 'on duty in the trenches' is always trying, whether in the actual front trenches under more or less aimed fire, musketry and artillery; in the supports (trenches or farms or dug-outs), where by day we cannot go outside, are liable to be shelled and very often are shelled, and by night only issue forth at a certain amount of risk from flying bullets; or in reserve in Kemmel which latterly the Germans have shelled every day. During the whole time the Battalion is 'in the trenches' one is never out of sound of that pop-pop and the heavy guns, which ends by getting on your nerves, to say nothing of the actual business of being fired at or shelled. So at the end of our time on duty we are all more or less 'done in' and it's 6½ miles from the trenches to West Outre; Oh! I wish I had some of those drink fanatics in my Company.

I've another man for a firing party. He has just been told off for a FGCM, and he should be sentenced to death. I told him he had better spend his few remaining hours in prayer and touching him on the chest, I told him, that's where the bullets would hit him. Brutal, I know, but I've no sympathy with a cur. He is always evading coming into the trenches and I hear, ever since he came out here with the Battalion last August, he has scrimshanked all he could to get out of the firing line. I expect and certainly hope he will get shot. Several men have been executed for less, lately.

We were to have been sent to Ypres, but the order was cancelled at the last moment, and another Brigade, from goodness knows where, marched through Locre two days ago on the way there.

'Grandmama' is all ready, and we passed her last night close to Locre, well muffled in tarpaulins as befitted a dame so valuable. We also passed the two petrol-driven tractors which brought her up. Huge engines with driving wheels 11 or 12 feet in diameter. A man told me yesterday we should be here till September, still doing this job; that by then all our guns and ammunition will be ready and we'd begin by simply blowing away everything in front of us for two or three miles; we'd advance and do the same again, and so on to Berlin, presumably.

Also I hear that directly K knew war was imminent he sent over to the United States and bought up their supply of rifle and gun ammunition for three years! So we have any amount of ammunition, and all we're waiting for now is rifles, I believe, and fine weather. I fancy a big move and a successful one: one which will possibly end the war, will be made within the next 4 or 5 weeks: from all I hear there are many hundred thousand of English troops in the country not yet in the firing line, waiting; and they say the French have over a million troops in reserve. Well, Germany has just 'got to hold her hand out' and she is going to 'get it' too, whether she likes it or not.

Just returned from a topping bath at Bailleul Lunatic Asylum. Officers are allowed to bathe there on Fridays. Four baths in a room, and a huge bath sheet issued free gratis. The door of the bathrooms (there are two) are invariably left open as some fellow enters or leaves, and the old nun who hands out the towels toddles past quite unconcerned, and I didn't notice even a downward cast or a pretence of a blush. However, as we all said, if she didn't mind, we didn't.

Rumour (lying jade, generally) has it that two women walked into the Wilts lines the other night, coming from the German lines. I have a real bed to sleep in: very short, so I lie crossways in it; but all the beds here are very short, and after all there are some big Belgian men. Sheets coarse calico, but jolly good, and twelve hours out of those accursed trenches, away from the incessant firing, the blue flares, the excitation of the imagination, works wonders in one, and I feel a different man, and as if there was no such thing as a war going on, no trenches, no close horizon lined with stark khaki mounds, only distinguishable with glasses from the surrounding mud by the black upturned boots and the slate grey patches which is all that now stands for face and hands. Looking back one seems to have lived in a nightmare, a dream we can now afford to laugh at. It's odd how one forgets, and what a blessing!

March 9th

Nothing of any note has happened since we came out of the trenches on Sunday 7th. We had an hour and a half's parade in very wet weather to practise the attack on a trench; and the following day we did it again; this time it did not rain, but there was a wind cold enough to freeze the toes off a brass monkey.

At 4 pm we paraded for trench digging beyond Kemmel; left about 5.15 pm and although we only had 5½ miles by the map to march, we never got to the ground (some 1000 yards from the nearest German lines) before 8.30. As we moved off our stretcher bearers came along, and we could sympathise with jockeys, who just as they are mounting, see the ambulance being wheeled down the course 'in case'. However, we later heard that the previous evening, the Battalion who had been digging, had two killed and two wounded; and three nights before, the Royal Engineers marking out the trenches had four men wounded by 'Fly-by-Nights'. But we were very lucky as I don't think I heard a dozen sing over my head the whole night. My Company had to dig about 250 yards of trench 2½ feet wide and 2 feet deep. And each Company had about the same task. It took us an hour and a half and we were home again by 1 am. But what a perishing march it was! My legs ached (I've had a touch of flu', I fancy, the last two days and I got in just cooked to the world, and the last three miles my legs were merely mechanical. I hear all along our line we are digging these support trenches, well in rear of the first line; to act as points in which troops can be massed, fairly safe from artillery fire, until they are launched in the attack. So we are evidently preparing for a forward movement.*

* Later we learnt these 'concentration lines' were dug solely for the purpose of letting the German Huns know we intended to attack them at this point, to prevent their sending troops to Neuve Chapelle. Their air scouts could not miss these trenches.

The RE Officer told me that the Germans in front of us all along this western line are no stronger now than we are, and that they have come to the last of their available reserves. 'Grandmama' has been firing the last day or two, but we haven't noticed the worst here. They say that in spite of her size she don't make a very big noise.

Went to Locre Convent this afternoon to buy some lace and had a long talk with the Mother Superior. When she saw 'Grandmama' (which she pointed out to me, from a window, calling it 'Grandmère'), being put up, she went to the General 'Oh, Monsieur le Général, the Germans always respected me and my Convent, but you English for whom I have done so much, and whose wounded I am nursing, are you going to destroy all the windows in my house?' However, the General reassured her. But she said four masses for her windows; and when she found Grandma's voice broke none of them, she said four more in thanksgiving and then topped up with another four for the safety and succour of us and our Allies and our Amis.

Jane and Pepper's tobacco arrived today only, and it must have been sent off the middle of January. Just heard over the telephone from Brigade Head Quarters that Colonel Du Maurier of the Royal Fusiliers was killed this morning by a shell which blew up Alston House, the old farm which is always used as Battalion Head Quarters when the Battalion is in the trenches. I haven't heard what other casualties there were. He was the author of 'An Englishman's Home', the brother of Gerald Du Maurier and the son of the artist. The Germans blew up the Head Quarters of the Royal Sussex Regiment a few days ago. It appears as if they are systematically destroying all the farms behind our line. Hope they'll finish before we go in. He and his Regiment are in the 85th Brigade which were sent back from Ypres, so cut up. I hear that they were awfully slack in the trenches and the enemy used to stroll up and look over into their trenches, so to speak, and when our Brigade went up there, they stopped all that nonsense, and they have quite calmed things. Pray these blessed regiments haven't been playing the fool in our trenches to give us all the worry and trouble of replacing matters 'in statu quo'.

Rifleman Drennan one of the two heroes which every halfpenny paper in England and Ireland made so much fuss of recounting their story of the 'intrepid flight through the German lines' and their escape to England has just returned to us as a deserter. To give him his due he is a very brave man and behaved well all through, but being put in the Guard Room for some little crime or other, he escaped and fled to England, a no mean feat, by the way. He has just been tried by Court Martial for desertion, but the evidence given as to his bravery will undoubtedly get him off the death penalty.

An officer attached to the Royal Irish Regiment which holds some trenches only 30 yards in places from the Germans, says our guns are giving them simply Hell, all day and night. Our trenches are in a hollow, the Germans live in a rise which prevents the enemy shelling our lines, and also allows our guns to shell theirs with perfect safety to our men in the trenches. He said the Germans were simply blown out of the trenches.

Gilliland and I went round to Head Quarters tonight to get a game of bridge, but we found our Padre (Rev Gill, S J) giving a selection on the gramophone which some firm he wrote to very kindly presented to the Battalion, with 25 records. He also received some half dozen penny whistles and some mouth organs. One of our men, I believe he came from the 4th Battalion, was up before a Court of Inquiry for injuries, the suggestion being that he had purposely shot himself in the hand. He stated that he had never fired a rifle before he came out here. And there happened to be no witness to prove that it was self inflicted. I know the 4th were very hard put to it to find men for their later drafts, but still it is criminal to send men out who have absolutely no knowledge of a rifle at all. It's rather unfair on us officers; I think sometimes the people at home don't sufficiently consider us who have to do the fighting with this poor material, and they refuse to remember the old saw about the battle which was lost for the want of a nail in a horse's shoe. Great events hang on little points. Sir John Moore's Army would have been surrounded and captured, had not a French officer taken enough wine to make him quarrelsome and Dr Jameson would have got to Johannesburg if one of his men sent to Zeerust to cut the telephone wire, had not got drunk.

We go into the trenches on the 12th instead of tomorrow. The Brigade now in the trenches owes us two days, so I suppose that is the reason we are getting this rest; and if we have to do eight days, well, as we at present arrange the reliefs in the Battalion it will not hit my Company any harder than it did last time. But... we shall be spending St Patrick's Day in the trenches. The first St Patrick's Day I've ever had with an Irish Regiment, and now I spend it in the trenches. Well, at least I shan't wake up with an appalling head on the 18th, as I surely should were the Battalion at home.

We had a bottle of Heidsiek Sec (10 francs) tonight at dinner. Horrid stuff, like sugar and water. But over here one can't buy the dry Champagne we are used to and which is all exported to England, for which it is specially made.

Up to midnight we heard our guns thundering and well on into the second hour I lay awake listening to the crackle of musketry from the direction of, I fancy, St Eloi. I think there must have been something up last night. It was very dark and required little imagination to picture those poor devils of Bavarians huddling together in their trenches, just waiting for death to come sharp and sudden out of the black velvet around them, all their nerves strained by the shattering devastating explosions of our lyddite far beyond the normal tension of a dark night and an active and resolute enemy within a hundred yards of them.

March 10th

Baker (my late 1st Whip), now a Lance Corporal in the Royal Engineers despatch riding section, has just paid me a long visit and we talked over the old pack and decided that next season must see us both in command of the Tiverton or West Somerset. He confirms the rumour I had collected this afternoon, of the surrendering of 300 Germans to the King's Royal Rifles somewhere St Eloi way; and also of the capture this morning by the Indians (Meerut Division) of 150 of the enemy, not more than twenty of whom, it is said, are over eighteen years of age.

The heavy bombardment and musketry last night was to the SW, the preliminary of an attack by the 6th Division and the Meerut Division, and at 8.30 am today they captured some two miles of German trenches. This took place on the line just below Armentières. Our 1st Battalion is with the 8th Division.

In Locre this afternoon I met Major Large of the Middlesex. He used to be at a crammers with me.* We swopt yarns. His brother, Adjutant of his regiment, was killed the other day. There are some extraordinary escapes from bursting shells due to the upward burst of the very high explosives used by the enemy. An officer and his servant and three men were sitting in a trench round a fire. A big shell plopped right into the centre and exploded. When the officer recovered he found himself upright at the bottom of the crater made by the shell, his servant on the parapet round the crater top and the three other men blown to atoms.

In another instance, an officer was sitting in his dug-out when a shell came through behind him and went into the ground at his feet and exploded. He was quite unhurt; though the dug-out was wrecked.

The Doctors in Locre Field Ambulance showed me the head of a 3″ shell one of them had taken out of a man's chest. It was resting on his heart, and the doctor couldn't take it out with forceps, but had to actually twist it out. The head is some 2½″ or more high, and 3″ in diameter at the base. It has ploughed an 8″ furrow from the man's armpit, across his left breast and was actually resting against his heart. The poor fellow lived for twenty-four hours, strange to say.

* He was himself killed a few weeks later at St Eloi.

I hear Colonel Du Maurier was the only man killed in the house; he had just ordered everyone out and into dug-outs outside and was waiting in the house for his Sergeant-Major to report that everyone was in safety before he took cover himself. Baker tells us there is an attack planned for Friday night up St Eloi way. Bavarian prisoners say they are all in a dreadful state, and hundreds would surrender but for the fear of being shot by their own officers, and of the report spread by their officers that we shoot our prisoners.

Gilliland hears from Derry of the floating petrol base in the Channel; our Royal Navy examined a Dutch Smack, found her full of petrol, put a prize crew on board and waited. Result, two submarines captured and one sunk.

Large, who was with his Battalion during the rather disastrous (to both sides) attack on February 21st and 22nd at St Eloi, tells me that the Buffs took a trench, and they and the Middlesex were relieved by the East Surreys. One Company of the East Surreys relieved a Company of the Buffs in the captured trench. This trench was recaptured by the enemy later, and the Company of the Surreys completely vanished. Neither officers nor men, he says, have turned up, and whether they were all wiped out, or were all captured, no one knows.

It appears there was some uncertainty as to whether the trench was completely captured, or whether the Buffs occupied one half, and the Germans the other half, and as it was at night it is quite likely the latter case was what happened.

In general orders sent round today, I see a man of some English regiment was tried for desertion; sentenced to death, and shot at 7.05 am on the 6th instant.

March 11th

Information just come in this morning from the 2nd Corps to say that all points to the enemy holding entire front from River Douve to the Ypres-Commines Canal with the 2nd Bavarian Corps alone; and that there are no signs of any large reserves.

Our 1st Army has inflicted great loss on the enemy (yesterday 3-11) taking 942 prisoners at no great cost to ourselves.

We move off at 3 am tomorrow morning as our Division is attacking Spanbrook Farm with two Battalions of our Brigade, we and the South Lancashires are in reserve. All of us officers have to wear the web equipment and to carry rifles, horrible!

March 12th

A very close morning when we started off and all of us arrived at Lindenbooke about 5.45 am very fagged out. The Battalion was placed in dug-outs and deep well-dug trenches some 2,500 yards from the front line. Day broke, misty, and there was no bombardment. At 8.15 am 'a rattle of musketry brought us out of our dug-outs'. The attack's begun we said, 'God help all our poor fellows'. Like a policeman's rattle the turmoil continued for a quarter of an hour and then ceased. Later a signaller told us that some of the Royal Fusiliers in the trenches to the left of the attack had been caught digging in front of their lines by the enemy, who have opened on them and wounded four sergeants and given them other casualties. The Fusiliers had not noticed the mist lifting.

The attack and previous bombardment did not come off owing to the mist. During the course of the morning a message arrived to say a *Battalion* of the 6th Division had taken a post of the enemy by the bayonet. But the Battalion was not mentioned. Why? There seems no reason for this absurd secrecy.

2.45 pm. Our guns had been firing intermittently towards our left, but at 2.45 the gunfire increased and at 3 pm a heavy rattle of musketry broke out somewhere opposite the K trenches, opposite the enemy's position and running N of Wyschaete. Their rifle firing ceased at 3.25. A message came to us that the expected attack was to commence at 4.10 pm. The weather up to now had been misty, clouds coming over thick now and again, but it had now begun to clear a bit, and through our glasses we could see the line to be attacked.

At 3.30 a battery of 18 lb field guns, and 60 lb howitzers, just behind us, commenced a heavy bombardment along the front of E and F trenches round Spanbrook Farm, and 'Grandmama' joined in. A hoarse whistle, slow, and as if the shell were veering now this side, now that, a whisper of 'that Grandma' 15; 20; 30; 40; we waited, and then on the sky-line it seemed as if a tremendous convulsion had taken place. To us, 2,000 yards away, it looked as if some 40 yards of trench had been blown up bodily, the straight spurts of the explosion going up some 200 feet and a huge volume of green grey smoke hung like a pall over the place which had once been the foundations of the Spanbrook Mill. Shells were now poured in fast; one burst short over our heads, the head of the shell ploughing into the field 30 yards to our front. I counted 21 shells fired in one minute, and in some minutes the rate of fire was heavier. The position attacked is some 800 yards extent, and into that line some 700 to 800 shells were poured, preceding and during the attack. Shells with high explosives, and shrapnel. 'Grandmama' fired four or five, one of which failed to explode, and one of which exploded behind one of our trenches blowing up several men. The position was wrapped in smoke – white feathery clouds mixed with the thick grey-green masses of the lyddite; and a message reached us that the enemy evacuated their trenches with heavy casualties. This is most probable, but as we also learnt later, behind their trenches were regular bomb proofs in which their reserves took cover. At 4.10 the attack was launched; the day had grown very grey, and I could see nothing. The Germans threw a few shells our way searching for us in Reserve, and for our guns but they did not get very close and did no harm. A very heavy musketry rattle broke out in front as two Companies of the Wilts dashed forward on the left, while two Companies of the Worcesters assailed on the right. Here they had some 400 yards to cross; on the left the distance was less than half this. In 15 minutes the rattle, a sound like the continuous working of a policeman's rattle, ceased, only a few dropping shots breaking the silence which could be almost felt, between the now slower fire of one big gun, and, so certain were we of the result, that we all said 'Thank God, they've got the trenches'. I personally felt it quite a strain, listening, and knowing that every moment took some poor fellow across the Styx. And then 20 minutes later some wounded turned up; no arms, no equipment; they'd not been in the attack; had been holding the trenches, and our shell fire had caught them mostly. Two or three had been hit by shrapnel; a Sergeant had two bullets through his right arm. All had tales to tell; mostly different except that our guns had fired into our own men. And more wounded dribbled through, all excited; every tale unreliable, a mass of inaccuracies, of exaggeration, but all taken in by their listeners avidly.

March 13th

And the story, as far as I can now reconstruct it, is one of failure; a failure due entirely to our artillery; who is to blame for this, I do not know, and it is to us at present, immaterial.

The Wilts went forward 50 yards and lay down to take their breath; a very heavy fire was poured into them and they refused to rise and go on. And really, human nature being what it is, this is natural. The first rush should have been carried right through when the start is anywhere within 400 yards of the enemy, or men, once they get down, will never get up again.

The Worcesters, of one Company, some twenty-five men, were held up at some point; the remainder of the Company 'disappeared' according to their Commanding Officer's telephone message – whether captured, killed, or what happened I do not as yet know. The other Company had to rush over a forward trench. As they rose they came under heavy fire, and passing over or through the trench in their front, I hear many remained in the trench and would go no further. However, the Worcesters did get up and into the German trench, and held both flanks of it till 8 pm under heavy flank fire from the enemy. The enemy blew up part of their trench, hitting some of our men. Our artillery, for some reason, instead of lengthening their range, still went on shelling these trenches and our men in them, and they eventually forced our men to leave the trenches they had captured, with the exception of two bits on either flank. These bits of the trench were evacuated at 8 pm. I hear one Company got up to the trenches with only five casualties, but another Company had all its officers casualties; three killed, two wounded and one missing. The Worcesters had in all 154 casualties; no great loss out of some probably 380 men, more especially when a very large proportion of these casualties are said to have been caused by our own guns. I hear the Germans were yelling out, 'Come on Wilts, come on Worcesters'; if this is true, they must have learnt of the attack. The casualties in the Wilts, are, it is said, about the same, slightly heavier, if anything, and our artillery caused considerable damage among Middlesex and East Surreys holding our trenches. The 5th Division on our right, I hear, did not make any attack. I cannot understand why we and the remainder of the Reserve Battalion were not ordered up and *at once* thrown at the Germans; we'd have taken them and held them.

But all admit that the failure is to be attributed to the artillery. In justice to them I must add that I now hear they were very averse to firing yesterday at all, owing to the state of the atmosphere being too bad for good observation.

Cuthbert, in a letter today, tells me he heard Joynson Hicks say that seventeen submarines have been accounted for since February 18th, and today's summary mentions submarine U12 sunk about the 9th by one of our destroyers; eighteen submarines in twenty-three days, not a bad bag.

March 14th

Yesterday my Company played football for the first time since I've been out. Some employees of Mackie & Sons Foundry, Belfast, sent them a football. They christened it by beating C Company 9–3.

143

March 15th

Instead of returning to our own old trenches, the Brigade took over some trenches of 5th Division around Wulverghem, and we marched off at 4 pm through Locre and Drain Outre.

After halting and marching, stopping and halting for everlasting, a motor cyclist despatch rider brought us word that all plans had been changed; that the Brigade was to return to its billets and that it was to act as the 2nd Army Reserve.

The Battalion billeted in Locre returned there, but we went into billets at Drain Outre, a village similar to Locre and West Outre. During the afternoon a heavy bombardment of the enemy's lines somewhere round the Spanbrook position took place, and about 5 pm there was a heavy crackle of musketry as if an attack was on. A gunner told me later that the 7th Division had taken a place called Aubers, South of Wyschaete last week, that our attack on Spanbrook was only a feint to keep reserves from being sent up for the counter attack on Aubers, and that last evening the Germans were apparently attacking again. The musketry seemed to be just north of Petit Bois. It died down after half an hour, but the bombardment lasted over an hour and was very heavy. They also fired some shells at Kemmel, and we saw in the clouds the faint outline of a Zeppelin, like a fish swimming in very thick water. All night long and this morning still, the guns are thundering as if to mark the minutes, and we here, so keen to know what has happened, and is happening, knew nothing. Our road back to Drain Outre was blocked by a battery of four 7″ guns (4 of them) which they were placing in position during the night; within half a mile is a battery of 60 pounders, and a light field battery, and in fact, the *whole* of the rear slopes of Mt Kemmel is strewn thick with our guns, and despite their daily attempts, the enemy has not as yet damaged one.

My Company was all billeted in a large farm, and some half a mile away, at the other end of the village, we got into rooms. I had a bed, but no clothes and had to get the blankets from my valise. Gilliland shared my room; he also had only a mattress. We got in at midnight, very tired. I pushed open our door and found a man and his wife (I trust) in one bed, and a couple of children in another. Apologised and vanished, hastily. But what a rotten life for these people; fancy their anxiety had we acted as it appears the German officers are accustomed to act. After all we do apologise for the trouble and bother we give 'em. Woke up a baker at 12.15 am to buy bread! He was sold out. An old man in a night-cap and his thick flannel vest and drawers toddled down to talk to me; I regretted I had awakened him for nothing. 'Oh! Monsieur, pas de quoi', and off he toddled back again. They're all very patient, but the innkeeper where I am feeding has a face a yard long, that three of us with our servants should feed in his place. However, our soothing influence is having its effect.

I hear that we have had heavy fighting last week at La Bassée, 10,000 casualties. We have suffered, and we found 4,000 dead Germans in the captured trenches. The information just come is that the Germans broke through our lines and captured St Eloi yesterday; that we counter-attacked and re-took part of the trenches, but that St Eloi is still in the enemy's hands and the preparations are being made to attack them. I fear there will be heavy losses then; also I hear a probably quite unauthentic yarn that we took the Medlestede position and Petit Bois, round Wyschaete yesterday. We did not go into the trenches last night, as the firing was too heavy for the trenches to be relieved.

Met Captain Hallowes RAMC who used to be at Ballykinlar as medical officer. He tells me everyone blames our artillery for the debacle last Friday, and that Smith Dorrien visited the Worcesters and told them they'd done well and that only our artillery caused the failure. The Wilts had just 100 casualties; the Worcesters 150 odd, and two or three other units suffered slightly. The East Surreys who should have co-operated, refused to leave their trench (it is said) and the Worcesters got into one trench of the Germans, found it vacant. But they at once were enfiladed by machine guns from either end. They held the trench despite this fire and the fire of their own artillery, till dark when they were ordered to retire. They lost nine officers out of thirteen.

March 15th

Hallowes also told me we'd suffered heavily, La Bassée way, putting it at 11,000, but then we had some 160,000 troops engaged. I met Brigadier General Boyle as we were marching through Drain Outre yesterday; was with him when he was a Major in SA. He gave up command of the Munster Fusiliers two or three years ago and I was always running across him at the Rag.

'Hullo Burgoyne' he says, coming up to me, 'Hullo Colonel', says I 'what are you doing here?' (I didn't notice he'd the crossed swords on his shoulder straps). 'I'm commanding the Brigade', (i.e. 83rd Brigade) says he, and then seizing hold of my arm and giving it a cheery little shake, 'Getting on', says he, 'Getting on', meaning his promotion.

Hear the 18th Royal Irish were terribly cut up at St Eloi. The Germans came on at night after sending up three flares as a signal. They came on in huge masses, and simply rolled over our men into the trenches; numbers of the enemy were in civilian clothes.

March 16th

Left West Outre at 5 pm and marched to the hutments on the Drain Outre road to Locre where the whole Battalion is billeted.

We and the South Lancashires are at present Army Reserves, the Worcesters and the Wiltshires of our Brigade having gone into the trenches.

St Patrick's Day

Very heavy bombardment up to midnight of St Eloi, which I hear this morning, is still in the German hands.

The 'Mound', a small rise in the trench line, captured by the Germans, is, I am told, now occupied by seventeen machine guns. Our attack in Spanbrook was a feint, and was purposely well advertised to prevent the Germans reinforcing at St

Aubers. Yet that is all poor comfort to the relatives of those who died in this 'feint attack'. We return to our old trenches H1, 2, 3, 4 and I1, 2 tonight, close to Wyschaete.

An artillery officer tells me the Germans have brought up a large number of guns; that three weeks ago we knew where all their batteries were, and that now we do not. However, it is certain that no troops could be cheerier than ours, and their men don't seem to be in very great heart.

March 18th

We left Locre to march to the trenches last night, St Patrick's Day, an absolutely sober Irish Battalion, and so earned the praise of our Commanding Officer. I did not tell him that I had not paid my Company for over a fortnight and that few men in the Battalion had any money.

We have to 'worry' the enemy now. I hear the Germans so 'got on the nerves' of the 27th Division that, had they but known it, they could have walked through our line held by them; and now we have to 'do likewise' and officers are encouraged to send in schemes for annoying them. We have to dig 'saps' from our trenches forward, to eventually creep close to the German line; bombard their trenches with grenades, send out reconnoitring patrols, etc, and generally stifle that apathy which Haldane (our Divisional General, brother of our German Lord of that name) says had laid firm hold of his Division during the winter months.

We are today in support, one platoon is at Battalion Head Quarters, another at 'Irish House', and I have two with me at 'The Support Barn'; it is now a regular shell trap, and the Germans will undoubtedly succeed in blowing it up one day. I put in three hours last night digging a shelter trench 2½ feet wide , by 3 feet deep, in the field some 80 yards from the house, whither we shall all flee directly they start shelling the place. We dug in the dark, by feel, tracing the outline of the ditch with bits of paper, and getting occasional light from the blue flares sent up from the forward trenches 500 yards in front of us.

I kept 'em at it till 1 am and then let 'em run in, and I laid down on my clean straw too, nothing but my coat to cover me, as McKeown (my servant) has lost my waterproof sheet. He says I am to blame. However, I've told him he has to find me another one. Very cold, and got no sleep, up at 4.45 am and out digging again; really we had dug some 60 yards of quite presentable trench last night in the dark. Deepened and improved it till the clouds began to clear, about 7 am, when I ordered all men into the house for fear of aeroplanes. If the Germans knew we were here for certain, their JJs would be fairly hurtling round us now. The field in which we've dug the trench is scored with shell holes; one big shell hit a tall tree about 5 feet from the ground. It has snapped it like a carrot, splinters and slithers of wood 6 feet to 10 feet long are stuck into the ground all over the field. After breakfast, as the weather got thick again, Gilliland and I and a couple of men went out and did some further digging in our trench. The 'Allemands' started to shell the fortified farm (S4*) some 350 yards from us, and put in about 20 JJs all round it, without, as far as we could see, hitting it, or doing any harm. But we were thankful for our trench. Directly we heard the scream, in we popped like rabbits, and sat on our heels on the clay floor. Bang! Up went our heads to see where the beast had hit, and then down again and we cuddled the bank for 60″, then a rattle like a cheap watch going off, and fids of iron hurtle into the ground all round us. One man picked up a bit a good 2 inches square flung quite 400 yards by the explosion. But it was strange what a time these bits took to reach us, whizzing and wheeling through the air before they went 'plunk' into the ground just in front or behind us. The remainder of the day has been very peaceful and quiet, though the front trenches are now (5 pm) just beginning to wake up and shoot and a stray has just dropped into the garden in front.

* S4 means Supporting Point No 4. Behind in the first line of trenches are a number of strongly fortified farms or blockhouses, as Supporting points on which troops can rally.

March 19th

We relieved the trenches at 10 pm last night, pitch dark and very difficult to get about. I had to take over a new trench J3. One which the Royal Scots captured from the Germans on December 14th. It is as bad now as it was then. A mere ditch alongside a weak hedge against which are a few sandbags piled up here and there, where they haven't slipped into the bottom of the ditch. The rear parapet which, of course, was the Germans front parapet, is better, but not much. The ditch is an ordinary wet ditch, now ankle deep all along in mud; in some places I sank in half way up my leg; two or three times I found my feet slipping on rounded substances I at first thought were logs but they were the dead bodies of the gallant capturers of the trench, which still lie there in the bottom, unburied, but sunk in the mud, and I was slipping and sliding on their limbs, their faces possibly! There are several corpses still lying about the rear parapet. I can only think the Regiment which has occupied this trench for the last three months has been very slack in not burying these bodies, although when they were first killed it was impossible, as the enemy had rifles set on each corpse and men attempting to move them were wounded. This J3 is only 40 yards in one place from the German fort at the edge of Petit Bois, and it was not a nice walk, or rather crawl, getting to the trench.

The enemy have a trench mortar here, which they use to bombard J1 and J3. They also fired grenades in J1 and last night I had one man killed and five wounded in that trench, and the company I relieved had several casualties too.

I see by the summary the attack by the 7th Division on Aubers took place on the 14th, the same date as our attack on Spanbrook which was merely used to prevent heavy reinforcements being sent up to Aubers.

I hear that a huge mass of cavalry had been collected just in rear of our lines when we attacked at Neuve Chapelle, and but for the misty weather they were to have penetrated the gap in the German lines and cut at their communications. Rumour has it

we are to be relieved tonight and that the whole of the 3rd
Division is to be withdrawn to our right (southwards), a fresh
Division taking our place here, where a strong attack is to be
pushed home. It snowed last night a bit and the country is all
white this morning in the sunlight.

March 20th

We were relieved at 9 pm last night, but I never left my dug-
out till at least half an hour later, as I had to wait till all my
platoons had reported their trenches had been taken over.
Eventually after a long talkee-talkee with the CO at his Head
Quarters, Gilliland and I got to our own billet in a wayside
estaminet outside Kemmel just before midnight. A mattress,
very dirty, on the floor next to the stove and our overcoats and
two sandbags for each leg were all our creature comforts.
However, despite the sharp frost, we were fairly warm but my
poor devils overhead must have suffered a bit, as this house had
been under shell fire, and all the windows are shattered, and are
battened with their shutters which keep out the light and let in
the wind. The inkeeper and his wife are, however, very kind and
go out of their way to assist us. I had two more men wounded
yesterday, in J3 this time. On the rear parapet lie several corpses
of the Royal Scots, killed when they captured this trench on
December 14th, and one of our own men, killed about
December 16th or 17th, when the Rifles just held this trench.
There they all lie, festering in the daylight and poisoning the air,
and it is dangerous to bury them, even by night, as the enemy are
continually sniping across. But the worst is the corpses lying in
the bottom of the ditch and rising up through the mud, corpses
on which men walk and stand. It is difficult to imagine the
horror and disgust with which any man is filled, when he finds
himself standing on some poor fellow's face, or his foot slipping
off the rotting flesh of arm or thigh. I have never before heard
my men grumble, but they did at being in this trench. And it can
be made no better, it is of no use, since the trench 40 yards

behind is equally useful, but the General refuses to blow it up and abandon it. These Staff Officers never come into such trenches and so don't know – 'Strafe 'em'.*

Casualties in my Company in 24 hours: 7 wounded, of which one died yesterday. The man I stated was killed in the trench, was only seriously wounded and may recover.

A beautiful sunny morning to cheer us all up. On arriving at Head Quarters on St Patrick's night, the platoon I sent there found half a jar of rum left behind by the men they had relieved and the Sergeant and Corporals polished the lot off getting beastly drunk. But I'll have it in for 'em, the swines. What disgusts me is the hoggish selfishness which made them drink it among three or four, instead of giving each man in the platoon a tot. But the selfish spirit, this want of 'pal-ship' is an extraordinary trait among Irishmen, at any rate among these in our Special Reserve. We've had so many cases of men thinking only of themselves, where food, and especially drink, is concerned.

I hear we had over 500 casualties among officers alone, in the big attack round Neuve Chapelle last week. One Regt., the Scottish Rifles I believe, lost all its officers (14 killed and 8 wounded), with the exception of the Quartermaster and Transport officer who were not in the attack.

March 21st

Just before lunch a Corporal in the Artillery reported that a man, wearing a tommy's jacket, with Captains' stars on his shoulderstraps was enquiring about our gun positions, and that he had sent a man to follow him. We have been warned about spies and told it is better to arrest an Ally officer than to permit a spy to go free. So I sent a Sergeant and two men to fetch the man back. And back he came, all my men very excited. He turned out to be a Captain Maxwell of the Cheshires, two Companies of which are in Kemmel and he was collecting brass shell cartridge

* J3 was blown up by us some time in April I heard.

cases as curios. However, to make certain and much to his amusement, I sent him back to his billet escorted by a Sergeant. Later he and another Captain came down to us, and we had a long chat. His Battalion has just put in three weeks in the trenches at Ypres and he says he prays he may never go there again. They had practically no sleep all the time, and the enemy were attacking at least every other day and sometimes much oftener. Prussians they are, and very active and very brave.

In one big attack these men advanced across some 100 to 150 yards of open ground at a steady march, *arm in arm* and all singing.* As the lines were annihilated, others came up in the same splendid manner, and when at last the retreat was ordered, they retired, *arm in arm* at a steady march, despite the volume of fire poured into them. Maxwell had nothing but admiration for such extraordinary splendid pluck.

The trenches round Ypres are veritable nightmares, for besides many of them being very shallow, lacking in cover and exposed to handgrenades fired from enemy trenches not 50 yards away, the French who first occupied them, and after them our troops, never took the trouble to get their dead out of the trenches but buried them inside, all over the place, in many cases only a spade-full of earth over them. It is impossible to make a loophole as it means cutting through a corpse; the men walk on corpses, there is no part of the trench where a sandbag can be filled, on account of the dead; and in front of the line, in one part particularly, the dead lie in thousands.

Maxwell said it was too awful, after an attack, to watch the wounded in between the lines of trenches moving and calling for help – and to be able to do nothing. Two men who crawled out to get one of their wounded subalterns in were wounded, and the poor fellow had to be left out there – to die. Even at night it is

---

* Medical officers have told me they have distinctly noticed prisoners smelling of alcohol, and often in a comatose condition, as if recovering from some drug; and we hear the enemy are dosed with a mixture of ether and brandy before they make an attack. This makes them absolutely reckless.

Freepost Plus RTKE-RGRJ-KTTX
Pen & Sword Books Ltd
47 Church Street
BARNSLEY
S70 2AS

DISCOVER MORE ABOUT MILITARY HISTORY

Pen & Sword Books have over 4000 books currently available, our imprints include: Aviation, Naval, Military, Archaeology, Transport, Frontline, Seaforth and the Battleground series, and we cover all periods of history on land, sea and air.

Keep up to date with our new releases by completing and returning the form below (no stamp required if posting in the UK).

Alternatively, if you have access to the internet, please complete your details online via our website at **www.pen-and-sword.co.uk.**

All those **subscribing to our mailing list via our website** will receive a free e-book, *Mosquito Missions* by Martin W Bowman. Please enter code number ACC1 when subscribing to receive your free e-book.

Mr/Mrs/Ms ....

Address...

Postcode.......................... Email address...

Website: www.pen-and-sword.co.uk Email: enquiries@pen-and-sword.co.uk
Telephone: 01226 734555   Fax: 01226 734438
Stay in touch: facebook.com/penandswordbooks or follow us on Twitter @penswordbooks

impossible, as the Prussians are so well supplied with flares that no movement can be made between the lines.

The Cheshires have taken their badge of rank off their sleeves and put them on their shoulders, where they used to be, to assimilate the officers' jacket to that worn by the rank and file. All nonsense, as the enemy always try to shoot the leaders – in whatever kit they are clothed.

To the S of our lines, round by 'Plug Street', as the Army call 'Ploeg Straate' (close to Armentières) they tell me things are very different, as this is opposite the Bavarians. There our troops have fine trenches; in one of them they saw the subaltern in charge, in a fine dug out, lying in an armchair, and watching the front through a window, and every now and then, just to keep things going, one or other side lets off a maxim, previously shouting the warning, 'Look out, we are going to let off our Machine Gun'. The troops in that part have been doing 4 days in the trenches, 4 days in Brigade Reserve, and 8 days rest in Bailleul! and they rarely have any casualties.

March 23rd

A quiet day yesterday in the trenches. On my left in the Js 1 and 3 the Germans threw in rifle grenades at night and wounded, I hear, several men.

A perfect day all yesterday (Passion Sunday), sunshine; a lark singing just overhead; just the day for a walk in the country and I could, even inside the mud walls of my trench, almost forget where I was, but for the constant 'tang' of a bullet hitting a certain iron loophole. Some German sharpshooter, 200 yards away, evidently had a sporting rifle. He hit the plate 5 times out of 6 shots; the 6th shot always ripping up a sandbag and sending a shower of earth over us standing near. Just at sunset they sent a halfdozen field gun shells, commonly known as 'whizz Bangs' over us at our fortified Farm, but I don't know if they did any damage. Reliefs never arrived till nearly 10 pm.

My Company returned to the Support Barn and Irish House:

frost at night and very cold.

All yesterday the French had no less than 3 huge stationary oblong balloons in the air, and there was a huge yellow sausage glistening in the sun behind the German lines. Aeroplanes were darting about like big houseflies, looking very pretty with the sun shining through their wings and striking on their aluminium fittings.

March 23rd

Last night I took over J1, 2, 3 and 10 and H4. J3 is much improved to what it was on my last visit; several hundred sandbags have been built up into the parapet. I didn't walk along it as I wasn't for stepping on any more dead men. Got my men to bury several dead lying about.

Later I posted a listening-post in front of J1, and about 80 yards from the German Lines, but they reported having seen and heard nothing all night.

At 4.30 this morning a fusillade along my front, and it became so hot I got up. Found J1, 2 and 3 a mass of flares, which were curving up and crossing those from the German lines. Perfect pyrotechnic display; both sides firing off grenades, those from the enemy's lines bursting badly, and well in front of our parapets, while most of ours appeared to be inside and just on the enemy's parapet. A devil of a rifle fire, which would have been far hotter but that, owing to the dirt, some 80% of our rifles were jamming. Presently an excited rifleman with a bandage round his head, rushed over to me from J1, saying they badly wanted ammunition and that the Germans had rushed out as far as our wire. I had just sent over to Gilliland (in J1) for news, and my orderly returned at that moment to say it was simply an outburst of 'panic' firing from the German lines, and that Gilliland had seen one German outside their lines running like blazes to get in, and that the whole thing was nothing at all. However, it sounded quite bad, so much so that one battery chipped in with a few rounds. By 5 am all was quiet again. I fancy we gave the Hun 'What for' for waking us up, though. We are being relieved tonight, and as we have a good supply of rifle grenades in our trenches, we are going to give him a farewell tickle-up with them as soon at it is dark.*

The man who was wounded, was hit by a bullet which entered the underside of the fore-end of his rifle, and bored a hole right through into the barrel, bending the barrel. I fancy a splinter of either the bullet or the wood hit the man. I should never have believed a rifle bullet would pierce a rifle barrel.

About 5 pm last night there was a regular fusillade from the German lines at an aeroplane of ours, and shortly after we heard cheering. Whether the Germans were cheering at the news of the sinking of one of our warships in the Dardanelles or our side were cheering at the capture of Przemysl by the Russians, I don't know.

March 24th

I had one man killed and another wounded in J3. This trench, when held by the Wilts, used to be manned entirely by volunteers from the Battalion and called the 'DSO' trench. It was entirely their own fault it was so bad, as we got it fairly safe and comfortable very quickly. My subaltern found a lot of German kit about the place, and in one of the packs he came across a lot of ammunition where the tips of the cartridges had been filed off, and the marks of the file are plainly seen. Such a bullet entering the body would give, in nearly every case, a mortal wound. I sent one clip of these cartridges to Head Quarters and hope they will forward them to the Brigade.† We

* Later I heard that so hot was the rifle fire that all the troops in Kemmel turned out and stood to arms. My platoon did splendidly, to our surprise. Every man standing up and aiming quite coolly on the parapet.

† Some week or so later an Army order came out to the effect that any persons captured with ammunition on him which showed signs of his having tampered with it, filed it, reversed the bullet etc, should be tried by a hastily convened Drumhead CM and shot. Proceedings to be forwarded to Head Quarters afterwards.

were relieved about 10.30 pm by the 5th Cheshires. TF and I never got away till 11 pm. We marched to La Clytte; not more than 2½ miles, but a terrible march. It was a very hot night, with rain showers, and all the road (and pavé most of the way) greasy and slippery. We had an extra mile to our farm from La Clytte village and arrived about 1 am 'done in' completely, to find the officers' rations had not arrived, and our servants, whom we had sent on to get everything ready for us, had been able to do nothing. The farmer and his wife curmudgeons, everything filthy; we slept in our 'flea bags' in preference to the dirty, filthy bed in the room. The farmer's wife won't lend us a brush to sweep the floor, or to clean up, and everything is perfectly beastly. We managed to get a bit of bread from one of our men, and we had some cocoa with us, so we had a meal of sorts, of cocoa, bread and butter and jam and a slab of very heavy rich iced cake. However, even that did not spoil our sleep. We turned in just after 2 am. I woke about 6 am and dozed off and on till 10 am when I forced my servant to bring me in a bucket of hot water, and I wanted it as I'm getting itchy in one of my arms and am 'afeerd'.

March 25th

La Clytte. Very heavy rain last night; and the fields and roads greasy and a sea of mud, and it was bitterly cold.

With regard to our attack on the 12th at Neuve Chapelle I heard we broke through the German lines completely, but our troops were 'done' and could go on no further, and there were no reserves to go forward, and complete the operation: presumably the gap was not big enough to send a huge mass of cavalry through. During our last tour in the trenches we lost some 60 men, 20 of these were sick, the remainder killed and wounded. Very few were really seriously hurt, but I had two men killed (one killed, one died of wounds) and 9 men wounded in my Company. We had one officer wounded slightly. A bullet struck a sandbag close to him and cut his face and neck with bits of gravel. Another officer looking over the parapet to see the effect of a rifle grenade he had just fired, got a bullet through the top of his cap, cutting the wire rim.

March 27th

This morning my orderly told me that the Germans were shelling La Clytte and that I couldn't go down there (our farm is about three quarters of a mile from the village where our Head Quarters are).

However, information from excited men is notoriously unreliable and Gilliland and I toddled off down, just in time to see their last shell fall in to some transport lines three hundred yards behind the village. I don't know whether it did any harm. One shell had actually dropped on the road harmlessly, and I believe they only fired four shells altogether. An aeroplane has reported that the Germans shifted four field guns into Petit Bois yesterday, and our artillery are going to give them 'what for' for doing so.

This afternoon Gilliland and I walked into Poperinghe, about six miles from here; that is to say we got a lift in a motor ambulance for the last 3½ miles in, and the last three miles out. But we got some exercise anyhow. Poperinghe is, I am told, the only town in Belgium that has never been shelled or in any way suffered from the War. Larger than Bailleul it is now quite gay with French and English and Belgian troops. The shops such as one gets in any English town. Nothing to do there, of course, and by the time we'd had tea, we'd seen enough. Went into l'Eglise St Berten, where the organ loft and pulpit and sounding board are beautifully carved, same style as Grinling Gibbons, very heavy and massive. This and one other old Church and two or three other old buildings are distinctly Flemish in their solidity and architecture, but the rest of the town is like any French town. The Chateau (now Hospital) and the private houses, examples of what monstrosities architects can design when they really try.

The car which brought us back was driven by the gentleman who owned it, and who has, at his own expense, brought out the Isle of Wight Hospital; a name 'Beattie', presumably his own, was on the car. He came over here with the first lot of Canadians, but like many other men among the Canadian Contingent, he was so disgusted with the disgraceful behaviour of the men and officers, and so ashamed of belonging to the Contingent, that he left and started this motor ambulance and hospital at his own expense. Rather sporting of him. He has been carting typhoid patients about and wouldn't let us inside the ambulance.

Two of our servants who went into West Outre this afternoon tell us that a Zeppelin flew over the village at 5 am this morning, and dropped about 20 bombs, but it did no damage.

March 29th

Last night the CO and all we Company Commanders went out to look at the new trenches we are taking over this evening. I took Gilliland with me and we walked, the others riding. About 5 miles from the trenches. We take over from the Worcesters, and the trenches are about three quarters of a mile South of St Eloi. When the Germans made that attack upon St Eloi the other day, their left just came across the left of the trenches we shall occupy.

It's all low lying country here, and in wet weather very wet, and the trenches are really parapet; we use the word 'trench' here as the Irish use the word 'dyke' and both may mean either a hole dug into the ground or a bank raised from it. Here the parapets are built up above the ground; the trenches being not more than from 1 to 2 feet deep. They look very safe and I should think they are quite impossible to rush. The German trenches are on the rise just a little above them, and from 100 to 150 yards off. They have no trench mortars, we have several used by the RE, and generally the enemy seem very quiet. The last six days the Worcesters have had one man wounded only, not counting a man last night.

We all met at the Worcesters' Head Quarters, a much shattered farmhouse. Gilliland and I arrived first and found a dead farm. Knocked, no answer, the front all pitted with rifle and shrapnel bullets. 'Must be a mistake, let's try that farm over there.' On our way 'over there' met a telephone linesman who directed us back. 'They're all in that farm, Sir, but you go in by the back.' Eventually we found the Colonel and his Head Quarters Staff fairly dug in between walls of sandbags in the interior of the farm. He gave us orderlies to lead us to the trenches; one man took us along. 'We calls this "Slaughter Corner" Sir, *they* comes over very 'ot at times, and several's been 'it just 'ere.' We tried not to quicken our pace past 'Slaughter Corner', where luckily 'they' were not coming over very much, and we got inside into the trenches quite easily, although it was a very brilliant moon. But it is difficult to see a man in khaki at 100 yards in moonlight.

The reliefs left hurriedly while we were in the trenches, and when we came out we found a man lying in a ditch being tended by two or three others. He'd just got a bullet through his jaw.

The field Paymaster told one of our Captains last week (and I heard this too from another source) that at Neuve Chapelle our Artillery accounted for a lot of our own casualties and that two gunner Generals had been sent home over it. As an RA officer admitted – the gunners *are* rather casual, but it's disgraceful all the same and is destroying the confidence we infantry had in our artillery. I hear an aeroplane was brought down today close here, but don't know whether it was a German or an English aeroplane.

March 30th

Elzenwalle; a tiny hamlet of a few houses and a large chateau all of which are now shelled, the chateau being a mass of crumpled wall and brick heaps. Two Companies of the Battalion holding this sector of the trenches, are kept here in reserve.

Head Quarters and two platoons of one Company in the cellars of the Chateau, the remainder of the men and the Headquarters of the other Company among the ruined walls of the village. By day no man can come outside his hide-hole, as the place is in view of the German lines 2,000 yards away, and yesterday, because some of the Middlesex Regiment Territorials were seen wandering round the Chateau grounds, the Germans put 30 shells into the Chateau.

We are in a house in the village, and the three other officers of my Company and myself sleep and live in a tiny room 13 feet by 12 feet. On the floor are a double mattress and a single mattress (for Father) and the boy sleeps in a corner huddled up in a teaspoonful of straw. However, he is young and has only just joined. They are very anxious to put our bit of line in a decent state of defence, the preceding Brigades seem to have done nothing, and there is very little wire out, and every night a large part of the men in reserve have to bring up wire, and other pioneer stores, to the firing line, and last night I led a party up, carrying wire, tressels, planks etc. I put the stuff down some 200 yards from the front trenches and went on into P2A to tell Norman, who is holding that trench, that I had done so. On my way up, I saw a dead German lying face down in a little muddy ditch. Fancy he'd been there some time, as he was covered with slime and mud. Got a man to shovel some earth over him. Several dead cattle lying about. Very little firing against our trenches last night, and we have very few bullets over us, but if the enemy do get a panic and fire much, they would make the relief impossible till they had finished, as the reliefs have to cross quite open ground rather higher than the line of the trenches and bullets could pretty well sweep it nicely. However, there is a good deep communication trench, through which, in case of necessity, we can splash our way in safety.

Something seems to have gone wrong with the Neuve Chapelle success, as I hear that one of the Divisions came up late for the attack and one Divisional Commander has been sent home. No water in this district fit to wash in, and every drop has to be brought up in petrol tins, so there is no washing. However,

I intend to have a mess tinful heated for a shave and a sponge over my face and hands. It's something, even if very little.

March 31st

My Company took over their trenches last night by 10 pm and we got in with no difficulties. The enemy appear to be peacefully inclined opposite us, and if we don't annoy them they won't annoy us. Just as well, as if there was any volume of fire, the relief of the trenches would be almost impossible.

'A' Company caught the Germans relieving their trenches and let them have it, and naturally if they caught us doing the same we would deserve all we got. We were working up to 4 am filling sandbags and building parapets: digging communicating trenches; putting out wire, though owing to the full moon it was impossible to put the wire out in front of our advanced trench where it is most wanted. There are no officers' dugouts in my trenches so I at once started to make one in the trench I hold. I cleaned a patch about eight by five feet on the flank of my parapet, put on some men to dig down about 18 inches, and then to build a wall of sandbags around it. I had brought down, for the purpose, six sheets of corrugated iron sheeting and some stakes.

The Germans have a working party out, but as they were not bothering us we didn't fire at them; an ill-conditioned fellow some 400 yards along their line, however, catching sight of the new sandbags forming the wall of my dugout, which glistened white in the moonlight, let drive a couple which dropped into the bags under my servant's nose. About 4 am the palace was complete. A sheet of corrugated iron on the very damp floor; a couple of armfuls of unthreshed wheat straw and my servant and I turned up; but as we all had to 'stand to' at that hour, I just sat up and watched the greys of the morning chasing away the silver blue of the night.

Close to St Eloi, and some 800 yards from us is the Mound, in appearance, a tumulus, which the German captured three weeks ago, and which they garrisoned with many machine guns. At 1.30 am this morning, having been previously warned, I heard a heavy report from behind Elzenwalle, and saw, tracing in red sparks through the sky, in and out of the clouds, a red comet, describing a huge parabola. I watched it fall into or very close to the Mound and a huge report and a vast column of black smoke shot into the freezing night air. It was a mortar firing a very high explosive bomb, which, I am told, had a back blast of 400 yards. Half a dozen times this mortar fired, and about 2.30 a rattle of musketry which increased in volume and lasted about ten minutes made me wonder whether our fellows had retaken the Mound.

In so small an area I cannot imagine anything living after that visit of a couple of such bombs.

I paid a visit to the Company on my right, holding a trench (P1 and P2) running along the outer edge of a small wood between the junction of the Wyschaetebeck and the Diependerbeck. The latter stream divides P1 and P2 (this wood is, I believe, shown on the map I sent you, dear; the enemy's line runs along the north west edge of the oblong wood just south of it). This trench is in places eight feet or ten feet deep, galleried in and out of tree trunks and huge roots, beneath which men have built commodious dug-outs. A veritable warren, sliding round corners, ducking under the trunks of fallen veterans, escaping by a miracle a false step into a hole, at the bottom of which a glowing red eye lights up the faces of two or three men. An extraordinary number of cattle are lying about dead, around this sector of the trenches.

One had thought it had been worth while herding such cattle and driving them off, instead of allowing them to fall victims to shrapnel or bullet. We have buried all the dead in the vicinity, but a few little heaps of blue, red and khaki in front tell the pitiful tale.

The last Brigade here must indeed have been the limit. The lines immediately at the back of our rear parapet are a mass of indescribable filth amongst which rise three small crosses:

evidence that some Battalion had no care as to where they laid their dead. Indeed, it is quite possible they never even troubled to bury their dead, as one cross is marked 'a British soldier lies here, name unknown'.

I put a working party on this morning to clean this horrible plague spot, and a sharp eyed sniper catching sight of a head, fired and killed one of my poor lads, quite a boy. Shot him through the back of the head and made a horrible mess. He lived for six hours in spite of it but he never spoke a word and was unconscious all the time. We could do nothing but put some sandbags under his poor head.

This at 10 am just as I was going to have breakfast, but one gets callous, perhaps even selfish, and I think the dominant feeling is one of relief that it is not one's self.

An hour earlier I was standing at the same spot where this lad was hit, explaining something to my Sergeant Major, and a sniper, twice quickly, cut the top of a sandbag in a line with the top of my head, which he evidently spotted. I thought I was hidden as I could not see the German lines.

When one is permitted to live and learn, one does not forget; out here, at any rate.

All this afternoon the Germans have been shrapnelling Elzenwalle, and this morning they put six or eight shells into the Chateau. I fear they have seen men moving about the village.

April 1915.   *The Times*. 20/4/15

> Now, day by day, with labour oft unseen
> The year fights through to summer; here and now
> The pale bud slowly bursts the blackened bough,
> Casts off the husk and stands up straight and green.
> Long, very long, the winter months have been:
> But God with need of waiting doth endow
> His gift of patience, and would teach us how
> We too must pass through months of hardship lean,
> Waiting and striving, till with dauntless head

We stand to greet life's summer. Day by day,
Often complaining, we are surely led
To greet a deathless beauty – what time they,
Who have accomplished, the all-glorious dead,
Shine forth like stars, and point us out the way.

H R FRESTON
Sec Lieut,
3rd Royal Berks Regt.

April 1st

Chateau of Elzenwalle. We were not relieved till nearly 11 pm last night and came up here in Reserve, where one platoon and the officers live in the basement of the Chateau; the other three platoons are in farm buildings close at hand. It's an awful shame the way this place has been simply shattered. It is a big building, two stories and a basement, and surrounded by a moat full of water, but saw nothing more than a huge sewer, full of debris, tins, bottles, floating planks, bricks, slates, masonry from the roofs, and walls, straw, old mattresses and offal of all descriptions.

Our quarters in what was evidently the kitchen, defy description. A kitchen table and a round hall table; several kitchen and drawing-room chairs, three sofas, more or less wrecked, and a pile of straw for us to sleep on. A large brazier is our cooking range. The front walls are cracked and bulging and a bit of the ceiling has given way under pressure of a bit of shrapnel. Above, every room has been completely destroyed, and what floors are left are covered with masonry, torn books and broken ornaments, and furniture. The only solitary complete piece I saw was a small cabinet silver table. Of course, the place has been well looted and there is nothing left worth carrying away.

We woke at 10 am and got breakfast at 11 am. I previously managed a 'sort of' a wash and a shave; the others washed after breakfast. We lunch about 3 pm, tea about 8 pm and off to the trenches again about 10 pm. An odd life. Yesterday I had only two meals, breakfast about 10.30 and dinner about 3 pm. I asked for some tea about 7 pm but I was told there was no more water. The machine gun section had stolen my water can and emptied it almost before I had found it. But I punched one man under the jaw, and emptied another man's bottle on the ground, and before I've finished with those men they'll be sorry they stole my water, not because it was mine, but because it is water. I'd be as annoyed had it belonged to any boy in the Company. But some men are so mean, they'd steal the milk from a blind baby, or the pennies from the eyes of their dead mother.

Captain Thursby, 3/60th Rifles, is buried in the grounds of the Chateau. He was killed at St Eloi on February 15th.

I continue to hear bad accounts of the Neuve Chapelle action. From Boulogne some 12,000 wounded were sent to England in two days: of course, these include the wounded of the three actions at Neuve Chapelle, St Eloi, and Spanberg Mill (Kemmel), but the action at the former place cost us far too heavily, and Joffre is reported to have decided that no further forward movement will be attempted at present. We lost 860 officers. How can we afford to lose another like number?

I hear (probably the rumour is inaccurate) that two Divisonal Generals (not RA Generals as I at first said) were sent down and that Kitchener came over in a battleship three days ago for a few hours, and it is decided to court-martial these officers.

One Division was one and a half hours late at Neuve Chapelle. The names mentioned are Sir H Rawlinson and Major General Davies (the New Zealander); I know him personally. He was a Major in South Africa on the same column I was, and he is a real good soldier and good fellow, and one Division I heard mentioned is the 8th. But, of course, nothing is authentic, and all I quote is hearsay. But the Neuve Chapelle show was undoubtedly a failure, as it was intended the cavalry (all our cavalry, goodness and the authorities know how many squadrons) should go through to Lille where they would have

165

captured thousands of prisoners. Instead the gap was never properly made, thanks to someone's blunder.*

Our doctor refuses to live with us in our cellar and is domiciled in the Icehouse, an underground brick-lined chamber within a huge mound of earth. There he lives like a badger in dank chilly gloom. However, he feels safe.

I hear there are Alsatian troops opposite our lines, which accounts for their lack of energy.

Last night Leask and I carried out quite a lot of wire and placed two rows in front of our trenches, but, though the moon was bright, there was a slight ground mist, and though I expect the enemy saw us, for we were not more than 75 to 100 yards from them, and they could hardly have missed seeing us had they used their glasses, they did not fire. I found my Ross glasses fine for night work, showing up objects I cannot even suspicion up to 400 or 500 yards.

April 3rd

We came down to the trenches last night. Just as we were marching off, the huge barn outside the Chateau, where two of my platoons were quartered, caught fire. Some careless idiot had left his brazier among straw outside the place. This caught on fire, and within an hour most of the walls of the barn were down. A splendid blaze. Up came the Commanding Officer, to ask why and the wherefore, but he was quite happy, and he did not blame me, and I'd luckily already sent him a report. But the poor old Rifles will be 'for it' again from the Staff, I suppose. This is the second farm building they have burnt to the ground, and B Company set fire to their billets last Monday, (luckily

* Communications with GHQ broke down: Neuve Chapelle was taken at 11.30 and the troops, Cavalry etc in rear had orders to move forward at 2.30 pm and neither the Divisional GOC, General Chetwode, nor all the Cavalry dare advance before. At 11.30 the Germans had fled, by 2.30 when the second phase of the battle commenced, they were returning in great strength, and our morning effort therefore failed.

they got it out before any great damage was done) and C Company, who burnt the first farm at Kemmel down, set fire to their dug-outs two nights ago. Well, I wonder every building troops sleep in is not burnt out long ago. It is terrifying, or it would be at home, to see men lying on heaps of straw, smoking, and glowing braziers standing, possibly on a few bricks, in the middle of a hay barn.

On our way down to the trenches poor Corporal McClartney got shot in the stomach. He cried out 'I'm gone, I'm gone', and asked for the 'Captain', so I went up to him and gripped his hand and squeezed it and told him not to be so stupid, that he was not gone or near gone, and that he had got to pull himself together. He died that night or early next morning.

3.30 pm. Our howitzers are 'registering' ranges in the German trenches, and they are 'popping' off their guns in reply. I saw from my dug-out two shells burst in the ground about two hundred and fifty yards to the rear of me, but whether the enemy are trying to range on my parapet, or are trying to hit a secondary trench some three hundred yards behind us, and now occupied by some of the HAC, I don't yet know. Doubtless we shall discover in due course, but I don't care tuppence for their rotten little field gun shells (while we are in our trenches, bien entendu), but I do dislike their 'Krupps'.

The burnt out farm is still smoking. When it was reported on fire, I was just commencing *a very urgent* note and if the Chateau itself had been on fire, I would have finished that note first.

However, I had three other officers there doing nothing, and I sped them forth, joining them five minutes later. But I fear I hurried that note. Was it very illegible, dear? We are relieved on Sunday night by the HAC. We, or rather one of my subalterns, put out a lot of wire last night, and very close to the German lines. He found an old French trench blown to pieces, and full of French dead; he said the smell was awful. Just behind us is another old French trench, also blown to pieces by shell fire.

My servant, digging not three yards from my dug-out, came

on an arm and shoulder. He did not dig any further. We shall plant the body deeper this evening.

April 4th

Easter Day, and as usual, damp and cold. We are completing forty-eight hours in the trenches this time and being relieved tonight by the HAC.

Yesterday, about midday, one of my men, in the next trench to this, got hit in the head. Stupid fellow was sniping at a sniper, and after firing a shot, instead of ducking down behind the parapet, he kept his head up to see the success of his shot, kept it up for an appreciable time, and his target shot the top of his head off. He was just living when the stretcher bearers took him away at dark.

Corporal McClartney, who was shot in the stomach the night before, is very dangerously hit I hear.

The Germans put a few shells into the Chateau and behind us yesterday, and at 5 pm they started on the north with an apparently new trench mortar, which they kept 300 or 400 yards behind their line. They bombarded the trenches just behind the mound at St Eloi and blew one trench to bits; one officer said he saw men going up into the air.

We could see the bomb falling; a long narrow sort of shell, and filled with a most powerful explosive, for the bombs were falling 500 yards away, yet the earth of my dug-out trembled for a second or two after each explosion as if after an earthquake. And after each bomb, the Germans put over a couple of shrapnel, to catch any men running out of the trenches. Their mortar seems a more powerful one than ours and is, I fancy, something new in that line.

Part of 'B' Company is holding a couple of trenches on my left, and very close to the part which was bombarded, and they, and indeed we all are wondering whether the Huns mean to take us each in turn. If so, our howitzers must really speak seriously to them. My servant McKeown, got it in the arm last night, within 500 yards of my dug-out, on his way up to post letters and to fetch water. I fancy the Alsatians, or, at any rate, the troops which were in our part when we came here, have been changed, as there has been much more firing, both by night and by day the last 48 hours and I don't look forward to the reliefs tonight: a walk of over a 1,000 yards at least, over a bullet swept glacier. I hope there will not be much firing. And these inky nights, as last night was, it is impossible to hurry. The men slip about and fall; are old, clumsy, tired, 'fed up' and stupid, and if one hurries, half one's men get lost; and a toddle of 1½ miles per hour, with constant halts to make them 'close up', and with these 'fly by nights' singing past one (and by no means overhead) it is very trying to old and young. A yell, a clatter, and men hurry past one, 'A man wounded, Sir' they say as they rush by. They're horribly afraid of a wounded man and very few of them will go to his assistance. I think it is superstition and the dread of blood, they get terrified. The dark night, the filth under foot, the squirming writhing man, the general jumble up. I can't blame them after all. I hate it myself, and we are very apt to grow callously selfish out here. McClartney was left to writhe on the ground till almost three-quarters of the column of 140 men had passed him and a Sergeant and my Sergeant-Major reached him.

There are five little crosses within two yards of my rear parapet, and a sixth where I buried that man of mine three days ago, some twenty yards behind. We put up a fifth cross yesterday just outside my dug-out and came on an arm and shoulder. A corpse lying there, had just had earth piled on him. No one had even taken the trouble to dig him into a shallow trench. I piled some near stuff over and put up a small cross to prevent anyone else delving at that spot. But fancy a grave (and a body with less than twelve inches of earth over it) just outside one's front door at home. Some regiments here are callously lazy, as when we took over these trenches, one officer buried five or six corpses which had been lying close behind his trench for months; and the last Brigade to be here had not even troubled to chuck a few spadefuls of earth over them. So insanitary for one thing. But in this heavy greasy clay soil the bodies will never decompose but will, I fear, lie as they are now for years, and the plough will always be turning them up.

In a shell hole behind us lies the fleshless body of a peasant. It looks as if he had been wounded and crawled into this hole for shelter, and so died. And his family still wonder where he is.

Another danger to the farmer after this War will be the large number of 'blind shells' they will come across; shells which the plough may quite possibly explode. Agriculture here, next year will not be without its exciting moments.

April 5th

The enemy put in half a dozen huge 'Kr-r-r-rumps' behind our P1, but beyond knocking down a lot of branches in the wood I don't think they did any damage.

A message came from Brigade Headquarters to warn us against accepting any flags of truce, as apparently, the enemy in some parts of the lines had tried to get into conversation with our fellows. Eastertide, I suppose.

The HAC relieved us last night about 10 pm but we never got back here (La Clytte) till after 1 am, some three hours to do under six miles, but a most punishing march, slippery and slimy and horrid.

April 7th

We were relieved by the HAC on Easter Sunday (4th), and I got back with my Company to our old billets near La Clytte at 1 am on the 5th.

In the thirty-six hours duty actually in the trenches I had two men (one of whom died the next day) wounded, and a Lance Corporal of mine, on his way down to our trenches to rejoin his platoon after coming out of Hospital, was shot in the knee and bled to death. Poor McClartney died.

Last night we four Company Commanders were sent out to inspect our new trenches about half a mile South of those we have just come out of. All parapets, and one advanced trench, are within 70 yards of the German lines. We had an awful time going round them, for though we had guides, it was so dark, it was almost impossible to see them, and we wallowed in mud; shell holes; bridgeless streams, and strands of barbed wire. I find it is always barbed, when one gets hung up in wire.

Returning, I tried to find the short cut by which I had come; in the dark I missed it, and walked over half Belgium before I found my way; had I not had my electric torch, I should have been obliged to stay the night at the first cottage I bumped my head against. I knocked up a peasant who fortunately understood French, and who directed me vaguely, but as it turned out, sufficiently. I got back at midnight having started off at 6 pm and having walked most of the time, but ten miles across country out here in the dark is equal to twenty miles anywhere else.

Into Bailleul yesterday and again today about my ears. Doctors say it is a tiny inflammation due to cold in my head. Went into Bailleul Church; perfect specimens of heavy carving in organ loft, and out around pulpit. A very fine old Flemish Church.

We came on the South Midland Division marching through Bailleul on its way to Nieppe (Armentières). A band of some Territorial Battalion in Bailleul played them through the Market Square. Splendid lot of men marching with such a swing. The men impressed me more favourably than the officers. The North Midland Division has come up here and is billeted all round here. They brought up a Battery of 4.9 (four guns in a battery) with them. These troops are Territorials, not K's Army.

An aeroplane was eagerly watched by all the garrison of the place, circling and wheeling over Armentières last week. Suddenly it swooped down, dropped half a dozen bombs and flew back to the German lines. Killed some children and women, did no damage to any troops and wrecked the interior of a large brewery.

A Zeppelin has been hanging about Bailleul and I heard it buzzing above us the last night we were in the trenches on its way westward.

I hear that it was opposite the Kemmel trenches that the enemy have been hanging the White Flag, attempting to fraternise. However, we are to allow none of that nonsense. I trust there will never be any fraternising again with anyone connected with Prussia.

April 10th

We are being punished for burning that barn at Elzenwalle down, as in Battalion orders last night we read that, by order of the GOC no more straw would be issued to the Battalion, and no more for braziers. How the General expects men to cook I don't know. But he does not understand an Irish Militia Regiment, and that is all we are now, for the class of man we have in it now is a class which would not be accepted for the regular Army. Feckless, thoughtless, stupid and, on the whole, don't give one confidence in them; though I think my men would follow me forward, possibly because they'd be afraid to go back 'on their own'.

We go into the trenches tonight. Every night since we have been out some 400 men of the Battalion have been on fatigue digging a drain and communication trench. A five miles walk to their task; sickening for the men, and I have not once been able to see my whole Company since we have been resting.

April weather, sun, wind, showers, but the wind is drying up the ground. Heavy gun firing away to our left, about the French lines, the last two nights possibly to prevent the Germans repairing any damage done during the day.

April 10th

We are warned through a Divisional memo that enemy agents posing as wine, spirit, tobacco and provision merchants are around our lines, attempting to act as mess caterers to regiments, and all ranks are ordered to at once arrest any such persons and forward them to Army Headquarters.

April 11th

In reserve at a nice farm some 2,000 yards from the firing line, I heard a good yarn with, I fancy, a substratum of truth in it, as to the way the French relieve their trenches. They were to relieve an English regiment. The hours passed, and still they did not come. The officer in the trenches became more and more anxious. We sent out scouts to see if there was any news of the reliefs. Word was sent to him that troops were apparently massing in his rear. He went out personally to reconnoitre. He had scarcely got out on to the road, when he heard approaching him a motor, and giving him scarcely time to fling himself into the mud at the side, an armoured car fled shrieking and throbbing up the road, through his own wire entanglements, into the German lines, smashing their barricade to bits.

The French artillerists commenced to fire right and left from the car, a blaze of lights and noise broke out along the front; into it, out of the darkness, a mass of French soldiers flung themselves; rushing over our trenches, they burst into the Teuton lines, stabbing, shooting, yelling; took the German trenches, were driven out of them still fighting into the safety of our own trenches which were still lined by our very surprised men. The blue wave fell back amongst them and our trenches were relieved. I have heard from so many sources that, though the French have rather a casual way of doing things, they seem to be doing rather good things at present.

It was not a very dark night last night, but two Worcester guides were sent to take A Company into their trenches; the 'Ms' led them to the 'Ps'; then, saying they fancied they had lost their way they disappeared. Some idiots at the head of the column mistaking a party in advance for the enemy, passed down the word 'We are in the German lines' and thereupon the whole Company or at least the three platoons which were there, turned and fled as if the Devil and all his demons were after them. Panic-stricken, yelling, screaming through brushwood and old wire, over drains and trenches, they crashed their terror-stricken way. I am told the noise was wonderful. They were eventually held up by running into the surprised arms of a support trench who, it is a wonder, did not open fire on them.

I had to take some planks (bridges for these drains, etc), wire etc to the trenches.

We had no particular difficulty except in finding the 'M' trenches, which are out on a flat plain. Huge parapets, not trenches at all; ground far too wet to dig trenches through it. Dug-out in M2 where I am going, is the best I have ever seen. A table inside, and one can sit in it. It seems some five feet high inside and a real little room.

The enemy have not been worrying much, though yesterday, they laid out some half dozen Worcesters with rifle grenades.

The bombardment we have heard the last two or three nights to the north is, I am told (I accept it with some reserve, though it is quite possible), only the French getting rid of their ammunition which they don't want to take with them. They are apparently going south, and being relieved by one of our divisions.

The Germans were shelling Elzenwalle three-quarters of a mile from here this morning and ended by putting a few shells into the wood close to this farm, where some of my men were repairing the road. They had to be brought back.

April 12th

1,667 miles of front. The *Matin* of yesterday publishes the following details about the length of front on which the Allied

Armies are fighting, which the Journal declares are based on exact information.

'In the West the French occupy a front of 543¾ miles, the British 31 miles, the Belgians 17½ miles, making altogether 592¼ miles. In the East our Russian Allies have to hold a line extending over 856 miles, while in the South the Serbians and Montenegrins cover 218¾ miles.'

'This brings the entire length of the fighting front up to the enormous total of 1,667 miles.'

April 13th

We got into our trenches very nicely and quietly and we spent a most peaceful night. About 4 am the Germans, who at one end of my trench are not 80 yards away and at the other perhaps 120 yards, put a rifle grenade quite close to my dug-out, but it never burst, and so did not wake me up.

A perfect Spring day; hot sun, no wind, larks singing in the sky and the rest of the picture which is only spoilt by the tossed and torn earth of old and present trenches, the welter of sand-bags, and an odd cross here and there. Right in the fair-way behind my parapet is a little mound surmounted by a rough cross of splinters on which is the uneducated inscription, 'In loving memory of a soldier *unknown*'. I suppose someone dug into him one day. About 300 yards to my left front, in front of the North trenches, (I am in M2) is a perfectly straight line of blue-clad corpses, perhaps twenty; they lie just in front of our wire and they look as if they had been laid there. I suppose they were swept down by a Maxim. In front of M1, at present held by the 2nd Middlesex (8th Brigade), are also several corpses (French); black now and mouldering. These are relics of the attack on Petit Bois on December 14th, when the Gordons and Royal Scots were so cut up. We walked into Dichebusche yesterday after about a mile behind our Head Quarters barn; the usual Belgian little town. The church tower had been shattered right down to the bell joists, and the big hole in the roof opens the Nave to the rain and winds. But service is evidently held there, though some Batt. has its Quartermaster's Store inside.

I am told that the Germans no longer shell Dichebusche, where the Head Quarters of a Brigade are and where several Battalions are billeted, and our guns in return refrain from shelling a town similarly used by the enemy. I can't believe this though. We saw a ghostly shadow of an airship over our lines last night, and little twinkling stars now and again in its vicinity shewed our anti-aircraft guns were trying their skill at it. It passed over Locre, West Outre, La Clytte and Dichebusche, dropping, I am told, three bombs in the latter town.

The Middlesex have just heard over their telephone that Austria has declared war on Italy. We all gave three cheers just to hearten the Germans.

Just heard an amusing story which I quite credit since, at a part of our line not 100 yards from where I sit now, the German line approaches 60 yards of M1 trench.

It is told of a Lancashire regiment. A German yelled 'Hi, I say. Do any of you know Birmingham? I have a wife and two children there'. 'If you don't put yer . . . 'ead down, yer'll have a widder an' two orphins there'. 8 pm. Have just returned from a walk up our line to visit Norman and Hutchison (B and C Companies). Was recalled by hearing that one of my men had been killed, and on returning, found one of my new draft, who had only joined me the night before last, was dead. A bullet had hit him in the mouth as he was digging, behind his parapet. A stray bullet of course, as it was quite dark. A great rattle of rapid fire at St. Eloi, lasting a quarter of an hour, almost as though it were an attack. I expect it is probably the Germans panic firing. A regular 'Brock's Benefit' going on up there, but no guns or machine guns, so it's not likely it was serious. But directly the light fails, the acting changes with the change of scene. Rifles pop off more frequently, and echo through the coverts at our rear; bullets sing across our line more frequently, the hours are punctuated by the heavy explosion of rifles, grenades, or trench mortars and 'Very' flares replace the sunlight. It is extraordinary how little it disturbs one.

A hell of a Babel, to one's ears, is going on, to the right or left, but it's 'Hullo! I wonder what's up' or 'The So and So's seem in a bit of a funk to-night', and no more notice is taken of it. Perhaps we send up a flare ourselves, but the German flares are so excellent that personally, I prefer to let the enemy light up the ground for me, and while they are sending up lights, one is quite safe from attack.

Then as it sometimes happens in a room full of people, all the rifles and guns along the line cease talking, for a few minutes, to possibly break out into a clatter in some corner or other with renewed vigour. At present there is such a silence, and some man next to my dug-out with no bad voice is singing to himself 'My little grey home in the West'.

This morning rounding a traverse, I came suddenly on one of my gentlemen; very much deshabillé, deeply engrossed in 'hunting'. I told him as I passed to 'let none of 'em escape' and left him cheerily smiling.

Another heavy rattle at St. Eloi, this time I hear a maxim tap-tap-tapping. The rattle of rapid firing is indescribable. It is scarcely a rattle, it is rather one crepitating roar, and it is quite awful; it may always portend so much, and St. Eloi is our danger spot undoubtedly.

April 14th

A peaceful night, but cold, and to-day was typically April, with very cold showers. About 4 pm from Hollandeschur Farm the enemy started to throw bombs from their trench mortar into M1 and they eventually managed to kill one man and wound six or seven others. Our Artillery were at once asked to put a few shells into the farm.

A funny little gun, possibly a mountain gun somewhere close behind us, was whizzing a small shell over our heads this morning into the German line.

I sent up a party to fetch some straw for my dug-out last

night, and they did not get 200 yards away before a stray bullet clipped a man on the side of the head and stretched him out. I think he will live alright, as it's only, apparently, a graze.

When the Armour Sergeant inspected our rifles last time, just before we came into these trenches, he said of 'D' Company's rifles, that no one would ever think after seeing the rifles, that the Company was on active service. He never had seen rifles in such perfect condition.

M2 is roughly 125 yards long; I have 100 men in it. It is now in real good condition; nice, dry and there is a perfect maze of sandbag shelters in rear parapet, and practically every man, but those actually on watch, has a dry shelter to lie in and sleep during the day. At night, of course, all the men are on the banquette, every other man standing up and watching.

April 14th

Last night the rattle of musketry we heard resulted in our capture of the Mound at St Eloi, a much battered, and I think rather useless heap by this time.

At 11 pm tonight a counter attack was made by the Germans. It started with a few shells and then a rattle of musketry broke out such as I have never heard before, while the guns of both sides thundered until the air even around us, three quarters of a mile away, was vibrating, and the dust was shaking from the roof of my dug-out. A star-lit night but very dark, yet away to our left, beyond a slight bend and hidden by trees, was the mound over and around which flares were lighting up the night; a red glare betokened something on fire, and a huge volume of smoke rolling slowly across the fields in the still night was, presumably, the explosions of the heavy shells which must have rained around. It is rather horrid listening to it, knowing men are being hurt, and badly, and, away out there in the night, too, there is the strain: it is not so much in these splendid trenches; and although the stars are out we cannot see five yards ahead of us, so all our sentries have to keep a sharp watch. The firing, but for a few shots, died out quite suddenly about 11.30 pm. I had a walk out at the back to Vierstraate at dusk, and took out some men to bury a couple of corpses I had noticed through my glasses. I found a third, possibly a Canadian. The other two were Frenchmen and were quite desiccated. 11.50 pm. The firing at St. Eloi has broken out again. It sounds at this distance just like a large flag whipping in the wind, but it is intermittent and scarcely seems to be an attack.

April 15th

Another fine day. This afternoon the Germans put an H E shell into one of our N trenches, blew in the parapet, wounded a man or two, and shook up 'Joy' of the 3rd Battalion.* Major Alston was shot dead this evening about 6 pm. He had spent the day in one of the N trenches, a charming gentleman, we shall all miss him very much. He died in a quarter of an hour.

My telephone operators caught this message being sent through to Headquarters. 'The Commanding Officer arrived M8 trench at 5 am this morning a.a.a. He was with me practically all day up to his death a.a.a. At about 4.45 pm I escorted him up to N4 and N5 trenches a.a.a. I then left him shortly afterwards and went down to N5 trench a.a.a. He went up towards the right of N4. At about 5 pm a man came and told me the Commanding Officer was hit. I and Mr Whitmore rushed up to him where he was lying at right end of N4 near to left of N3 trench leading to Sap Head a.a.a. He was moaning and bleeding profusely from the head. He was very badly hit on left hand side of his head above the ear a.a.a. I was with him until he died at about 5.15 pm. He never spoke. From R B Hutchison, Lt. Place. OCC Coy. Time 7.15 pm.

---

* A sandbag blown off by a shell caught him in the neck and gave him a stiff neck. He was afterwards killed in June, near Hooge.

April 16th

The Germans put a few rifle grenades and trench bombs
behind last night, one burst about 40 yards from my dug-out;
and a grenade landed close to my subaltern, but very luckily it
did not explode. I hear now it is all a cook house yarn about
Austria and Italy; the mistakes of a stupid telephonist in the
Middlesex Regiment.

Hear that the attack two nights ago was a German attack on
the Mound (St. Eloi) and that we lost twenty-five men and they
lost seven hundred. Sounds rather like a fisherman's story
though.

Another topping spring day. Have been digging a hole under
our parapet from whence, when it is finished, we can either sap
out a 'listening post' at our wire, or do a bit of gentle sniping.
Their sniping is distinctly good, at certain points which they
cover. At one such, I was pointing out some alterations and just
put my head outside; 'Flick' and a shot struck the sandbags at
my back, very sharp and quick. Went back and through a
loophole put a bullet into each of the three loopholes I saw
opposite; just to show them we can do it too.

Hear the shell which shook up 'Joy' sent a sand-bag into his
neck and knocked him nearly silly. He has a bit of a stiff neck
now. Word was passed down last night to 'look out' as an attack
by the Germans was expected at the salient N of Ypres, and they
feared the attack might spread down the line. But the night
passed off quietly as far as we could hear.

April 17th

Yesterday the enemy sent some eighty to one hundred shells
over the N trenches and wounded nine men altogether with
shrapnel; I had one man wounded in my Company in M3 but no
shells came in the trench I was in; we were too close to the
German lines. All a yarn about the seven hundred casualties, etc
around the Mound. We have never taken it. What really
happened was that the first heavy firing was panic, and the

heavy fire three nights ago was due to the Germans blowing up one of our trenches at the Mound and also a house where a number of our men were in the cellars. Altogether the Battalion there had sixty casualties and the enemy never left their lines.

Alston spent the day with Hutchison in his trench and only a few minutes before he was killed, he was writing to his wife in H's dug-out and he remarked 'to-day is the third anniversary of our wedding'. He had an awful wound in his head, and H thinks a bullet came through a sand-bag and hit him side-ways on.

We were relieved by the Worcesters comparatively early, but leaving our trenches for home it was pitch dark with a nice wetting rain driving in our faces. I had literally to tap tap my way with my stick in front of me, to avoid shell holes and trenches, and only by the lights of frequent 'Very lights' could we find our way; as it was half my Company got lost, and in recovering their route they picked up some men of another Company who were completely lost. We were told to go to the billets in Dichebusche via a narrow path round the southern part of the lake, a path built up through the shallow water and in places only a foot wide; under the circumstances I had barely gained the opposite shore when it was passed up 'Man fallen into the water, Sir'. I sent down that I was not going to save him from drowning, that if he could not get out of 18" of water by himself he could stay there. I had 150 men strung out over nearly ¼ mile in a single file and so dark I could hardly see my hands. We had two men fall in and my subaltern went in up to his hips, and also my Sergeant-Major and we all arrived in billets very cross. My temper was fairly set boiling by a heavy fall I took over a small irrigation ditch into a slimy greasy clay field. Our men are in wooden huts and we officers are in a small estaminet close by.

Drove into Poperinghe in the mess cart this afternoon to send off a cable to Herself, as tomorrow is her birthday, and to have my hair cut. Hear the French brought down a German aeroplane early this morning and captured the men in it. The 1st Battalion, R I Rifles did splendidly at Neuve Chapelle, and they say there were 20 'Michael O'Leary's' (the man in the Guards who got the VC for capturing a trench singlehanded) among them.

Rodney got a very bad wound shattering his wrist. He held it up to his men, 'Look what the . . . have done, boys — have at 'em'.

One of our fellows in hospital at Rouen met the interpreter who used to be attached to the IXth Lancers. He spoke of the charge the IXth made against some battery, in the early part of the War. They got the order to charge. Colonel Campbell reconnoitred and found the guns entrenched behind barbed wire. He rode up to General de Lisle and told him of the wire and the hopelessness of the attack. 'Charge, Sir', was all the answer he received. 'Sir, I will venture one more appeal. I will make the charge if you order me to do so, but will you come up with me and look at the position. The General refused and Colonel Campbell led his regiment down on the guns, and lost (as far as I remember) ¾ of them. Of course it was just possible that the General wanted to get a fresh target for the guns and to distract their attention from some troops elsewhere.

While N4 was being shelled (it's only 70 yards from the enemy) a voice from the German lines floated across 'Are you happy?' But they're in for it, I hear we are going to simply blow their whole line in, in a few days time.

We buried Major Alston at 6.30 pm. A party of 100 men, besides a firing party, followed, and of course all the officers. He was laid in the little military cemetery at Dichebusche, and we four officers (Company), the 2nd in Command and the Adjutant lowered the coffin into the grave. The firing party presented arms at the end of the service. We could not fire volleys or sound bugles as we were within sight and hearing of the German lines, and the 5th Division were going to have a bombardment at 7 pm. At 7 it started and for over an hour the air trembled with the noise, and their musketry broke us. I don't know whether the Division made an attack. They hold the line from St. Eloi to Ypres. Heavy Artillery fire went on till after 11 pm and our doors and windows are shaking. Not much of a rest for our poor nerves. We caught a spy in Dichebusche dressed in the uniform of an English Officer. Also the French brought down an aeroplane this morning and captured the pilot.

April 18th

The bombardment went on all night with less severity and I awoke at about 6 am with the big guns still shaking our windows. The Germans replied heavily to our guns too.

This morning news came that the 5th Division had blown up a German trench, and taken the first line together with a few prisoners, with slight loss to themselves, and heavy casualties to the enemy. Later news: a motor MG section fired two belts into two Companies of Germans, in close order with terrible effect. There has been some hard fighting and hand to hand fighting this morning and fighting was still going on at 11 am but we had the position well in hand and things were going on well with us. The Artillery fire stopped about 8 am.

Went to church in the evening: during the service (in the hospital) thought men were throwing heavy furniture about overhead. Found it was our guns and the Germans trying to remove bits of Belgium. They kept it up till quite late but nothing like so heavy as the night before.

April 20th

About midday yesterday the German guns threw several shells into Dichebusche, knocking down a few houses, amongst them the Post Office, blowing up the mail. I hear it was not our mail. A few people were wounded.

There were 1600 casualties at the attack by the 5th Division on last Saturday and Monday nights. The first line took the trenches with hardly a casualty, all the German resistance being destroyed by our bombardment, but our supports suffered very heavily from the enemy's fire from the big guns and most of the casualties were here and in resisting the counter-attack next day when there was a lot of hand to hand fighting. However, we gained and held some 200 to 400 yards of trenches and a bit more was taken on Sunday night. I hear too that if we lost severely the enemy lost very heavily. It is said the attack was merely to keep the enemy busy, as all our guns are concentrating about Bailleul and a rear attack will be pushed forward through Armentières within the next three or four days.

A Sapper officer who is always up and down the line told us that when the 27th Division were up here he was visiting the trenches and he suddenly noticed a German patrol inside our wire walking up and down and looking into our trench. He crawled up into this trench and found every man in it asleep and he had to wake them all up. Everyone gave the 27th Division up as perfectly hopeless. They were the last Division from India and simply refused to learn. The enemy did what they liked with them, and I fancy it was largely owing to their splendid example that the Germans are and have been showing such activity round St. Eloi, the last two or three months, and the 3rd Division had to send the 8th and 9th Brigades up to replace the 27th and restore some sort of 'Discipline' among the enemy's patrols, as they were getting really quite out of hand.

In the shooting party of such men in the Brigade as are 'bad hats' our Battalion provided two men, who only by a legal quibble escaped a death sentence themselves; and at 4 am they shot a man of the Wilts for desertion.

The Times, 21/4/15

On the Rue du Bois

A distinguished officer writes from the British Head Quarters in France: 'I venture to send you these beautiful lines, written by Canon F G Scott, of Quebec, who is doing duty with the 3rd Brigade of the Canadian Division and whose impressions which brought about the writing of these lines were gained from actual experiences in the trenches. It seems to me that such words as these should be made known to the public, for, apart from their

intrinsic beauty they are full of comfort to those who are sorely
stricken in this terrible War'.

> O pallid Christ within this broken shrine,
> Not those torn hands and not that heart of thine
> Have given the nations blood to drink like wine.
>
> Through weary years and 'neath the changing skies,
> Men turned their backs on those appealing Eyes
> And scorned as vain Thine awful Sacrifice.
>
> Kings with their Armies, children with their play
> Have passed unheeding down this shell-ploughed way,
> The great world knew not where its true strength lay.
>
> In pomp and luxury, in lust for gold,
> In selfish ease, in pleasures manifold.
> 'Evil is good, good evil,' we were told.
>
> Yet here, where nightly the great flare-lights gleam,
> And murder stalks triumphant in their beam,
> The world has wakened from its empty dream.
>
> At last O Christ, in this strange darkened land,
> Where ruined homes lie round on every hand
> Life's deeper truths men come to understand.
>
> For lonely graves along the country side,
> Where sleep those brave hearts who for others died,
> Tell of life's union with the crucified.
>
> And new light kindles in the mourners' eyes,
> Like day-dawn breaking through the rifted skies,
> For Life is born of Life's self-sacrifice.

> Holy Week, Northern France.

April 21st
    Came into the trenches last night. On our way down one of

my men close behind me was hit in the neck. He yelled from sheer fright like a wretched child. I ran back to him, (most of my men were hurrying past him as if he were stricken with plague), and shook him by the shoulder and told him to 'shut up'. Had to, as only some 500 yards away was a German machine gun I knew of, and many German rifles. Assured him he couldn't be badly hurt or he wouldn't yell like that; and a Sergeant bandaging him up, we left him lying there until a stretcher came for him. A man in one of the other Companies was shot through the lung on his way down; he died.

The 4th Battalion East Lancs on our left loosing off the rapid fire every ten minutes. On our way down such a burst broke out and half a dozen of my men at rear of the column started to bolt, panic stricken. However, luckily my Sergeant Major knocked one man into a ditch with a blow of his stick on the side of the head, and stopped it sharp and quick. It was lucky for the man that the Sergeant Major did so, as another NCO had loaded his rifle and was on the point of shooting the man. If he had done so I should have considered the action justifiable, – and so would any Court Martial. The East Lancs went on panic firing all night. They told me over the telephone they were firing at a working party of Germans working in front of the German lines. But as all the flashes were directed heavenwards I think the working party must have been working in a Zeppelin among the clouds. There seemed to be a little scrap round St. Eloi, as that wave of rapid fire which betokens an attack broke out about 2.30 –and the guns of both sides joined in. There was also a night bombardment of the line in the East of the Canal where an attack took place last Saturday.

On my way along my front trenches this morning a man fell over at my feet yelling like a heathen. However, he wasn't badly hit, a bullet snipped through a sand-bag and cut a deepish groove along the top of his head, but he never lost sensibility, so he's all right. About 3 pm Gilliland turned up at my dug-out with his face bound up. We'd both been using a periscope in his trench this morning and the trench isn't 80 yards from the enemy who are holding the edge of a wood at this point. They took no notice of our periscope then, but later when I'd left him they put a bullet in a sand-bag alongside it and when he removed it along the trench and looked through it again a bullet hit the top glass with such force that the fragments of the top glass smashed the lower glass and splashed into Gilliland's face cutting his nose and chin about, but nothing serious of course. He's the second officer we have had wounded by having his periscope shot through.

In front of one trench lie the row (16) of Frenchmen I remarked last week and up a road, across which another part of my trench goes, lie mouldering over a dozen blue clad corpses; their faces black now, two of them lie half sunk in the wet ditch at the side, the others are huddled against the bank as if they had crawled there out of the centre of the road and the direct line of fire. There are a couple of bodies behind our trench which will get buried to-night. The Germans threw some 20 or so shells at our line this morning but they were evidently not trying for my particular trenches. They got in a pretty shot or two at No 2 though I don't think they did any harm, but most of their shells burst into the empty fields behind, their Artillery evidently shelling some old trenches under the idea that our supports were there.

A small spring runs just outside my support trench, and some 80 yards behind my forward trench. This stream is open to flank fire from the enemy's trenches on our right.

Contrary to orders, one of my men, as soon as my Sergeant Major and I had turned our backs, hops out of a small trench cut as a drain through the parapet of a communication trench to this spring with his water bottle. A bullet immediately hits him in the arm and enters his body below the waist. He drops yelling, 2 or 3 men, one a Sergeant, Tweedie, rush down from behind their trench 80 yards away out into the open and pull him into my dug-out. But one man of the rescue party is shot in the arm and both legs and another who went to bring this last man in gets hit in the head. A fine bit of work on the part of the men engaged. The poor fool, I fear, will die, the other wounds are I think not dangerous.* The Germans had evidently noticed men going there before and were on the look out as they opened a burst of rapid fire.

April 22nd

Beautiful bright spring day after a very cold night. The enemy threw a few shells behind us at a support trench some 200 yards in rear, and dropped them in the fields harmlessly in front of them. About 3.5 pm a very heavy bombardment started away to the North of us; it was far enough away to sound like peals of thunder, but it jarred the ground inside one's dug-out and gave me a head.

Had another man wounded in the head at 'Stand to' this evening. Bullet came through a single sandbag blocking a gap in a bad bit of parapet. All my men just reporting they are suffering from bad eyes, can't think what it can be. Have sent them back to their work, though. I went out and noticed a curious sweet smell like marigolds and certainly my eyes began to smart. I 'phoned up the Head Quarters and I hear that all along the line we are noticing it. Presumably it is the fumes of the heavy explosives, Turpinite, or what not, which is being used in the bombardment, the guns of which are still at 9 am thundering away to the North of us. The Suffolks on the right report that the Division on their right again have reported that the Germans have been letting loose obnoxious gases into their trenches. I had read of this invention of a German Chemist-Soldier, and the idea crossed my mind, and it is quite probable, but at 90 yards no gas is likely to do any harm beyond, on a still

---

* He died three hours later. I reported the names of Sergeant Tweedie and the other man to Headquarters – Becher, who was temporarily in command, refused to forward the names. Said the men were engaged in rescuing a man shot through disobeying orders and he couldn't forward their names! He is a real old fashioned type of 'Foot-slogging' muddle-headed officer.

day as today was, giving us petty inconveniences; sore eyes, or headaches, I have the latter at present.* The bombardment to the North seems to have died down now, at 10.45 pm.

April 23rd

From about 11 pm onwards guns sounding like very heavy howitzers were going all night up to about 2.30 am. The Germans have been throwing 15″ shells into Ypres this last week and to me it seemed as if they were shelling the unfortunate town again.

I woke up at 3.30 to a very heavy rattle, and going out found our shrapnel and the enemy's bursting all about the mound at St. Eloi. The rifle fire went on hard for over an hour, so it looks as if the Germans had another push at us up there.

Watched one of our very early birds flying down the German front. They sent some 40 shells after him. Tiny cloud bursts very pretty against the pinks of the rising sun.

A beautiful day till the afternoon; and about 3.30 a field gun sent a few shots all too close to our heads into the German trenches; in fact, one of our shrapnel burst over one of our support trenches on my right and possibly sent a bullet or two into 'A' Company's backs.

Our Artillery seem to make a hobby of firing into us, and they admit that practically they cannot make a certainty of always getting within 70 yards of their target: that is the margin outside which they say we are safe, and so it's no joke when they persist in shrapnelling the enemy who are only 70 to 80 yards from us. Of course, with high angle howitzers it is different.

Heavy firing to our left (NW) again.

Our scoff box arrived last week and we brought it up to the trenches with us; a box fitted with plates, cups, coffee pot, etc,

---

* We heard later it was gas used by the Huns in an attack on the French, North of Ypres, some 7 miles away. It floated all down the line and, of course, was very weak when it reached us.

for six. A 'Joy for ever' is the Primus Stove with which I have been playing, and blackening my dug-out with smuts. Water seems to take twice as long to boil over a Primus as over an ordinary coke fire, but I fried my own bacon ration on it with some success and also 'hotted' up my meat ration.

A thunderous bombardment of Ypres from 6 to 7.30 pm with huge howitzers; the earth here, 4 miles off, was shaking from the explosions.

April 24th

All last night, all this morning, the German guns away to the NW have been thundering at Ypres, and at our line N of the town. I hear they have concentrated huge masses of troops about there to have another 'go' at capturing the town.

I was up again at 3.30, took my field glasses to see if I could see anything of the fight going on certainly within a mile of us. But I could only hear the roar of rapid fire and see the white fluff balls bursting against the Mother of Pearl sky. About 6 pm my subaltern and I retired to my dug-out for cocoa and ration biscuits and honey and cake. Such a meal for that hour of the day; and when he returned to his dug-out along my far trench, he witnessed an Anti-Aircraft gun bring down a Taube, or rather hit it and force it to come down within its own lines.

'A' Company's trench had a shell in it, blew in the signallers' dug-out and cut all their lines but did no other harm. They also had 7 casualties from rifle grenades fired into them. The Germans again shelled the trench where 'A' Company's supports are and cut all our telephone wires and we were, I'm glad to say, cut off from Headquarters for a few hours.

Just as we were packing up, anticipating relief, a message came to say relief is cancelled; the Worcesters who relieve us are doing a big digging job and it has to be finished at once, and so they are doing it tonight and relieving us tomorrow.

The French were driven back 3 kilometres on their line N of Ypres and the Canadians on their right were forced to retire a bit, too, owing to the French retiring; I hear 130,000 Germans are massed about there.*

Ypres is in flames which are reddening the sky; all the people have cleared out of it, and the terrible shelling it has had the last three days must have almost levelled it, for the big guns were going most of today, too.

Poperinghe has also been shelled for the first time in the War.

There are printed orders all round West Outre, Locre, La Clytte, etc, warning everyone that all the roads must be kept clear of all traffic next Tuesday and Wednesday and that all civilians must remain indoors.

Large number of Cavalry passed through Dichebusche going Northwards last night and this morning; a Division, at least, my CQMS tells me. Also no mails today; he says there is a rumour that the mail boat was sunk.

April 25th

Very heavy fighting heard beyond Ypres at 3 am and musketry and artillery were going hard till about 8 am when things quietened down. It is said that the whole of the German lines from Kemmel to the river Douvre are mined; this is, I suppose, Petit Bois, a farm we call Peckham, and further South other prominent or well fortified points d'appui close to our lines. Big things are promised next week.

A quiet day for us, but about 5 pm the Germans commenced to shell the Companies on my right, and plumped some shells not only into the parapet but actually into the trench; unfortunately from the Huns' point of view that particular trench happens to be empty. They have also thrown a few trench bombs round our fire trench.

Am very glad we are being relieved tonight – five days too long in one spell, as one can't get properly clean, and I see my men hitching their shoulders or their arms, scratching their legs and bodies or, horribile dictu, searching their shirts. And I myself

---

* This was on the day when we smelt the gas in our trenches.

am irritating all over, but this I think is rather the effect of 5 days sedentary work on one's blood than due to 'little things'.

I had almost written that we had had no casualities since the first day, but just now a rifle grenade drops into my right trench (6.30 pm) and slightly wounds two men in the legs. We saw the German machine gunners at work on their parapet this morning and managed, I am told, to get a couple of 'em. They apparently retired hurt; Sergeant Byrne says they were wearing Glengarry caps. By the by, all our Highlanders out here are being issued with Tam O'Shanters as the stock of Glengarries is used up, and the clothing department cannot procure any more, as these caps were all made in Germany! (So I heard tell.)

April 26th

Returned to the hut camp at Dichebusche last night. I hear the French General whose troops gave way N of Ypres says he's 'got the situation in hand'. It is said they lost 1100 prisoners and 30 guns, and that they put up no sort of a fight at all. The Worcesters were busy night before last completing some trenches of a third line behind St Eloi. All along the front there are no less than two lines of trenches we can get back to should we be pushed out of our forward trenches. The enemy put some shrapnel on the road our transport follows bringing rations to the trenches, and got some men and horses the other night, and a Taube dropped a bomb within a field of our present camp. Things seem to have quietened down a lot three days ago; all troops here were 'standing to' to move at ½ hour's notice to Ypres and we only just escaped being kept in the trenches indefinitely.

April 26th

In hut camp at Dichebusche: on my return this afternoon from Locre where I had gone for my weekly bath, I found four bombs had been dropped by an aeroplane on our camp and one of them, landing between two huts, had knocked out 16 of my own men and one man belonging to 'B' Company. The 17 included two of my best Sergeants, one of whom I fear will not recover, and such a good chap and only been out here a fortnight. Sir John French was motoring round here at the time, a lucky thing his car was not hit.

A very heavy bombardment going on NE of Ypres, probably in preparation of a counter attack on the line captured the other day by the Germans, from the French. All night the windows and doors of our billets were shaking at the heavy explosions of the German 17" shells which were landing at Ypres.

April 27th

Yesterday afternoon the enemy threw some shells into Dichebusche and the HAC, clearing out of their billets for safety into shelter trenches in rear, were caught by shrapnel and had one killed and 16 wounded. This afternoon about 4 pm we found small shells, a number of which failed to explode coming into Dichebusche from the N, NW and NE and we heard later on that it was an armoured train firing from where the railway crossed the canal, about four miles North of Ypres; they must have had long range 4" guns. They killed a number of civilians in the village.

April 28th

Took a digging party of 200 men out last night at 8 pm, didn't get back till 1.15 am. Digging trenches behind the P's, close to St Eloi, we were from 600 to 1200 yards from the German lines, but bullets were coming on us unpleasantly and I had two men hit; one man working at the furthest range got a bullet through the centre of the chest; he died in half an hour and was buried at Vormezelle; the other through the ribs and back. I was talking to a private in the Lincolns. Apparently all 'Bells' in the Army are nicknamed 'Daisy'. He informed me he was sometimes called

'Daisy' (and what a Daisy, too), but he had a brother in the heavy Battery always known as Daisy Bell. The other day a shell burst in the gun and Bell and the Sergeant were both blown to pieces. Bell's neckscarf is still to be seen hanging on a branch of a tree 30′ from the ground. The gunners buried the bits of indistinguishable debris in two graves and then left the place to get their guns mended without putting any crosses up. They returned in two days' time with two nicely made crosses, and since there was nothing to show which was which when the bodies were buried, were for sticking them in haphazard, but on arriving at the tiny clay mounds, they saw a daisy growing on top of one, all by 'its lonely'. 'That's Daisy's grave', they said, and stuck up his cross at the head. His brother told me he considered it a 'mericle'. The present Daisy, a huge, burly, very ugly, very dirty gentleman, with kindly, pleasant eyes, is doing Storeman to some RE Stores at Vormezelle, the first job he has had he told me, since he came out here in August.

April 28th

A perfect summer day, very warm and, best of all, for 12 hours not a sign of War, beyond the crowds of soldiers all round. A regiment of Bengal Lancers is camped next to us. They sent out a Squadron last night to round up all the loose horses which broke away from various transport lines during one shelling of this place yesterday evening. At 7 pm the perfect peace ended, and a half hour's violent bombardment, from I hear, some 200 French guns, broke out, the preliminary to the attack by the French on Steenstraate Bridge over the Ypres Canal, which was in the hands of the Germans, captured by them when they crossed the Canal last Friday. Under the terrific fire we heard poured into them, it seems impossible that they can hold it against an attack of any kind whatsoever.

Major Weir from the 1st Battalion joined today to take over command.

April 29th

The weather still the same, hotter if possible. Inspected the two Anti-Aircraft guns which are close by our billets. They are only 13lbs Horse Artillery Guns with the trails cut off and mounted on a horseshoe mounting on large trolleys, the chassis of which, made in America, cost our Government £1000 – chassis which should have been made at home at a third of that price. But all the motor works at home now are busy, if not making shells and guns, then working at gun parts, etc. The German yarn that their fleet over-ran the North Sea last week without our knowledge is, of course, nonsense. Not a ship of theirs moves out of port, but that we know of it within 12 hours. I understand our spy system is perfect, the more so that one hears nothing of it or about it. At the time of the Scarborough raid, we knew about their coming, and a fleet from the Thames, and one from Scotland came down and formed a ring right round the German boats. Then a fog came and under its cover the enemy slipped through. The luck of War.

The gun which was shelling Dichebusche the other day was a 5.4' mounted on railway trucks, and it must have been firing at a range of over 5½ miles, and as all the shells fell into a very small area the gun was shooting very accurately. A gunner officer has just told me that some three months ago long before there was any mention of operations in the Dardanelles, a lady told him (in the Albert Hall at a concert of all places) that there would be land operations there and they would have at least 300,000 men engaged. I suppose some shining light at Headquarters told his wife the secret. The Convent of the Black Sisters at Ypres has been burnt, also the Convent of Les Dames Anglaises, where hung the Standards of the Irish Brigade which fought so well in the service of Louis XV at Fontenoy, as they did in the days of his father at Malplaquet, when the Royal Irish Regiment with Marlboro's Army, beat them. Everyone has left Ypres now, and most of the people have cleared out of Dichebusche.

Passing through Vormezelle the other night, the whole place is wrecked and that side of the church facing the German lines about 1000 yards off is blown clean out, and of the church only one wall and bits of the two ends remain while the graveyard is a mass of shell holes, broken and jumbled crosses and stones and twisted railings.

I was talking to our Belgian interpreter today and he was telling me about the German atrocities. He keeps a note of three Regiments of Bavarians who are responsible for the atrocities in Dinant and he told me he would give no mercy to any man of those Regiments who fell into his hands. He knows of one case of a Belgian Officer who was captured by the Germans close to his (the officer's) home. His wife and their six or seven children went to the German Major and begged for the Father's life, and the wife pointed to all her children. 'You have too many', said the Major, and then and there before the mother and father he had two or three of the kiddies shot. If one did not know such stories to be authenticated, one would almost be sorry for the Germans, when the French and German troops get into German Territory. My Subalterns (another joined me today getting his commission from 'Queen Victoria's Rifles')* and I had a bathe this afternoon in a ditch about 200 yards from our billets, a ditch with a spring in it. We could just get it up to our chests, very cool and very refreshing.

All billets now have to be paid for; for regimental officers the rate is 1 Fr. per night. For men, 35 cents, so I don't suppose we shall do more billeting than we can help.

The Germans got through the French lines last week entirely by the use of asphyxiating gas which terrified the Zouaves and African tirailleurs holding the trenches there. They got frightened at what they didn't understand and made but a poor resistance. Just before, too, a whole corps of line troops had been withdrawn, and so the first line had no backing. I can't help thinking the French Generalissimo in this sector (General Foch), who commanded all the Belgian, French and English

---

*He got wounded later, in June: in the attack on Hooge.

Armies from the sea to the end of our line about La Bassée and whose Headquarters are at Cassel) made an error, as he must have known at least a week before the Germans were massing troops opposite Ypres. However, we all, the Allies, did a splendid bit of work in putting such an immediate full stop to the German effort; for all our guns in this part of our line had been sent southwards. Of course, they were immediately hurried back.

This evening (7.15 pm) the whole of the northern horizon is clouded with purple pink smoke, from Ypres, which above that town is rising in a long streamer.

I have just heard one of the finest things that have happened during the War. Young Pike, a son of the Pikes near Ballincollig, has for years been paralysed from his legs down. Unable to do anything but motor, he has joined the flying corps, is helped into and out of his 'plane, and though a cripple is able to do 'his bit'. Rather a fine example of spirit, I think.

April 30th

Battalion went to the trenches this evening, 'D' Company being in reserve at Gordon House. Gilliland rejoined today from the Convalescent Hospital on Mont Noir; Messing 2/- a day and Port and Champagne at dinner every night! Two motor ambulances to take patients out and horses for riding. Worth being wounded – slightly, of course. A number of officers who have been fighting at Hill 60 and at Ypres were there completely broken down. One Major came in and burst into tears. Gilliland had never seen men so broken. He heard the French simply bolted, their penal Battalions going strong – to the rear. Some of their artillery teams were found in West Outre next morning (after the German attack) traces cut; the men simply galloped panic stricken away. Our Canadians appear to have been simply fine; men and regimental officers, but their staff was shocking; simply lost their heads or else were ignorant.

The Companies who first charged Hill 60 only had five

casualties; the heavy losses coming after from the counter-attacks and the shelling, when the supports suffered so heavily. The French Artillery stopped the German advance until their infantry could be brought up, by simply placing a sheet of shell fire in front of the German advance. Their fourteen batteries (4 guns each) of their famous 75's fired no less than 79 rounds per gun in 10 minutes; over 4,300 shells in 10 minutes and, of course, our guns were going too; and this did not by any means end the Artillery action.

Our counter-attacks occasioned us heavy losses, partly because two battalions were launched at 3 pm across 1,000 yards of open country without any artillery support. It was wiped out and the remnant dribbled back. The next advance a couple of hours later was supported by our guns and was successful in its object.

The whole affair of the Ypres battle is most discreditable to the French Staff. Apparently, as we all knew 10 days ago, the Germans were massing troops here. Something must have gone very radically wrong. An officer in the General Headquarters Trenches, our last and third line of trenches, said the Germans advanced to within 300 yards of them and there was no trench dug at that point. Luckily there was a very fine barbed wire entanglement in front. As a matter of fact, it appears the Germans never thought they would have been so successful, and had made no preparation for a push right through, and also they naturally could not believe there was no strength behind the French and our lines and so they never went on as well as they might have done.

German spies appear to be still very numerous. Last week a lady in Poperinghe came up to a Belgian officer and told him there was an officer in English uniform staying at her house whom, she thought, was not an Englishman. The Belgian went back with her, covered the officer with his revolver and took him prisoner. He spoke very broken English; wore both the South African Medals and had been in Poperinghe for three weeks. I suppose he's shot by this time.

We apparently thought a German gun had got through our lines as our Cavalry patrols were all round West Outre searching yards, etc, for a hidden gun, the day after the Ypres attack. A good yarn of the Neuve Chapelle show: a grenadier, clambering into a German trench, looked into a dug-out; 'How many of you in there?' says he. 'Four', yells out a terrified Teuton. 'Then share this amongst you', chucking inside a hand grenade. If the story is true I hope the grenade did burst, sometimes they don't.

I see Major Large of the Middlesex Regiment with whom I was cramming, was killed at Ypres. His brother was killed last March and I met him only a month ago convalescing at Locre, from shattered nerves. A little Scottish Doctor in the RAMC was at the Mont Noir for a rest. He was at St Julien where all the heavy fighting has been for the last few days. He says our Motor Ambulances got up within 700 yards of the fighting. Two ambulances filled up, and, though really it seems incredible, *took the wrong turning and drove into the German troops.** He swears this is a fact; this may be so, there was absolute chaos behind our lines for a day or two, so they say.

May 1st

I hear General Foch wants us to give up the Ypres Salient. He says he does not mean to waste men in pushing the Germans out of the new line they have so strongly fortified. Of course, I understand, he admits his troops ran, but there seems to have been faults on both his and French's part.

We moved all our guns to the Armentières side; the Germans knew of it, and naturally took advantage, though probably the opportunity offered before they were completely prepared; hence the failure, for it was a failure to them, though they did so

---

* It is a fact. The two drivers and one conductor were shot. What happened to the wounded, we don't know. The German advance disorganised the whole line, so that it is not to be wondered at, that our motor drivers drove in among them.

much. I fear it has cost us more dearly than Neuve Chapelle. There were so many of our wounded that they were lying in the courtyard of the hospital at Bailleul.

Everyone is cursing Churchill for starting the Dardanelles show; we want the men here, which is the chief area of the War and history should have taught him the stupidity of dividing his forces. We want up here the 300,000 that are ear-marked for the Dardanelles.

A perfect May-day, one of the very few perfect, hot, sunny May-days that I can remember. I'd sell my jacket now; as a rule, May-day is the Day on which one buys an overcoat.

Clouds, and apparently rain is blowing up. I walked down to N8 and paid a visit to Hutchison who has just been made Captain.

When the French bolted at Ypres, the Canadians prolonged their line to the left till it became so thin they could prolong it no further. I hear our boys put a few, a good few bullets into the flying Frenchmen just to show their disgust.

We are wondering whether the French will use their new explosive Turpinite which is poisonous on explosion and, therefore, prohibited by the Geneva Convention. They tried it the other day on a flock of 800 sheep. Put two 75 shells into them, and killed and suffocated the whole lot. Now the Germans use Asphyxiating gases, I see no reason why the French should not use Turpinite.

I heard an amusing and as it happens an authentic yarn, about one of our air pilots. Some months ago his machine came down within the German lines close to Lille. A large number of German soldiery rushed up to capture him, but somehow or other, he managed to escape into the city where he found a French family who took him in and concealed him.

He lay with them for some three weeks, the whole town plastered with his description, and with rewards for his capture.

At the end of that time, in a suit of civilian clothes, he walked out of the place, got across into Holland and thence home. Returning here he promptly, on the first opportunity, flew over

Lille and dropped a sarcastic message telling the Germans that the man they were after presented his compliments to them. All of a sudden something went wrong with his engine, and when on the point of falling again into the Germans' hands (and would they have not have had the laugh on him), he by some means righted himself, and just managed to get to our lines. But it was a narrow shave.

Last week a second lieutenant performed a plucky deed. Alone he flew off to drop a bomb on to Courtrai (I think) Railway Station. In a perfect hail of fire he descended to 300 feet and let loose his bomb. The explosion he felt even at this height. Severely wounded and with a large gash in his thigh, he flew off, and to gain speed descended to 100 feet, at which height he flew over the German trenches. Again they fired at him and a bullet ripped up his abdomen. Instead of descending into the German lines, where his life might have been saved, he flew over Ypres and back to the flying ground, where he was lifted out of his machine and died.*

May 3rd

In M3 and N1 there were thirty-two casualties, the majority slight, but we had six killed, all from HE shrapnel. Had the men's shelters been splinter-proof on top, most probably we should have had no casualties at all. There was a very strong whiff of chlorine gas all over the place, right up to Dichebusche they smelt it, yesterday afternoon. Most probably it had come down wind the six to eight miles from the German lines north of Ypres. All men are now issued with muslin or Gamgee tissue, or flannel respirators, to be soaked in a mixture of washing soda and water, the mixture being kept handy in jars in the trenches.

Our draft of twenty-six last night does not quite fill up the holes caused by the Huns. This morning at 4 am a tremendous

---

* His name appeared in the next Honours Gazette as a VC.

bombardment was going on north of us, and later in the day we had a message that General H. Plumer and his Division (the 5th) had repulsed a German advance from St Julien, and also that the French had been unsuccessful further on our left.

A German stationary observation balloon broke loose last night and drifted westward over our lines, and we also brought down one of their aeroplanes into our lines.

Another message says just in from Norman's trench that he has had two more killed and eleven wounded today from shell fire. At present the wires are cut and we cannot hear anymore.

May 4th

Two or three heavy showers which made all the countryside greasy and slippery and almost as beastly as ever. Luckily a warm rain.

Some heavy firing away to the north but nothing else.

Our Battalion came out of the trenches tonight, and returned to camp in Dichebusche, but D Company remains out in bivouac in a wood close to Gordon Farm, as Brigade Reserve; our duty, if our front line should be forced, being to occupy the Subsidiary Line, a line of trenches running about a 1,000 yards in rear of the first line.

May 5th

A topping night for camping out. Black velvety sky studded in stars: nightingale in full song; everything perfect if it was not for the Hun. He has got the idea that our transport uses the road running the front of this wood at night, and so from 9 pm to about 1 am he shells it regularly every ten minutes. As I lay in my flea bag I saw the little bursting stars some 400 yards off, then came to our ears the wicked hiss of the beast, and the ear-splitting explosion, the short sharp crack of the HE shrapnel, and, of course, all the time, all the night the rifles were going continually, and though our front line is quite 1,000 yards away, the echo through the trees makes it sound as if men were firing just on the edge of the woods.

I awoke about 8 am to the heavy cannonade and rifle fire to the North of us; I think it may have been round Hill 60. At nine I resolutely arose, pulled on my gum-boots and awoke Leask to accompany me for a bathe in Dichebusche lake. But when we got there we found a 'flying sentry' who told us he was guarding the lake to prevent all bathing, so went to Gordon House where the Worcesters, who have taken our place, gave us hot water for shaving.

Hill 60 was captured from us by the Germans early this morning.

At 4 pm we got an order to be ready to move at a quarter of an hour's notice, and all the Battalions not in the trenches are 'standing to'.

They say we are going to support the 5th Division in their counter attack.

May 6th

Awoke to a hot summer day, and directly after breakfast Gilliland, Leask and I, started to on the new dugout we are building for ourselves in the old GHQ line in this wood. A palatial place where four officers can sleep, with a sort of verandah under which we shall set our table.

To Dichebusche to attend office. Returning I found the Huns shelling the place, and half a dozen shells bursting round the church, along the side which my path back to camp lay. Approached with some trepidation, and half way down a shell arrived. Luckily it burst some 40 yards off.

Reached camp very hot, as the sun is simply pouring down on us.

A few moments later, a perspiring cyclist Orderly brought word for me to be at Brigade Head Quarters at 2 pm and for the Company to 'stand to' and be prepared to march at once.

It was now 1.15 and no hot water. However, I rolled up my

valise, packed my kit, and started Gilliland on to the Primus. The damned thing, of course, refused to work. Eventually, got half a cup of tea and a piece of biscuit and jam, and off to Head Quarters in Dichebusche. It began to rain as I started; far too hot to put on my 'Burberry', so I trudged on and arrived fairly wet. Found Becher and the other three Company Commanders there, and that the Battalion was taking over some trenches East of Ypres, and we were to walk on and inspect them by daylight. Off we went. Becher, with a very hazy idea of map-reading; and as he'd not allow anyone else to help him we made very heavy weather of it. We advanced very slowly, very hotly, up the Ypres-Dichebusche Road, turned off to the Chateau South of Kruisstraat, close to which we crossed the Canal, and thence to the forked roads North of Trois Rois. This point we were told the Germans shelled heavily, as they always hoped to catch transport on the march, and we didn't stay to look about us for long. The few roadside houses here all shattered, the trees cut in half like carrots, or with limbs torn off and hanging down.

As we were waiting, we heard a tremendous explosion from Hill 60, a big eminence in this flat country, though really hardly distinguishable as a hill. We saw an enormous volume of smoke rise, and surmised it was a mine. Our Artillery were plastering the place with shells, and some lucky hit either exploded a mine or an ammunition cart.

As we dropped down alongside the railway embankment, we quickly came on the debris of the heavy fighting round here; for, burrowing into the embankment were, first a dressing station of RAMC and then a battalion of the Rifle Brigade, the litter round this latter, filthy beyond description, and I cannot understand any officers allowing their men to live in such insanitary and disgusting conditions when it was quite possible to have a camp clean and sanitary.

In front of the dressing station we saw three dead bodies, awaiting burial, evidently died of wounds, and, within a very few yards more dead but no effort at burial. The men walking about amongst the corpses callously.

Apparently no one's job to bury them and no one cared.

After a very muddy and disgusting trudge we reached the Head Quarters of the 13th Brigade, in a farm (see map I. 21.a) on the West side of Zillebeke pond.

We soon discovered something was up. The South Lancashires were to accompany us, but they were going into reserve that night; we were to relieve the Bedfords who had been 25 days in the trenches. We also heard we had an attack on that night. I often wondered how I'd feel if I were ordered to attack, but to my surprise I just felt a curiosity as to what would happen to me, though I had no thought that anything more serious than a wound would come my way. A guide met us at Brigade Head Quarters, and taking us across country round the North end of the pond, and through the Tuilleries, a brick field ½ a mile East of Zillebeke village, we eventually arrived at the Head Quarters of the Bedfords where more guides met us to take us to the trenches.

With intervals of 50 or 60 yards between us, so as not to attract the enemy's attention, we followed our guides, keeping as much behind hedges as possible, as we were within rifle fire from Hill 60. After some ¾ of a mile we came to a large communication trench which led us out to just behind the support trench of our Fire trenches; here there is a miniature graveyard;* and we saw several poor fellows yet awaiting burial, and a huge pile of clothing, arms and equipment off the dead, waiting to be carried away. A Major of the Bedfords led us into the trenches. A shell had blown in the left and he suggested we need not visit that part as there was a horrid mess there. I believe there were a number of poor fellows lying dead, horribly mutilated.

These trenches had been gassed, and all the grass and foliage around was bleached white, or a sickly yellow; all brass buttons turned black, and it even affected the bolt action of the rifles, corroding the steel apparently and making them stiff to work.

---

* It is here Gilliland was buried the following day.

205

The trenches were dug very deeply and had huge parapets, while dug-outs and shelters for the men were plentiful. These trenches 47, 48, 49, 50 and, I think, 51, were more or less enfiladed from Hill 60, and every few yards huge traverses were built right across the trench, archways some 3 feet high under them permitting the passage from one part to the other. We were shown 48, and 47 pointed out to us, but we couldn't go into either, as half way up the communicating trench to 48, the parapet had been blown in and had not been repaired, and it was impossible to reach 47, as on one point of passage the Germans had a MG trained. The Bedford Major promised to have the gap built up before we took over, and also a traverse built to safeguard our passage to 47. We then returned to Battalion Headquarters, dog tired and very hungry.

Managed to get a few mouthfuls of tea each and a piece of cheese, and then a message came ordering us to meet the Battalion at Brigade Headquarters. So back we tramped there. The Huns were by this time, indulging in their usual afternoon 'Hate'; sending shells along the embankment of the Zillebeke pond. We came in for a shower of them en passant; to escape we had to cross a broad ditch full of water. One guide and Becher, both went in up to their middle to my secret joy. Our guides appeared to have lost not only their way, but their heads, for soon after they were stopped by another ditch. They struggled across it, getting still wetter. I remembered a plank by which we'd crossed on our way up to the trenches. I went over it, and Becher, who is rather blind at dusk, once more fell in. I didn't wait to listen to him.

A struggle through absolute filth along the pond embankment, over the roofs of dug-outs, into one of which Hutchison fell, and after much hard language, we again brought up at Brigade Head Quarters, where we were regaled on wine.

Yet still, no food, and I was hungry. Had had no lunch and it was now about 8 pm. Heard the Battalion was coming up under Major Weir* so we waited. I met the Divisional Motor MG

* Of the 1st Battalion.

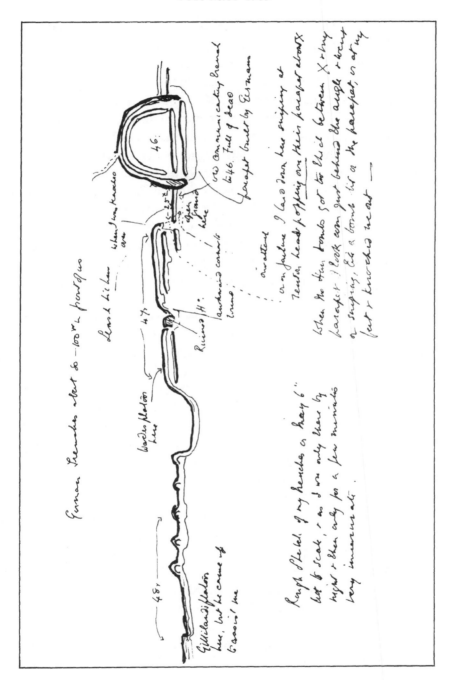

Officer there. He has a flat, bathroom, bedroom, sheets! in Bailleul, but the Germans had not let him see the place for the last fortnight. He and his guns were present when the Germans broke through in April, and the Canadians and our troops saved the situation. He said he'd turned some of our guns on the flying 'Red Breeches', just to help them run, and also that he really did not know which was the worse, the German gas, or the Canadian gas!!! He said their Staff arrangements were simply appalling.

The Brigade bomb officer showed us some bombs he was going to use this morning, huge spherical affairs like cannon balls, about 7″ or 8″ in diameter; he also showed us, what up till now we'd only heard of: the 'jam tin bomb', a tin the size of a 1 lb. tin of jam, with a piece of fuse at the top and on the fuse a cardboard cap, which the operator forced down giving it a sharp turn; this caused a friction spark to ignite the fuse which was timed to burn five seconds.

All this time we four officers and several other officers and men were waiting in the scullery of the farmhouse; some of us lucky to get a seat on a chair or a case. We four were very hungry, weary, worn out, and there was no sign of the battalion; it was now about 9 pm and pitch dark, and every now and then an ear splitting explosion shook the house, as the enemy 'whizz-bangs' shot along the embankment, exploding within a hundred yards all round the Headquarters. The Germans knew the dug-outs on this railway embankment were full of troops, and every night they plastered the ground with shells to catch men moving outside the cover of the ground, and they evidently knew this farm was occupied by us, as they seemed to give it special attention, most of their shells bursting outside the front door, between the house and a barn some 20 yards away. We all used the back entrance; in fact, the front of the house was more or less sandbags, doors and walls being blown in, and through some of the interstices of the sandbags the shell-bursts seared the eye like lightning.

At last about 10.30 pm Major Weir arrived to say the Battalion was up; and after he had spoken to the Brigadier commanding the 13th Brigade to whom we had been lent, I was called in, and the General told me that trench 46 had been captured by the Germans. That another attack on Hill 60 was planned, but that Hill 60 could never be held while trench 46 was in the hands of the enemy (in fact, this was the reason Hill 60 had been taken from us two or three nights ago). He went on to say that two battalions, the Westminster Rifles and another battalion were making a frontal attack at 2.30 am on the 7th, that the Suffolks who were holding the trenches on the right of 46 had mined the sandbag parapet separating 46 from their trenches and were to blow it up and rush up to the trench to the apex, while I was, at 2.30 am sharp, to cooperate in the attack by rushing the sandbag parapet between 46 and my trench 47, and rush round to the apex of the trench to meet the Suffolks; that it was quite a simple job. 'How many men? oh! yes, 14 or 15 men quite enough, just a few men with grenades and a few bayonets'. So easy, so simple – in the room and over a map. The General had in course of a previous conversation told me it was just wasting life to attempt Hill 60 again, as no one could hold it, and that in any case, now the foliage was coming on the trees, the Hill as an observation post was negatived; but, he said, Army Headquarters wanted it re-taken and so he had to do it. But just take trench 46 – I was rather proud old Weir had picked me out, a compliment to my Company, which was certainly, by a long way, the best in the Battalion, and admittedly so: but then I had topping good platoon leaders and a rattling good Sergeant Major.

Now to find my Company. I had luckily sent a message to Gilliland to send our 'skoff box' back to the transport. Couldn't risk that in the trenches so close to the Huns. A guide met me at the scullery door, and loaded with respirators for my men, and with two boxes of grenades, he led me and two orderlies to where the battalion was halted under cover of the embankment.

We just reached them when a shell burst over us, just missing us, thank God. A very nasty corner and shells coming over frequently.

209

To my surprise the men were firm, but then since last February our drafts have been improving both in quality and training, and we've got rid of all our wasters, and I had some 155 quite useful lads under me; a small company, but quite good; none better in Flanders outside the Guards. I called up my platoon leaders and explained to them what we had to do, put on my pack which I had left behind with the Company, and which a man brought up for me; issued the respirators, and marched off, in the order each platoon would be in my line of trenches. I was told off to hold 47 and 48, all parapets more than trenches; 47 well enfiladed from 46 – Jolly Leask, who was my Company grenade specialist, I selected to hold 47 and to make the attack with his grenade throwers. He, quite happy about it. Gilliland, I put in 48 with a youngster who had just joined the Battalion from the Westminster Rifles. Altogether, four platoons (70 men in 47; 85 in 48) held these trenches.

May 7th

We marched off, in file, which in places became single file, the remainder of the battalion following as their Company officers came out of Headquarters. Mayne's Company to the reserve at the Tuilleries; Norman's and Hutchison's Companies to occupy the trenches on my left.

Getting clear of the embankment we got out of the zone of the fire; a starlight very dark night, no moon, but clear. We had to halt every hundred yards to close up. Marched through all that remains of Zillebeke; a dead village, not even a wandering cat to disturb the silence. It was about midnight when we set out, and about 1.15 am we reached the support trench and entered the deep communication trench leading to 50 trench. A march of perhaps 1½ miles. But my poor fellows were very tired; a long march from Dichebusche in greatcoats; a heavy muggy day, and some of my fellows carrying boxes of grenades, ammunition. We filed along into 50, and got among the Bedfords. I sent Leask and Gilliland on to their trenches, and stayed behind to see the rear of my company up. After some half an hour we got through to our own lines; no easy job as we had to take off our packs and thread our way in single file under these traverse arches.

As I passed up my line, I posted my platoons and sections, taking the place of the Bedfords, who are, without exception the rottenest crowd I have ever met. They had a rough time of it, yet no battalion should have got into such a demoralised condition.

Eventually stumbling and slipping I came to 47; and found at the dangerous corner, where the Bedford Major had ordered a traverse should be built, nothing but half a dozen sandbags placed in position, and the breach in the parapet he had ordered to be mended had not been touched.

It was 2 am. Trench 47 full of Bedfords and my men, no one able to move. The subaltern in charge told me his Captain had just been killed and 'I'm awfully sorry but I'm afraid I'll have to leave you to bury five of my men'. I managed to swallow my wrath. The blighters, couldn't even bury their own dead; and by jove, they had not even removed their identity discs or papers. Told the poor fool to leave a sergeant and half a dozen men behind to collect their papers and bury them. (Directly the

going up the trenches

shooting started, these beauties hooked it!) The Bedfords would not clear off; it was 2.10; 20 minutes to arrange my attack and I couldn't move. The subaltern couldn't get his men out. At last they cleared, and at 2.20 am I told Leask to collect his men grenadiers, or the bravest men he could get hold of in the dark and get ready.

Gilliland now joined me to help; absolutely invaluable. Leask got the boxes of grenades open and found they were of the 'jam tin' pattern which no one but myself had ever seen before. Tried to show them how to work them, but, of course in the instant I could spare, neither he nor any of his men grasped it. There were some handgrenades ready fused, left in the dug-out. These he got hold of and he, heading his men, waited. My watch had been synchronised with that of the Brigadier. At 2.30 am I showed a flashlight to the rear, to mark the right of my trench, so that the main attack should not rush us; and I sent Leask forward. I cannot quite remember what happened. I know I saw Gilliland very busy 'setting' handgrenades and generally helping. I saw from the black wall of the parapet (German) 30 yards in front of us, flashes, and knew they were firing; I heard a scream, a groan, a thud, and my Sergeant Major told me, it seemed within a few minutes, that men were killed and wounded. Then I heard a shriek, and a 'Mr. Leask is kilt', and I saw Leask ploughing his way, arms and legs like a drunken man, fighting down the trench through the dead and wounded, for in this trench were three of the dead Bedfords at least, beside our own men. I rushed forward and caught him by the shoulder and dragged him under cover. Poor chap, he was just a bit shaken but like the plucky fellow he is, recovered at once; he had a bad hit in the back of the head, and was wounded in the ribs too. Told me the firing pins were jammed in his grenades, and he couldn't get them out. He crawled up so close, he could hear the Germans talking, and chucked his grenades over the parapet. 'Hullo,' says they, 'Here's someone coming'. So they opened fire and threw, in all probability, our own grenades back again, only they managed to take out the pins. Most of Leask's followers had been killed and wounded; now, I didn't know what to do. Had to make one more bid, so I rushed out to the back of the communication trench leading to 46, (where it was open ground, since one could not go up the bottom of the trench on account of the bodies) and yelled to my men to follow me. Three bayonets peeped round the corner and got a whiff of fire; hesitated, and stopped — in my heart I thanked God most sincerely.

The parapet which the Brigadier so casually said we were to knock down, loomed some eight feet high, very solid, what could I and three or four men have done, had we got up to it? My Sergeant Major joined me. 'Come on, you . . . ' he yelled; full of dash and go, but there was no one to 'come on' and so I told him we couldn't take it 'on our own'. I could have cried with vexation. I was so sure we could have done it, and promised the Brigadier. Of course, with the whole Company we might have done it, but I could not denude my front trenches, and we could not spare more men. So Courtenay and I went back and lay down and fired. I chucked a few 'jam tins', but I am bad at throwing the cricket ball, and was thankful to chuck 'em far enough away for them to explode harmlessly to ourselves.

Then the Huns commenced to bomb us. All the time there was Hell's delight from some 17 machine guns in 46, and I presumed the frontal attack had started, but I could hear nothing but this awful rattle, amid which the enemy's exploding grenades sounded like popping peas.

I saw their heads over the parapet and had some interesting shooting; but soon a heavy cloud of mist from the cordite expended on both sides almost hid their parapet from view. Their bombs were coming and bursting closer and closer to us. I took refuge behind the corner of my front parapet and went on shooting. Then a star shell behind the trench 46 went up; showing their parapet a straight black line, and there, silhouetted against the blue flare I saw a German figure, crawling over their parapet, presumably in order to drop down and creep up close to us and snipe. It was less than 30 yards. I took a pot shot, and he fell backwards like a shot rook. So glad I have one German to my credit. Bombs were bursting all too close to us. Suddenly a flash and something hit me in the eye and I sat down hurriedly, fortunately on a heap of sandbags. I put my hand up to feel my eyeball on my cheek, and was surprised to find it still in its proper place; but my hand was all sticky and I found I was bleeding like a pig. Courtenay ran up and bandaged me; nothing serious, and I returned to tell Gilliland I was all right, but would go down before dawn and get it dressed and washed, and return. There was no water in the trench, also, I badly wanted a sleep, and I thought I would get one at the dressing station at the Battalion Head Quarters. Gilliland turned round and said 'You'd better go at once, then' and looking up, I found the eastern sky alight and all firing had practically died down. It was about 3 am and so I made off down the trench, and it was rather pleasing to hear the remarks of my men, 'Sure, ye are not hurt Sorr', 'Don't leave us long Sorr' and 'Come back to us again, Sorr'. It rather touched me. I took two men with me, one hit in the head, another with his hand blown off. He was bandaging a pal, who was killed, when a grenade landed and blew his hand to bits. He very pluckily walked down with me.

Found the Bedfords had not all left the trenches even. A shocking lot.

Major Weir heard my story and said I could have no more, and then I went on to the Doctor. While there, a telephone message came down from Gilliland to say we had six killed and five wounded, out of, at the most, fifteen men engaged, and there I broke down and the Doctor seeing that sent me down the line. Going up the day before, I felt my legs giving out, and felt just 'done in'. My nerves were all on edge, and just this rotten little wound brought all the winter hardships to a head and made me really break down.

From our regimental first aid post, we were sent on to the Ypres Road, where the motor ambulances picked us up and took us to a dressing station near Kruisstraat where there were a crowd of wounded, and more coming in every moment.

Seated round a table three or four officers suffering from gas; and others I saw there very bad. All the wounded got an anti-tetanus injection and then we were put on motor ambulances and sent to Bailleul.

On my way to this dressing station, we motored round the South and East side of Ypres. Couldn't go through the town as the driver told me the roads were quite impossible for the traffic, and even the road we were on was heavily pitted with huge shell craters and required a most careful driver. At this dressing station one of the doctors said he knew of 10 officers of a Battalion making the frontal attack on trench 46, who were 'down', and numbers of wounded were coming back from it. We heard the attack was successful.*

I got breakfast at Bailleul, and about 11 am was put on board a Red Cross train for Boulogne.

Reached Boulogne, – (I shall never forget my lunch on board, and my first whiskey and soda for weeks), – in the morning; here the worst cases were unloaded, and the rest of us sent on to Rouen. Most comfortable beds were made up for us in the coaches, and we all travelled 'en prince'. Rouen about 8 am next morning.

May 8th

I was vetted at No 2 Hospital and the doctor ordered me home as I wanted a rest.

May 9th

Left by the Red Cross train for Havre, shipped on to a well equipped hospital ship, and got an upper deck cabin. Sailed in the afternoon.

* It was not successful, and up to date (August 24th) as far as we have heard, neither this trench nor Hill 60 has been taken from the Germans.

215

May 10th

Arrived by breakfast time in Southampton. Here a small medical board sorted all the sick, the various cases being distributed among the different hospitals; the 'gasses' patients to one place, fever patients to another; severe wounds to somewhere else etc. I with several other officers, either only slightly wounded or more or less mental cases, was sent to Osborne.

I stayed a week at Osborne, and then got a month's sick leave. At the end of the month my nerves were really bad, and the Medical Board gave me a second month. They told me that men coming home broken were generally far worse at the end of the month or six weeks than they were when they had just returned.

I rejoined the 4th Battalion at Carrickfergus on July 2nd, jolly glad to be back with them again.

Leask quite recovered, joined us a month later, and about the same time, Whitmore came to us from the 2nd Battalion, sent home broken down.

Norman and Hutchison both broke down within two days of my leaving the 2nd Battalion; bad nerves, they'd both had heavy shelling. Poor Gilliland was killed on the afternoon of the 7th. A sniper got him in the head from trench 46; and Wale, the youngster who joined us from the Queen Victoria Rifles took command of the Company, though within a few hours another Captain was sent up to it.

Whitmore who was in Hutchison's Company told me that while this show was on the Germans had an MG playing right down our line from the top of Hill 60 and that his Company had to lie down right in the open and wait. All the Bedfords in the trenches who were waiting to be relieved bolted at this and when Whitmore entered the trenches they found no one there but a machine gun officer who seemed more or less off his head. They also found about 30 dead and the next morning they discovered among them a wounded Bedford officer; the damned fellows hadn't even the esprit de corps to look after their own officers.

In trench 47 I came across a poor devil who had been there for four days with both legs broken. His pals hadn't the pluck to cart him down at night to the dressing station. Imagine the mental agony, let alone the physical pain, of such a man incapable of movement, dreading an attack by gas, or by the enemy in person, no water, little food. I knew they'd had a dreadful time in these trenches but nothing but a real rotten bad regimental spirit can account for the appalling state of this Battalion of the Bedfordshire Regiment. I hope their officers are proud of themselves.

My Company, I hear, did splendidly all through the very trying three or four days they stayed in these trenches, and well made up for the rotten state the Battalion was in during the bad months of the winter. But I had a complete new Company of decent young well-trained soldiers and top-hole platoon leaders and platoon sergeants and without them I could have done nothing. The whole of my little affair was a first rate example of bad staff management, and an example only too common. They were continually bringing men up and throwing them into an attack over ground they had never seen before, and with which they were unacquainted. It had been much better, seeing how late my Battalion was in arriving at Brigade Head Quarters, if we had been sent in reserve and the Bedfords had continued for another night, and done the little 'side-show'; it was a dark night and ignorant of the lay of the land I hardly knew even the direction of the attack.

The same thing happened in the case of the attack by the Gordons and Royal Scots on December 14th.

In the attack on St Julian this Spring a Staff officer brought up a Battalion and told them to attack the German lines. 'Where are they?' 'Oh, I don't know, somewhere in that direction.'

An Irish Battalion (I think the Dublin Fusiliers), at great loss, then took these lines; all the senior officers were knocked out and Captain Bankes (late 2nd Dragoon Guards) was left in command. Another Battalion was also told to attack the Germans. They were never told that this Irish Battalion had already taken the trenches. They formed for attack: Bankes saw them coming and stood up to watch their advance. They opened fire on him and he and many of his men were at once killed. Rotten Staff management and all caused by the Staff never coming near the trenches and keeping in proper touch with the troops under them.

The whole time I was out there I only on one occasion saw one of our Brigade Staff come round our trenches and I never heard of any of our Divisional Staff coming near them. The consequence was that the Staff were never in touch with the regimental officer – never in sympathy with him and appeared rather to look down on him for being shabby in appearance and at times very dirty, and nothing now irritates the Regimental Officer more than the sight of the Red Tabs, which have become the insignia of hopeless inefficiency.

Luckily there are exceptions to this, as to every other rule; but unfortunately, this is the general opinion of the British Army at present.

Carrickfergus,
August, 1915.

The following Summaries of Information and Extracts from Summaries are given, not alone for their interest, but to show the type of official news-sheet with which every British unit to Flanders was issued daily.

The average summary was merely a mass of more or less unpronounceable names, and Roman figures; and was, as a rule, an indifferent copy of the *Daily Express* we had received with our rations the previous day. Possibly for this reason, for it is an old Horse Guards custom that the importance of any subject is in inverse ratio to its sense or utility, these documents were considered confidential, and therefore were to be found lying about any billet and estaminet behind our lines, or littering the roads and fields, at the service of any spy with sufficient energy to pick them up. However, spies could always get the *Daily Express* with less effort.

2nd ARMY CORPS SUMMARY OF INFORMATION.

FOR GENERAL INFORMATION.

ALLIED FRONT.

The French continue to make steady progress in the VOSGES and CHAMPAGNE. No details have yet been received, but the fighting of the last week has resulted in a considerable French advance.

COMPOSITION OF NEW FORMATION CORPS.

The composition of the New Formation Corps (Numbers above XXVII) appears to be as follows:-

2 Divisions (XXXVIII consists of 75 and 76 Divisions and other Corps follow in sequence).

1 Telephone Detachment
1 Searchlight Detachment } Bearing the Corps number

Each Division consists of:-

3 Infantry Regiments (75th Division consists of 249, 250 and 251st Regiments and other Divisions follow in sequence).

1 Regiment Field Artillery (The 75th Divisional Regiment is the 55th and other Divisions follow in sequence).

1 Sanitary Company (bearing the number of the Divisional Artillery Regiment).

1 Reserve Cyclist Company
1 Reserve Pioneer Company   Bearing the Divisional
1 Train Detachment   Number
1 Divisional Bridging Train

GENERAL.

The untrained Landsturm of the XI Corps area appears to have been due to be called up about the middle of February.

RUSSIA.

The Russian official communique of February 20th, gives no news of the operations about AUGUSTOWO. It states that feeble German attacks have been repelled on the BZURA, NIDA and Upper VISTULA.

An Austro-German attack was repulsed on the DUNAJETZ, and German attacks in the Carpathians SE of the USZOV Pass were similarly repulsed.

Two sorties by the garrison of PRZEMSYL were repulsed.

No news of the BUKOVINA.

TURKISH PRESS.

The following is extracted from THE TIMES:-

'To judge from the samples which have reached Egypt of Turkish newspapers, more especially those published in Asia Minor, they are indulging in amazing flights of fancy concerning the progress of the War. It was the Hanumlar Gazettassi (Ladies' Gazette) of Skutari, Asia, that informed its fair readers that:-

"The harem of his Islamic Majesty William II, the principal officers of the harem, and the general staff are expected in

Constantinople early this spring. Ten of the most powerful of the captured British Dreadnoughts will escort the Imperial harem".

Another newspaper described in December how his "Imperial Islamic Majesty had just uttered a speech from the Throne in the former French Chamber of Deputies, and afterwards offered the Imperial hand to be kissed by French ex-Deputies, who were deeply touched by his magnanimity".

But it is the German Press Bureau in Constantinople that transports us most successfully to the days of the Arabian Nights. When we read that the "British Government has offered two thousand asses laden with gold to induce his Islamic Majesty to renounce his project of dispatching a mighty fleet against London", we may congratulate Baron Kuhlmann for having brought us back to the days of the djinns of Sinbad, Aladdin, and the good Harun-al-Rashid.'

No. 98 – 24th February, 1915.

2nd ARMY CORPS SUMMARY OF INFORMATION.

FOR GENERAL INFORMATION.

ALLIED FRONT.

On February 22nd the French occupied the greater part of the village of STOSSWIHR (18 km WSW of COLMAR, in ALSACE).

At EPARGES the French continued to make progress and now they occupy nearly the whole of the enemy's position.

Progress was also made on the front SOUAIN-BEAUSE-JOUR, where the French captured a line of trenches and two woods, completely repulsed two heavy counter-attacks, captured many prisoners and inflicted severe losses on the enemy.

The Germans bombarded RHEIMS very heavily on the night of the 20th, 21st and during the 21st. The first bombardment lasted six hours and was followed by another lasting five hours. About 1,500 shells were fired into the town; the cathedral was specially selected as a target and was badly damaged. Some twenty houses were set on fire, and twenty civilians were killed.

A Zeppelin bombarded CALAIS in the morning, dropping ten bombs, killing five civilians and causing an insignificant amount of material damage.

DISTRIBUTION OF THE ENEMY'S FORCES.

It is reported that one division of the XXII R Corps is at GHELUWE in support of the XV Corps (see below), otherwise there is no change in the distribution of the enemy's forces in the neighbourhood of the British Front.

STATE OF AFFAIRS AMONGST HOSTILE TROOPS IN OUR FRONT.

The following is an extract from information obtained from a prisoner of the 8th Bavarian Reserve Regiment captured near PETIT BOIS on the night of 22nd & 23rd February:-

'He had been with his regiment since beginning of the war, except for a period when he was sick. His regiment has been in neighbourhood of WYTSCHAETE since November.

His Company has one Captain and one Offizier – Stellivertreter. Another Offizierstellvertreter was killed two days ago. The Company has about 150 men. The average strength is 150-160; they have recently received drafts. The regiment consists of reservists, 1st Levy Landwehr, Ersatz Reservists and recruits of 1915 class. About 15 to 20 men per company belong to the 1915 class. The recruits shoot rather wildly and are apt to suffer from frost-bitten feet.

The 2nd Levy of the Landwehr was sent back Christmas for

Garrison duty in Germany, being replaced at the front by Ersatz Reservists.

TRENCHES.

His Company always returns to the same trench, which lies North of the PETIT BOIS, between the wood and the WYTSCHAETE BEEK.

The trenches are very wet and have to be baled continuously. Entrenching, drain-digging, constructing revetments and entanglements is practically all done by Pioneers. His trench has a stake entanglement, not knife rests; the entanglement is four or five rows deep. He had never been outside in front of the trench for making entanglement, only as a listening patrol.

Listening Patrols. Each Company after dark sends out a listening patrol (SCHLEICH - PATROILLE) of two men who lie or crawl about just outside the wire entanglement. They rarely advance further out. They are relieved every hour. This is not considered a specially dangerous duty.

Telephones. Each Company has a telephone in the trench connecting it to Battalion Head Quarters and to neighbouring trench.

Sniping. He had never seen or heard of a periscope. No regular system of sniping is in vogue. Rifles remain night and day on wooden rests (except when taken down for cleaning). The sights are aligned at the top of the parapet opposite. Loopholes are either of the wooden box pattern or steel plates.

Men fire only when ordered to, or when they think they can see or hear something. He does not think the Germans shoot as much as we do. Rifles are not laid on roads, gaps, etc, behind our trenches.

Machine Guns. His Company has no machine guns, and has had none since the fighting near METZ in August. Companies have usually one or two machine guns in the trenches. They are well dug in with good overhead cover.

Supply and Transport. The field cookers never come nearer than OOSTTAVERNE and MESSINES, so the troops in the trenches never get a cooked meal. They cook their coffee and bacon in the trenches. The rations are good and sufficient. The ration bread is brown rye-bread, the same as in peace time.

Condition of Troops. There is a good deal of sickness, rheumatism, etc, but very little foot complaint, except for newly-joined recruits. The Germans have good boots, and in the trenches wear wooden clogs over them.

The War will be over in three months as the Russians have now been decisively beaten. The troops hear nothing of Naval battles in the North Sea. Germany has enough food to last at least another year.

They don't like trench life at all. Several would probably surrender, but they are told we shoot all single prisoners captured.

Belgian Inhabitants. No Belgians are employed on work in or anywhere near the trenches, though they mend the roads. All their cattle and foodstuffs have been commandeered, and they are served out with army rations. They sell wine or beer to the troops at a penny a glass; Belgian beer is not so good as the canteen Bavarian beer. They pay the inhabitants with either German, French or Belgian money. He has heard of no sequestration of copper and brass articles.

OOSTTAVERNE is entirely ruined and uninhabited. His regiment used to rest at HOUTHEM, but this is now ruined, so they go back to COMINES.

Artillery. There are some heavy guns (not howitzers, he thinks) 20 or 22 cm calibre entrenched in the open near HOUTHEM.

226

Uniform. Reserve and Landwehr units wear a metal cap badge, bearing a cross with the national motto:-
    Bavarian — IN TREUE FEST
    or Prussian — GOTT MIT UNS.

General. British rifle fire is very accurate and the shell fire always does a lot of damage.

His diary contains the following entry under date January 22nd:-

'We were subjected to a severe shelling with high explosive; fourteen killed in the first platoon and eight in the ninth Company.'

No. 113 – 12th March, 1915.

ALLIED FRONT.

In CHAMPAGNE, on March 10th, the French consolidated their position on the ground captured. Several vigorous German counter-attacks were repulsed.

Later information shows that the number of prisoners captured by us at NEUVE CHAPELLE on March 10th amounts to 750, including nine officers. The action there continued yesterday but the weather was unfavourable for the observation of artillery fire. All the ground won has been maintained and a German counter-attack repulsed with loss.

Information received this morning states that the counter-attack on our trenches to the South of NEUVE CHAPELLE was repulsed with ease, the Germans, except for sixty who got into a communication trench and surrendered, retiring in face of our rifle fire. The counter-attack on our trenches to the East of the village was preceded by a violent bombardment but was equally easily repulsed.

The village of L'EPINETTE, three miles East of

ARMENTIERES was carried by us by a bayonet charge last night.

NIEUPORT was heavily bombarded by twenty-one centimetre howitzers on March 10th.

No. 117 – 16th March, 1915.

2nd ARMY CORPS SUMMARY OF INFORMATION.

FOR GENERAL INFORMATION.

ALLIED FRONT.

It appears by a letter found by the first Army on a man of the 6th Bavarian Reserve Division that that Division left MESSINES on the 8th March, and marched to ROUBAIX on the 9th.

The writer says that his last days in MESSINES were terrible and that his unit had never been subjected to such a fire. The doors and windows of his billet were blown in five times in one afternoon. He also states that the water in MESSINES is so full of typhoid bacilli that it cannot be drunk.

It was believed that the Division was to rest for a week at ROUBAIX and then go South – destination not stated.

NOTE. The bombardment mentioned above probably refers to the 5th Division shoot on the 7th instant. It would be a pity if the newcomers at MESSINES were to escape similar attention.

The following is a summary of information issued by the 4th Corps of the operations from March 10th to 12th:-

It will be remembered that at the time of our first attack, on the 10th inst, the only German troops opposed to us were the units belonging to the 7th Corps, which for some months past has held the line from the LA BASSEE Canal to in front of

BOIS GRENIER. The prisoners taken on the 10th belong to the 13th and 16th regiments, both of the 7th Corps, and to the 11th Jager Battalion, which has been with the 7th Corps for a long time. They all agreed that our attack was a complete surprise. Some active soldiers, who had been through the War, said they had never seen such terrible artillery fire. This undoubtedly had a great deal to do with our success. It caused the enemy very heavy losses and from some trenches his men, as soon as our troops advanced, came out with their hands up and surrendered. Another fact which told in our favour was that ranks of all three regiments, especially of the 13th, contained many young recruits and elderly Ersatz men.

An officer of the 16th Regiment, wounded and taken prisoner, had belonged to the 7th Field Artillery Regiment (14th Division, 7th Corps) and with five other officers from the same artillery regiment, had been attached to the 16th regiment. This suggests a shortage of infantry officers in the German army.

The following order of regiments was disclosed, from South to North 16th Regiment, 11th Jagers, 13th Regiment, 15th Regiment.

At the end of the first day, not only had our troops made an important advance, but it was evident from the numbers and condition of prisoners, that we had caused great material and moral damage to the enemy. The three regiments represented among the prisoners had all suffered very heavily from our artillery and our infantry.

During the course of the day, the Germans brought up as reinforcements for the regiments in the trenches, those Companies of the same regiments which were in reserve.

Early in the morning of the 11th, we began to capture prisoners belonging to those reserve Companies. Those of the 13th Regiment had been resting in FOURNES; were called out about 9.30 am and marched up to support their comrades in the trenches. They were under the fire of our artillery all the way up, and their counter-attacks were repulsed by our infantry.

During the night of the 10th and 11th, and on the 11th, the enemy brought up more reinforcements, more important, consisting of the 6th Bavarian Reserve Division. This Division had been for a long period in the trenches in front of part of our 2nd Army. It had just been withdrawn to rest in ROUBAIX and TOURCOING, when, after only a day and a half instead of the three weeks it had expected, it was ordered up here. It appears from captured documents that this Division was the Army Reserve for the 6th German Army, which occupies the front from before ARRAS to just North of the YPRES-MENIN Road, and is commanded by the Crown Prince of Bavaria.

From prisoners and documents alike, it seemed fairly certain that the whole of the Division was brought up and subsequently from captures made by the Indian Corps its presence in its entirety was definitely established. The troops left the ROUBAIX-TOURCOING-LILLE area during the afternoon and evening of the tenth (10th), detrained at MARQUILLIES, DON and WAVRIN and came into action on the 12th.

Further reinforcements, amounting to about 6 battalions, from different regiments, of the 19th Corps (Saxon), which is in the line immediately to the North of the 7th Corps, were also brought up, and also came into action on the 12th. The only other unit from which prisoners were taken was the 19th Pioneer Battalion of which 30 men were sent up from LA BASSEE, half joining the 15th Regiment and half the 7th Pioneer Battalion (7th Corps). They were sent mainly for the purpose of bomb-throwing. One of these Pioneer prisoners said that he and his captured comrade were the only men left unwounded.

The severity of the losses suffered by the German reinforcements was confirmed by men of two Bavarian Reserve Regiments (20th and 21st) one of whom, pointing to his fellow prisoners, said:- 'Almost all of my company that were not killed are here'.

A wounded officer of the 21st stated that he thought the German counter-attack must have gone wrong, as he and his men found themselves alone with no support. The organisation of the counter-attacks was evidently bad; communication between units was altogether bad; troops who thought they were in support suddenly found themselves under heavy fire in the front line, with no knowledge of the whereabouts of the troops they were supporting.

A man of the same regiment said that the Bavarians had surrendered because the 133rd Regiment (XIX Corps, Saxon) had left them in the lurch, having failed to attack when they should have done so. This suggests that possibly Saxons and Bavarians did not work very well together. Whatever the explanation, there is no doubt that the Bavarians had a most unhappy time. One of them describes in his diary his experiences whilst he was waiting to take part in an attack: 'There was a most awful noise of shells and bombs and crackling of rifle and machine gun fire. We sat in groups close to one another in an icy wind, hungry and thirsty. We had had nothing to eat for 20 hours. Such is war!'

Prisoners of the 15th Regiment stated that two companies of their regiment were ordered early in the morning of the 12th to re-take trenches previously lost by the 11th Jagers. They were at first partially successful, but eventually our infantry captured the disputed trenches and the men holding them. Other companies of the 15th Regiment were in the trenches North of the 13th Regiment.

Finally, it may be mentioned that many prisoners were allowed to send postcards to their relations, and all of them wrote that they were being well treated. In conversation the only thing that seemed to weigh upon their minds was their danger from German submarines during the Channel crossing!

April 1915.

GENERAL. *Statements by prisoners.*

It was stated that the XXVI R Corps possessed a detachment specially trained in the use of the asphyxiating gas apparatus, who wore the number '4' on their shoulder straps. The attack was planned for the 20th instant and a day or two earlier the pioneers buried the pipes and cylinders containing the gases deeply in the trenches so as to protect them from shell fire. One prisoner thought there were three of four nozzles to the length of trench held by his Company; these nozzles project some distance in front of the trench. Owing to the wind being in the wrong direction, the attack was postponed till the 22nd April. The gas apparatus was provided for the trenches in front of LANGEMARCK and to the East of it, but not to those about POELCAPELLE. On this signal being given the taps were turned on for 20 minutes. All the prisoners who had seen it concurred in saying that the gas issued from the nozzles and was not ignited. An officer of the 234th Reserve Regiment said that when they advanced, his men were not wearing mouth pads and the gas caused nothing worse than a smarting of the eyes. Other prisoners said that the use of gas was not a success as the enemy should be able to see the preparations and have ample time to retreat, while it obstructed the view of the German troops who also feared the gas might injure them.

The following official statement is issued from PETRO-GRAD:-

From the time that the Prussian General Staff had declared unequivocally that the Germans has taken from us three hundred cannon in the course of our retreat from East Prussia, the German official communiques continue to distort everything, particularly warlike operations. The Germans tried to pass off as a victory the operations of their army which lost at GRODNO ten cannon, two thousand prisoners, and a large part of their stores, an army which is prostrated by gastric diseases,which sought to throw its reserves againt PRASNYSZ, and was forced to withdraw in the SUWALKI region. All this happened in fighting against Russian troops which, according to the German communiques, ceased to exist after the retreat from East Prussia.

A German communique stated that the Germans had killed and seized the body of the Russian General Lachekevitch, the commander of a division, and they actually disseminated the news in the form of a proclamation among the men of the column in which the General in question was to be found in the best of health.

The last communique calls their retreat from PRASNYSZ on February 27th 'accidental'. It is interesting to remember that in this accidental retreat the Germans left behind several dozens of machine guns, twelve cannon, over a hundred cases of munition, and other booty, besides losing ten thousand prisoners. It would be more true to call their retreat from PRASNYSZ on the night of March 12th an accidental retreat when, independent of any action by our troops, a sudden and inexplicable panic occurred in the German lines during the night, and in the morning we found ourselves face to face with deserted trenches and with masses of arms and ammunition which the Germans had abandoned, while the German front had fallen back four versts to the rear.

1.5 pm

A telegram has just been received that the German cruiser DRESDEN, which escaped from Admiral STURDEE'S squadron after the battle off the FALKLAND ISLANDS, has been sunk by HMS GLASGOW, KENT and ORAMA off the island of JUAN DE FERNANDEZ.

233

No. 134 – 2nd April, 1915.

2nd ARMY CORPS SUMMARY OF GENERAL INFORMATION.

FOR GENERAL INFORMATION.

GENERAL.

It is reported that, at the urgent request of Marshal VON HINDENBURG, the Germans have given up sending recruits with only six weeks training to the Eastern front. In future at least four months training will be carried out before the recruit joins a service unit.

The Germans are reported to be manufacturing crows' feet in large quantities, for use against our cavalry and for impeding the progress of our motor-cars.

MAINTENANCE OF GERMAN TRENCHES.

The following translation of a German Divisional Memorandum is of interest as giving an idea of the constant work that is in progress in the enemy's lines.

13th Infantry Division.   WAVRIN. 8/3/15.
1.a.No. 611

SUMMARY OF POINTS REFERRED TO AT TODAY'S CONFERENCE

1. Cover trenches not more than 100 metres behind the fire trenches; in the first instance constructed in groups and afterwards formed into a connected line.

This and the construction of the front line trenches are the most important items of work. There must be simultaneous work on the most advanced fire trenches and the cover trenches. (The table of work must be suitably arranged to admit of this simultaneous work.)

2. Companies which are holding fire trenches are not to be detailed for work on approaches, but on principle are only to be employed on work in the fire trenches. In exceptional cases small parties may be detailed for work on cover trenches which are close behind the fire trenches. Steps must be taken to ensure that the men can at any moment be employed tactically to occupy the fire trenches. Work in the fire trenches should be carried out also by day. The distribution of work in a group should be roughly: 2 men on guard, 2 men resting, 4 men working. Time available should be thoroughly made use of: work should not be stopped at 2 am.

3. Work to be superintended by officers, who will go the rounds of the working parties. If necessary, officers from the supply columns, etc, should be detailed to superintend work in rear of the front line.

4. Selection of sites for the motor driven pumps which are being dispatched in a few days time. Discharge channels to be cut now. Each regiment will receive one pump, beginning with the 15th Infantry Regiment.

5. Flooded listening galleries to be rendered serviceable.

6. Machine guns to be placed in flanking positions.

7. Employment of hand-grenades; instruction in their use; safety precautions; hand-grenades not to be stored in shelters – stored in the pioneer depots outside villages. Approaches not to be too wide, passing places, traverses, exits to facilitate the offensive. Overhead cover in places for protection against shrapnel fire, to be extended later to the rear as far as the ridge AUBERS-RADINGHEM.

8. Shelters.

No. 135 – 3rd April, 1915.

2nd ARMY CORPS SUMMARY OF INFORMATION.

FOR GENERAL INFORMATION.

GENERAL.

It is reported, on somewhat doubtful authority that a new Corps is being formed at TOURNAI round a nucleus of troops withdrawn from the XVth and possibly from other Corps, in the front. These troops are said to have started assembling on March 14th and to have been joined by other troops which arrived from the direction of MONS, presumably straight from Germany. These troops are said to have been still at TOURNAI on March 26th.

It is reported that the first Guard Cavalry Brigade was at EECLOO, between GHENT and BRUGES, on March 20th.

It is also reported that the Germans are entrenching the line of the SCHELDT some ten miles East of TOURCOING.

According to prisoners of the XVth Germany Army Corps, the ZILLEBEKE front is provided with iron bottles five feet high, placed slightly behind the trenches, either buried or sheltered. These bottles contain asphyxiating gas. They have not yet been used, but pioneers have been instructed in their use, they are laid prone and the seal removed, when the gas escapes parallel to the surface of the earth. A favourable wind is necessary. The pioneers in charge are provided with a special apparatus fixed on their heads as a protection against the fumes. The inventor has been promoted to a lieutenant. (This is on the authority of the IIIrd Corps.)

FROM THE GERMAN PRESS.

Stern measures are to be taken to enforce the Berlin police order for the closing of tea-shops. The order was originally intended to restrict the excessive consumption of tea, bread and cakes, and General KESSEL, the military commander of the Berlin district has now prohibited orchestras to play at tea-time as it leads, in his opinion, to HALBWELTVERKEHR (immoral intercourse with the demi-monde).

In the Saxon district of CHEMNITZ, the police regulations enforcing economy in the use of flour have been disregarded to such an extent, that the baking of cakes has had to be altogether prohibited. In one house the police discovered that 29 cakes had been baked for a christening party.

No. 138 – 6th April, 1915.

2nd ARMY CORPS SUMMARY OF INFORMATION.

FOR GENERAL INFORMATION.

GENERAL.

A man was evacuated from TOURCOING on March 27th and reached France via Germany and Switzerland, states that very few German troops are to be seen behind the firing line in BELGIUM. What troops there are in the garrisons of LILLE, TOURCOING and ROUBAIX are Landsturm, and there are a few hundred young recruits training at LILLE.

The following are extracts from the diary of a German Reserve Lieutenant of the 133rd Regiment (XIXth Corps) which were holding the trenches between ST YVES and LE GHEER last December:-

20th October, 1914: Departure from ZWICKAU at 6.15 with

over 1,200 men. The men were rather undisciplined especially the volunteers and Ersatz reservists with about six weeks training, especially in the dark, and the idea of obedience is not yet familiar to them. The old soldiers, those who have recovered from their wounds, are no better. On the contrary they think they have done all they need do. Nevertheless they mean well, and when treated sternly know how to obey. The captains are rather shy about inflicting punishment, and so there is a good deal of swearing and scolding, although some of the junior officers try to get men more severely punished, but as a rule in vain. The excuse is that it is a large batch of men and there are too few NCOs, and of these not many are reliable or sufficiently trained. They are mostly Landwehr or younger reservists, not active soldiers.

In the RHINE provinces the inhabitants were enthusiastic; in BELGIUM, especially in the Flemish districts, tolerant, but in BRUSSELS they were morose and scornful. As they meet you in the street they sometimes make the gesture of cutting your throat; young girls are the worst offenders.

Before and after BRUSSELS it often happened that the children, between the ages of 6 and 10, cried out to us for 'bread'.

Arrival in LILLE at 10 am on 26th; the part of the town near the station in ruins; the inhabitants apathetic; few young people.

The inhabitants amiable and timorous. A nervous sentry fires at some willow trees mistaking them for the Frenchmen, another man runs round shouting, 'Help! Help', under the impression that he is being shot at. He is shot at and so are two men who are following him. I out with my revolver – a ridiculous situation; the man who called for help cannot be found, the sentry calms down and the rest of the company clusters round me – indeed a ridiculous situation.

The men are very lavishly fed and there is much waste of bread and preserved food – the inhabitants go round collecting it of a morning.

30th October: We have been in the trenches two days now, at

PONT ROUGE, North-West of LILLE. The English are about 600 metres to 800 metres from us and fire like mad, they do so it is said, as a form of sport. German and English shells thunder overhead; one soon gets used to it. We are only holding on, so we do not answer the lively and accurate firing of the English who are said to be conducting themselves bravely here under Kitchener's command.

We are in touch with the army from ANTWERP which is pressing down from the North and is meant to roll up the (enemy's) flank.

21st January, 1915: How long is it since I made an entry (in this diary)? In the meantime I was wounded. With me in hospital were Lieutenant Wankel (181st Regiment) who, in a state of nervous excitation, alarmed the XIX Corps with a false report (that the English had broken through the line, that all his company were killed, and he himself was wounded); Lieutenant Baltzer, 32nd Artillery Regiment, also with his nerves upset; he flung himself out of the window into the yard, broke a thigh bone and an arm and knocked his face about. He raved during the night and kept us awake by shouting stupid orders. It was very pleasant at Christmas and New Year; my comrade Schweitzer and I came in for much applause for our performances.

FROM THE GERMAN PRESS.

The price of sausage has risen in FRANKFURT, and the celebrated 'FRANKFURTER WURST' now costs 1/5d a pound. The less tasty delicacies known as 'BLUTWURST' and 'LEBERWURST' may, however, still be bought for a shilling the pound.

The price of beer in Germany is to be increased by 4d a gallon from the 1st April.

No. 141 – 9th April, 1915.

2nd ARMY CORPS SUMMARY OF INFORMATION.

FOR GENERAL INFORMATION.

ALLIED FRONT.

In spite of continuous bad weather the French have made good progress in the WOEVRE (COTES DE MEUSE). At EPARGES an important advance was made during the night 6th-7th March. A German counter-attack executed by a regiment and a half, which advanced in dense formation, failed completely with very heavy loss, leaving about 1,700 men on the ground.

All French positions were maintained.

Elsewhere only artillery duels took place.

Air reconnaissance this morning reveals no particular activity in the hostile lines. Some infantry were observed practising extended order drill East of MESSINES; our artillery assisted the extension movements and emphasized the advisability of taking cover.

GENERAL.

A German-French handbook issued to German soldiers contains the following useful phrases:-

'If you run away I fire. We want ten horses and twenty carts. Obey, march in front. Empty your pockets. Take off your boots and stockings. Tell the truth or you will be killed. You will remain here as a hostage. Show us the cellars. Where is the safe? Move off or I fire. Are you a spy? If you lie you will be shot. Are the inhabitants rich? Where are the big rooms? Hurry up. Every inhabitant with soldiers billeted on him must provide daily $1\frac{1}{2}$

lbs bread, 1½ lbs bacon, 1 lb meat, ¼ lb vegetables. All will be paid for later on. You must supply 11 sacks of rice, 15 sausages, 8 pigs, 30 litres of beer, 40 litres of white wine, 400 cigars and 200 blankets. Do not fear, we are very peaceful. The driver who takes the wrong road will be shot. We are not barbarians.'

The following extracts were taken from letters on a corporal of the 23rd Bavarian Regiment.

'I believe our happiest days are over; now there is grief and misery everywhere. If only the longed-for peace would come! That is our only wish.'

From a letter written from Bavaria on 2nd February:- 'We are now beginning to feel the pinch of the War. You will have heard already that the damned English are trying to starve us, and our corn has all been registered. There is said to be only enough for ½ lb bread for each person daily, and that is certainly not much but we have to put up with it. Let us hope that the tables will be turned on the English. Indeed it will not be a quick job to starve us out as we still have a lot of corn and potatoes. We all long for a speedy and honourable peace.'

April 15th, 1915.

SUMMARY OF INFORMATION.

GERMAN PEACE OVERTURES.

The following is a translation of two letters which were tied round stones and thrown into our trenches last night by the Germans:-

Dear honoured Comrades,
    As this war has now been going on for about nine

241

months, and whole villages with their inhabitants have been devastated, it is now high time to put a stop to it. We are all tired of this savage life, and you must be too. Our dear wives and children await and long for our return and yours must do the same. Hoping we may do some good by this.

We remain with friendly greetings,

The Germans.

Sapping Party,
11th April, 1915.

Dear French, English and Comrades,

It is now just about time you stopped all this, for I think you soon have had enough of your war.

Our losses are great and yours must be three times as great. Every day it gets finer, and it would be better if we could be at home with our wives and children who are waiting every day for us as yours are waiting for you.

Let us have peace on Earth before the cherry blossom comes out, but the sooner the better. Or do you want to go on sitting for ever in these damned trenches.

With friendly greetings,

The Germans.

To try and equalize the evident disparity in losses, our men this morning shot three or four Germans in the trench from which the above letters were thrown.

2nd ARMY CORPS SUMMARY OF INFORMATION.

FOR GENERAL INFORMATION.

ALLIED FRONT.

The following are extracts received from a part of BELGIUM at present occupied by the enemy:-

'Now something about the battle of NEUVE CHAPELLE: some people came here from TOURNAI on business and they said that on that day, and the days following the fighting, hundreds of German soldiers passed through the town *in the greatest confusion*, fleeing, without hats or rifles.

When the breakthrough does take place, then certainly the population will lend a hand, as they are very eager to do so. But for that the Germans will have to be in disorder, so that the people can see they are really beaten.

I can assure you that the German soldiers are deeply impressed by the heavy losses they sustain. They are not any more the fine, proud bodies of troops we saw before!

Truly they are still disciplined, well behaving, but their individual spirit has fallen very much, and there are fairly many cases of desertion.

More than once German officers mentioned the possibility of having to evacuate BELGIUM.

It is said even that the German Governor of ANTWERP has asked the Burgomaster if he, in case of a retreat, would remain responsible for the calmness of the population.

You may be assured that the Germans, though they don't feel themselves beaten yet, are far from feeling sure they will be able to keep their positions.

A tremendous number of soldiers passed through here lately going to Flanders. Probably they will try there a desperate attempt. But no first class soldiers, you may be sure!

"Bon courage! Vive la Belgique!" and against what the Germans say "God Bless England!"

FROM THE GERMAN PRESS.

A deputation of Bavarian peasants have asked that the bread ration should be increased as it is insufficient for agricultural labourers who are hard at work tilling the fields.

The reply they got was the following:-

'When a father has got 10 apples and 10 children and wants to treat all alike he can only give them one apple apiece. The supplies have been reckoned up throughout Germany, and it only works out at $7\frac{1}{2}$ ozs a day. We can't complain about that however hard it may seem. Think of the hundreds of thousands who work in factory or mine and need bread as much as the farm labourers. Why are these measures taken? We know now what the enemy's intention is. He evidently has lost all hope of beating us by force of arms, so he is trying to starve us out. England with its long purse and its dominant fleet has cut off all our sea-borne imports. We live as in a fortress, and just as the prudent commander of a besieged fortress counts the heads of his garrison, so we have to apportion our bread-ration for every head in our German fatherland.'

The Governor of Strassburg has made it a criminal offence, punishable with imprisonment, to speak French.

SUMMARY OF INFORMATION.

THE PIG-CENSUS.

On the 16th April the census of all pigs throughout Germany was commenced. In Berlin the census is being undertaken by the Statistical Bureau, and about 30 male and female pig-counters have been employed in visiting the different yards in order to fill up the requisite forms.

In view of the possible shortage of food supplies, the Town Council of NEUSTADT have increased the dog-tax, and are discussing the levying of a cat tax. Herr Kommerzienrat FREYTAG proposed to make the tax 10 shillings per cat, as there were 3000 cats in NEUSTADT and they drank a thousand pounds worth of milk yearly. The Town Clerk pointed out the difficulty of enforcing the tax as cats did not wear collars, and so the matter was referred for a decision to the financial sub-committee.

The following circular letter is being sent by a Berlin Matrimonial Agency to the widows of officers and men killed in action. It illustrates the delicacy of feeling of which a cultured nation like Germany is capable:-

Dear widowed Madam,

Last Sunday we inserted a notice in the papers announcing that we had as a candidate for matrimony a Post Office Official with a five-year-old daughter. As a result of this advertisement Mrs S G offered herself as a prospective wife. We therefore wish to call your attention to the fact that we are ready to undertake similar negotiations on your behalf.

In spite of the War, we have a great number of gentlemen (about 467) *desirous of marriage*. There are still a great many gentlemen who have no opportunity of making the acquaintance of suitable ladies, partly because they have not the time, partly because they live a retired and modest life. We have a large selection of gentlemen of all ages, from 21 to 70, also those who are not concerned about a dowry, and of every profession and class of society from workmen to officers, so that we are able to meet the requirements of any of our lady applicants.

No. 156 – 24th April, 1915.

2nd ARMY CORPS SUMMARY OF INFORMATION.

FRESH USE OF GAS.

On the evening of 22nd instant, the Germans made a strong attack on the line LANGEMARCK-BIXCHOOTE. The enemy using asphyxiating gases, forced the French troops opposed to them to fall back. According to prisoners the whole of the XXVI R Corps was engaged. Counter-attacks yesterday regained a considerable portion of the ground lost. No units other than those of the XXVI R Corps have so far been identified.

Two attacks about BROODSEINDE during the evening of the 22nd were repulsed.

GENERAL.

Asphyxiating gases. The enemy made great use of asphyxiating gases in his attack from LANGEMARCK on the evening of the 22nd. A prisoner of the 233rd R Regiment taken yesterday states that the gas is contained in metal cylinders about 4 feet long, which are sunk in the earth at the bottom of a trench. When required for use, pipes are attached to the cylinders, and the nozzle projected over the parapet. At a given signal the taps are turned on and the gas, which is of a yellowish colour (probably chlorine) drifts in clouds down the wind over the opposite trenches. The operators, who attend to the apparatus, wear rubber garments with special respirators. The rest of the troops are provided with cotton mouth pads which are wetted with a certain solution (probably bicarbonate of soda).

In the fighting on Hill 60 the enemy employed shell producing dense greenish fumes (probably some chlorine compound) which causes headache, violent sickness and temporary blindness.

FROM THE GERMAN PRESS.

Liability to serve in the Landsturm in Austria has been extended from 42 up to 50 years of age.

Extracts from letter written by German NCO in 105th Regiment, in the trenches on Hill 60, on 17th April, 1915, just before out attack began:-

Dear Ones,

I wrote to you some time ago that we thought we were going to Russia. So far, from all appearances nothing is going to happen about that – still one can never say for certain, for everything moves pretty quickly in military matters. Our Lieutenant of the Train who has been in command of our company since Christmas and understands nothing about it has already got two decorations but why? It is practically the same with all officers. If I had served as an Einjahriger, I should be a Lieutenant.

We brought some EINJAHRIGER Unteroffiziers with us who have already been made lieutenants, and at the same time have got the Iron Cross.

247

These people are supposed to lead us now: it will soon be as it is in Russia. War volunteers have also got on well – naturally the students. It is a pity that our regular officers are all away, and those that are at home do not come out again, with a few exceptions. Still we would put up with everything if we could only come home again safe and sound, and that right quickly. I suppose you know nothing about peace yet? As far as we can judge, this year will easily be over before it, if the countries can stand it so long. On the 14th April we could watch for the first time a fight between two airmen – a German and an Englishman. The German was making in any case for the ground from a considerable height without any idea of the enemy and owing to the humming of the motors failed to notice him. We had to look through glasses before we knew which flag they carried. The Englishman came suddenly over the German out of a cloud and opened fire immediately with the machine gun, which they nearly all carry. We had hardly heard the shots when the German came down in a rapid volplane, fortunately inside our lines. We learnt afterwards that the pilot was quite unhurt, but the observer had had three shots put into his upper arm and shoulder by those raghounds of English.

We are again in KORTEWILDE in wooden huts. One can now pretty often buy things, when one comes out of the trenches – because behind the front, canteens have been provided. At this moment the Artillery is beginning to fire. I hope it won't inflict any losses upon us.

With best love,
from
G.

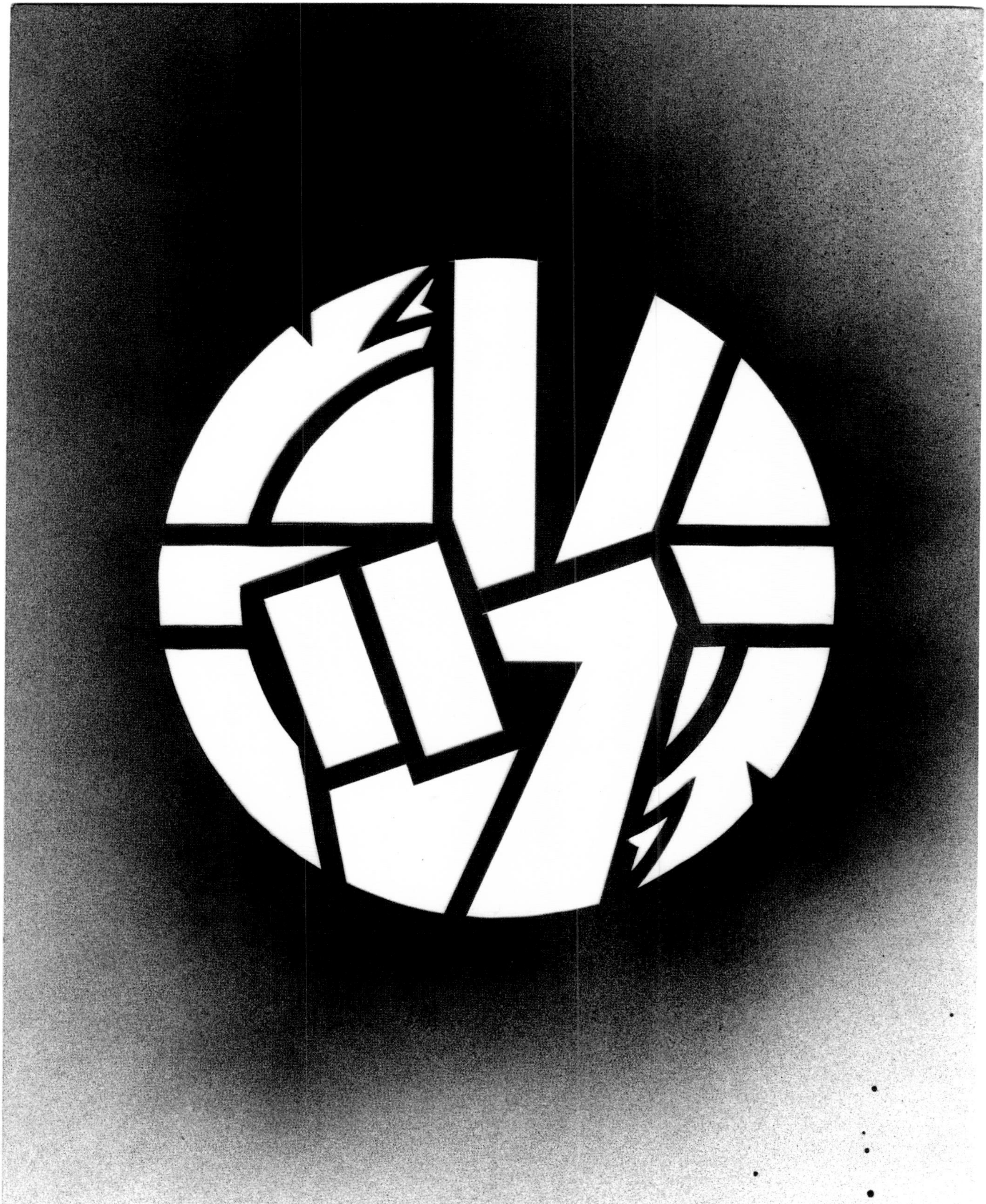

DAVID KING STENCILS
PAST, PRESENT & CRASS!

GINGKO PRESS / KILL YOUR IDOLS

GINGKO PRESS INC.
2332 FOURTH STREET, SUITE E
BERKELEY, CA 94710
GINGKOPRESS.COM

KILL YOUR IDOLS
PO BOX 48888
LOS ANGELES, CA 90048
KILLYOURIDOLS.COM

Published in the United States of
America by Gingko Press in
association with Kill Your Idols

DESIGNED BY
CLINT WOODSIDE
AND BRYAN RAY TURCOTTE

PRODUCTION ASSISTANT
MAX GOLDSMITH

PRINTED IN CHINA

FIRST PRINTING
10 9 8 7 6 5 4 3 2 1

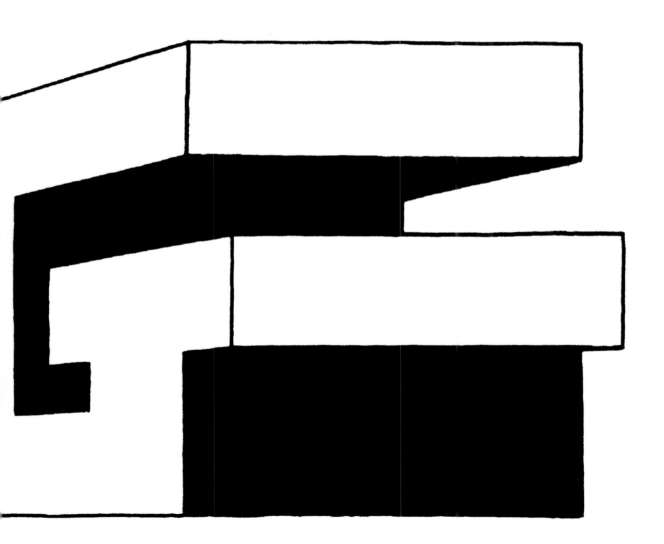

FOREWORDS

ESSENTIAL FORMS

MATT BORRUSO

There is a consistent aesthetic found in every-thing that Dave King does. It can be seen here in this book, running through every page. His work distills the world into a series of essential forms: silhouettes, monochromatic objects, frame grabs from films, photographs of shadows, repurposed logos. Inspiration taken from art, advertising and comic books is boiled down into only what is necessary. While there is always humor, there is nothing baroque. It is a world reduced to the least amount of information needed to describe itself.

I met King in San Francisco in the early 1980s when he was part of the band Sleeping Dogs. Back then I was very interested in his artwork, especially the Sleeping Dogs posters that had appropriated images of Mickey Mouse and the Batman logo. In San Francisco at that time the typical punk flyer utilized a rough shredded and torn graphic approach. The Sleeping Dogs flyers were so different—they felt cartoony, clean and tight. Later I realized that he had designed the Crass symbol, which was becoming more and more conspicuous in the Bay Area, tattooed on bodies, and stenciled on walls and studded leather jackets.

In a way the Crass symbol, for which King is best known, is an outlier amongst the rest of his work. He is typically focused on a singular easily readable form, but the Crass symbol integrates multiple loaded images—cross, serpent, cir-cle-backslash—into its final design. And its subversive quality stems from this juxtaposition of well-known images that morph into something wholly new. It is both enigmatic and familiar.

The stencil, in general and as seen here in this book, is a primal and effective tool. The positive space of the stencil itself is cut away, but then magically reappears as paint is blown through it onto the intended surface. Think of prehistor-ic cave paintings of hands, achieved simply by holding the positive hand on the cave wall, filling a mouth with pigment and spitting onto the "stencil." The result is the image of the hand, but also an image of negative space.

The stenciled pieces presented here are a lot like the work that King has made in other medi-ums—high contrast, graphic and readily visible from a distance. He is obsessed with the shapes and outlines of certain forms, and their contours and volumes repeat themselves again and again throughout his investigations. In this book we can see both process and result, a working and reworking of the same forms to create subtle repetitions and variations on a theme.

King attended art school in South East Essex outside London in the 1960s. He later went on to work in advertising in London, first as an art director and designer and then as an illustrator from 1967 to 1977. His work always reflects this professional graphic design history, and the specter of advertising is apparent in everything he has done since. In fact, according to King, the design of the snake's head found in the Crass symbol reflects a promotional design piece he had done for a client, Yorkshire Television, for a series of TV plays called The Seven Deadly Sins. In this piece the snakes grew more twisted with every sin.

Like many British artists of his generation, King has an obsession with a certain type of American visual culture—much of it relating to the post-war period. There are many examples of this im-pulse in others: J. G. Ballard, Eduardo Paolozzi and Richard Hamilton of the Independent Group, to name a few. At the same time there is some-thing undeniably British about King's aesthetic. After living in America for the last 40 years, it's as if he sees British visual culture the way that he once viewed American visual culture. Where-as once it was Mickey Mouse, now it's the teapot creeping into the Crass symbol…

In the late 1970s King dropped out of the London advertising world and went to live with some former art school friends in a communal living experiment in the countryside. This project would take the shape of what we now know as Crass. It is not a stretch to compare King's journey from advertising to punk, to that of the fictional character Don Draper from Mad Men— exiting Madison Avenue for the West Coast and Big Sur's Esalen Institute. As utopian dreams fade and new nightmares emerge, symbols and images of earlier promise remain as potent reminders. The Crass symbol is one of these. It combines powerful elements into a simple form meant to express something expansive. It is the distillation of a feeling—the promise of freedom, and the rejection of a system that never cared about you anyway.

STEVEN HELLER

Logos do not exist in a vacuum and their power (or lack of it) is fueled by external forces. Logos are designed as reminders of a product or an idea, and the best logos act like time bombs, exploding the public's perceptions without warning.

The logo for the punk band Crass (1977–1984), designed by Dave King in 1977, does just that. It is explosive and memorable. He equates his design with the ubiquitous Campaign for Nuclear Disarmament (CND) logo, best known as the "peace sign," inspired by Bertrand Russell and designed in the UK by Gerald Holtom in 1958. The peace sign echoes an early Christian-era mark called the crow's foot and it became the primary ban-the-bomb protest symbol in the early 1960s. (Another origin story posits that the CND symbol is the combination of two semaphore signs for N and D, implying the crow's foot was a coincidence.) The symbol later evolved into the emblem for the emergent anti-Vietnam War peace movement and has retained its vitality for over 60 years. The Crass logo has a similar trajectory. It is a "peace symbol for punks," King told me. "In fact I discovered years later that the peace symbol nestles within the Crass one," he said.

In 1977 King originally designed the symbol for an agitprop pamphlet railing against the British church and state titled "Christ's Reality Asylum." Fifty copies were run off on a Gestetner copier. The type and logo were spray-painted on a gray cardboard cover using hand-cut stencils. "The design was specifically wrought to be stenciled," he explained, adding, "what lends it resonance I think is having a double-headed snake and the strong, negating diagonal at the heart." Later the same year the pamphlet's author, Penny Rimbaud, co-founded Crass and applied the mark as the band's symbol. "It fit neatly and dramatically on the bass drum," King said.

King's design deliberately takes chances with double-edged symbolic elements. An alternative version of the mythic ouroboros, a snake eating its own tail, is rendered as two legs of a sun-cross, intertwined with a symmetrical (Celtic or Christian) cross also commonly found in ultra right-wing emblems. In the war of ideological signs and symbols, this can be a confusing signal—but the result, like a vaccination, uses some of the disease to create immunity. This is why King's logo, like the peace sign, has achieved the transcendent status he very much wanted.
King designed the Crass logo to attack the very

images it co-opts. The band advocated anti-fascist, anti-capitalist, anti-establishment, anarchic action, and King's work in general, through prodigious stenciling and spray-painting, is an antidote to the symbolic bombardment from the middle and far-right.

Although Crass disbanded in 1984 (a sly reference to George Orwell's dystopian novel) the polemical music is accessible for latter-day disaffected generations to discover. The symbol remained: It acquired a ubiquitous independence as a sign of protest—and became a very popular tattoo motif, too.

King continued to evolve variations on the original design. A few years ago for an exhibit in San Francisco, where King now lives, he resurrected the unused variations, adding as many new takes as he could. This book derives from that show, and other work is included which was made using stencil techniques. Many original cardboard stencils used for spray-painting are shown on the following pages.

In the 1980s, King mused on the similarities, not differences, between the US and USSR. His "Mickey Mouse as the hammer and sickle" stencil explored what a joint flag would look like if the countries ever merged!

King's visual critiques effectively employ familiar tropes in surprising juxtapositions, among them an arrow-like, streamline swallow, shot from a bow-like sickle; a robotic head with death-ray eyes under the title DESPOT; and the universal sign-symbol known as the running man, escaping from a maze of color forms. Each has a quality consistent with the stencil protest genre—they are graphically strong yet confounding and enigmatic.

Funny, powerful, articulate and impactful, King's graphics defy authority and continue the legacy of political and social commentary in the process.

Steven Heller is America's preeminent graphic design historian. He is the author, co-author or editor of over 180 books on the subject.

A PEACE SYMBOL FOR PUNKS

SEVEN THESES ON DAVID KING

HOWARD A. RODMAN

1. Stencils are as much about absence as about presence, what Manny Farber would call "negative space." A stencil is an outline of what's not there, or, more precisely, what's not yet there. It's a presence-through-absence: an absence that causes a presence, or intends to. One thinks of Rachel Whiteread's Ghost (1990), a plaster cast of the interior void of a Victorian parlor. It is not a reproduction of the parlor, but a literal concretizing of all that the parlor is not. David King's stencils are, at one and the same time, machines for making art, and the art itself.

2. A stencil is, in effect, a machine (with no moving parts) that enables its user to incite images. The user may be the artist, or may be someone else. The easiest way of thinking about stencils is that they enable the mechanical reproduction of a work of art. Yet as with silkscreens, each use of the machine produces a (slightly) different effect—the vague bloom when there's a gap between stencil and ground, the razor-sharp line when there isn't. It's where the machine fails in its mission to create exact, reproducible replicas that we find its glory.

3. The image that David King cannot escape is, of course, the Crass logo: David King chased it and now it chases him, like a snake eating its own tail. One has seen the logo stenciled by an anonymous public artist on the signage surround-ing the Lake Hollywood reservoir; one has seen it tattooed on a shaven skull. Its ubiquity is at one and the same time the index of its success and the hallmark of its exhaustion. (If something is everywhere, it's nowhere; if it's available to all meanings, then its meaning disappears in front of our eyes.) If to some it's an ouroboros, to others a swastika, to others an anti-swastika, to others a cross, to still others a CND peace sign, can we say that it's become depleted of meaning? Perhaps it's best approached without any attempt to fix its meaning at all. As Don DeLillo puts it: "If you stay too long, you wear out the wordless shock. Love it and trust it and leave." For David King, the Crass logo has become an object of endless fascination, occasional perplexity, reproduced and varied, shallow and deep. Can we say that this logo is for him what the swimming pool is for David Hockney?

4. And if so many meanings—barnacles on its hull—have become attached, what does the Crass logo mean now? I would maintain that as this book so admirably and convincingly shows, the true art of the logo only emerges when the interpretations fall away, and we gaze upon the thing itself. Magisterial and disturbing. Symmetrical and off-kilter. Like the stencil that created it, at once a presence and an absence. King confounds the issue by integrating the logo into other pop culture settings. Crass logo as 45 rpm record adapter. Crass logo as Bat-Signal above an 8-bit Gotham. As Superman shield. As hammer-and-sickle crossed with Mickey Mouse. And, of course, as teapot—that most domestic and reassuring of British objects ("I've just put on the kettle, my dear…") rendered strange and then again familiar, ultimately reassuring in stenciled slashes that more than suggest shattered Spode.

5. Some of the images in this book are literal, some abstract. Some deliver their meaning straight up, staring at you with all the subtlety of eggs on a plate. Some can be but glimpsed through the fog, a quarry about to turn the corner and disappear into a Conan Doyle mist. Some are superflat, others tease at a third dimension. Some are black and white in a way that implies a third color, others are lurid, ranging from tropical lushness to warehouse-fire intensity. What we are watching is an artist whose limits are his liberations. Working within the stencil's narrow technical framework, David King finds his independence. As André Gide puts it, "Art is born of constraint, lives in struggle, and dies in freedom." David King's stencils both incarnate and transcend their X-Acto origins.

6. In the middle of the 20th century, stencils became a way of allowing graffiti to be made by anyone—regardless of age or skill level—who possessed a spray can. Signage without signature. Stenciled public wall art found its flowering in Paris in May '68, during the heady days of poetry-must-be-made-by-all-not-by-one, Lautréamont's sentiment incarnated in red, writ large. And so it's not surprising that David King's work consists of words as well as images, letters deployed not just for their graphic beauty but for their meaning. BRAVO FOXTROT OSCAR: stencils both imitating and instantiating government-issued cargo. A single, cryptic uppercase word: ORIGINS. Or: DESPOT. One cannot deny the politics inherent in David King's stenciled alphabets, the revolutionary impulse lurking just beneath the Lettrism.

7. Like his stencils, David King is both a presence and an absence: a king but also, and always, a citizen. His work has insinuated its way into the sign language of the world so pervasively that we forget, when looking at that world, how much of it he has created, or taught us how to see. Working with the humblest of means—a knife and a piece of stiff paper—he has populated the landscape with his images and disappeared into the landscape that he himself incarnated. Which is why David King (like the elusive Fantômas) is everywhere and nowhere. David King has deliberately practiced the arts of invisibility. But even he can't disguise the fact that one of the great artists of our time is working in plain sight.

Howard A. Rodman is a celebrated screenwriter and educator. He is the author, most recently, of the novel Great Eastern.

GRAPHIC SENSIBILITY

BARRY MCGEE

It's a great pleasure to write a few words about an extraordinary artist. I met David in my formative years at the San Francisco Art Institute. We were studying there in the early 1990s. We both attended a relaxed Friday evening life drawing class. I always sat across or at an angle from him, so I could see David working away in the frame with the model. David's strong features, along with a crisp button-down shirt with the sleeves rolled up, always made for a better composition. Often I would crop out the model and just go straight into drawing David. He is a generous, kind and stylish man.

What drew me to David's work decades ago and still draws me today is its bold yet simple graphic approach, using stencils cut by hand with all the elements of problem-solving and chance still intact. We made a connection through our mutual love of simple line drawings, whether on a fruit carton found in the street or a cartoon by Mad Magazine artist Don Martin.

David's iconic symbols were a badge of authenticity in the underground scenes across the globe in the pre-internet era, recognizable at 65 mph on the back of a squatter punk meandering down an alleyway at four in the morning. What symbol has even come remotely close to so immediately showing one's allegiance to an ideology or attitude?

An immediate link forged by graphics.

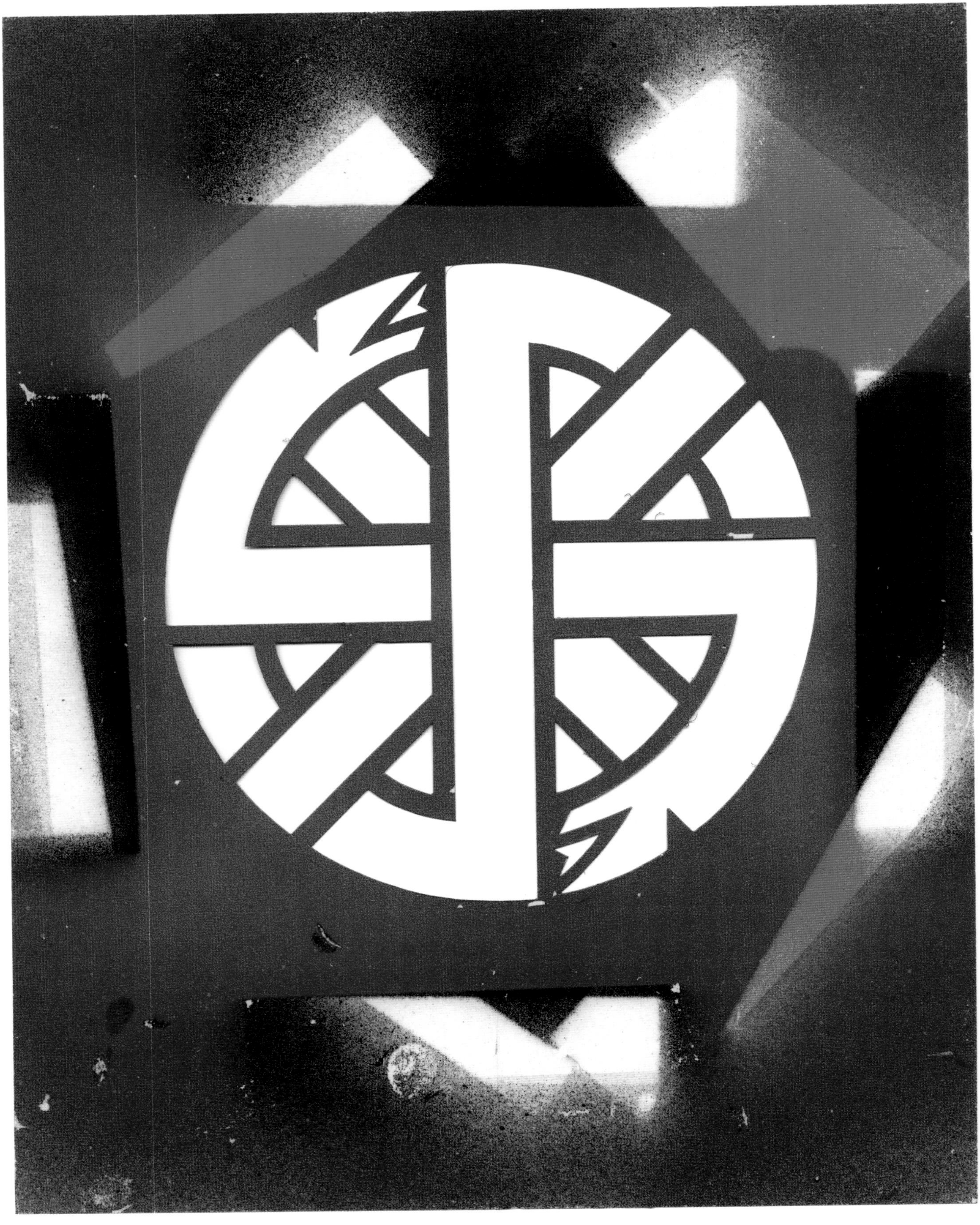

NEW IMPROVED   DK'11

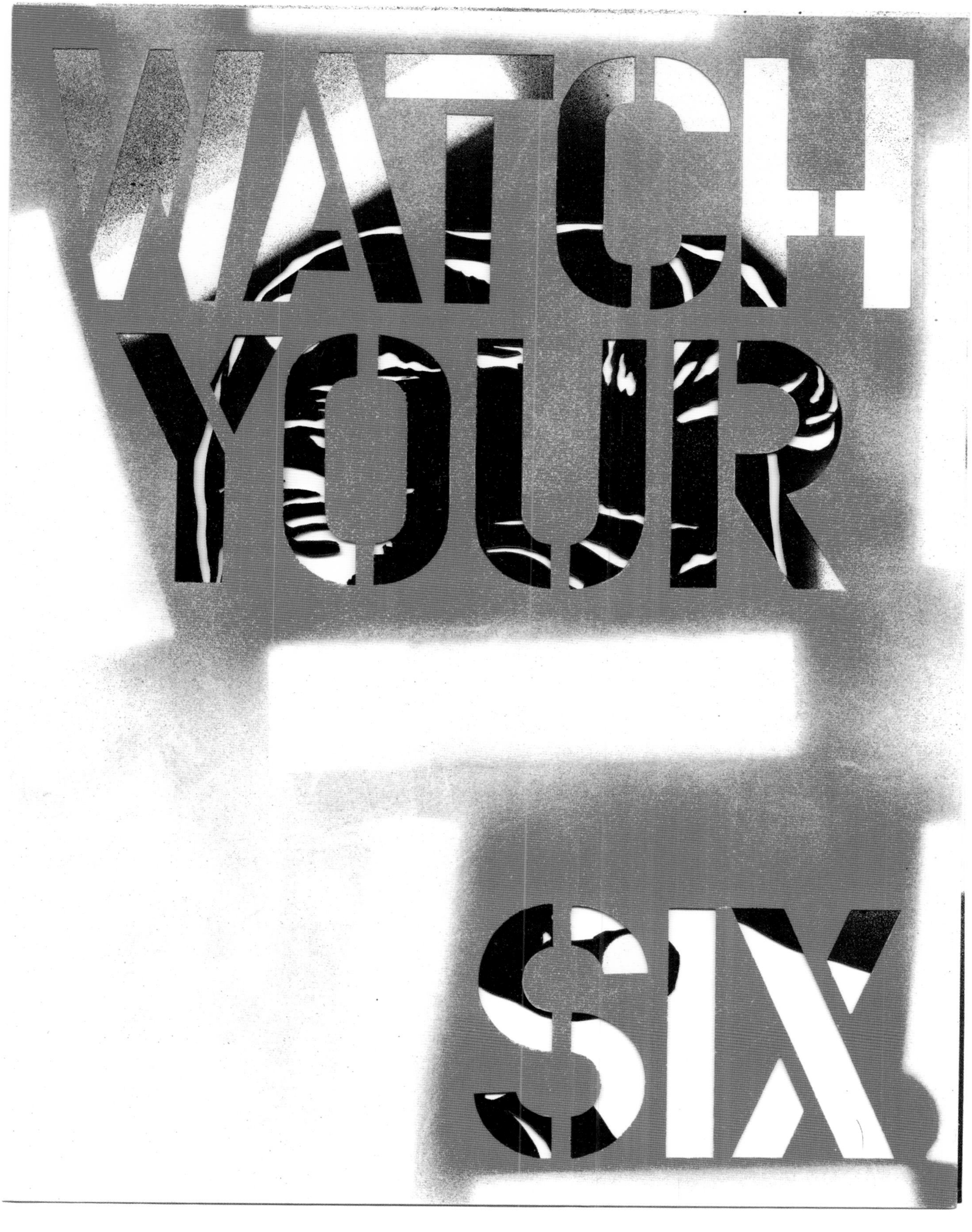
WATCH
YOUR
SIX

BRAVO
FOXTROT
OSCAR

BLACKPEACE   DK/13

MAKE TEA, NOT WAR   DK'11

ORIGINS

DK'13

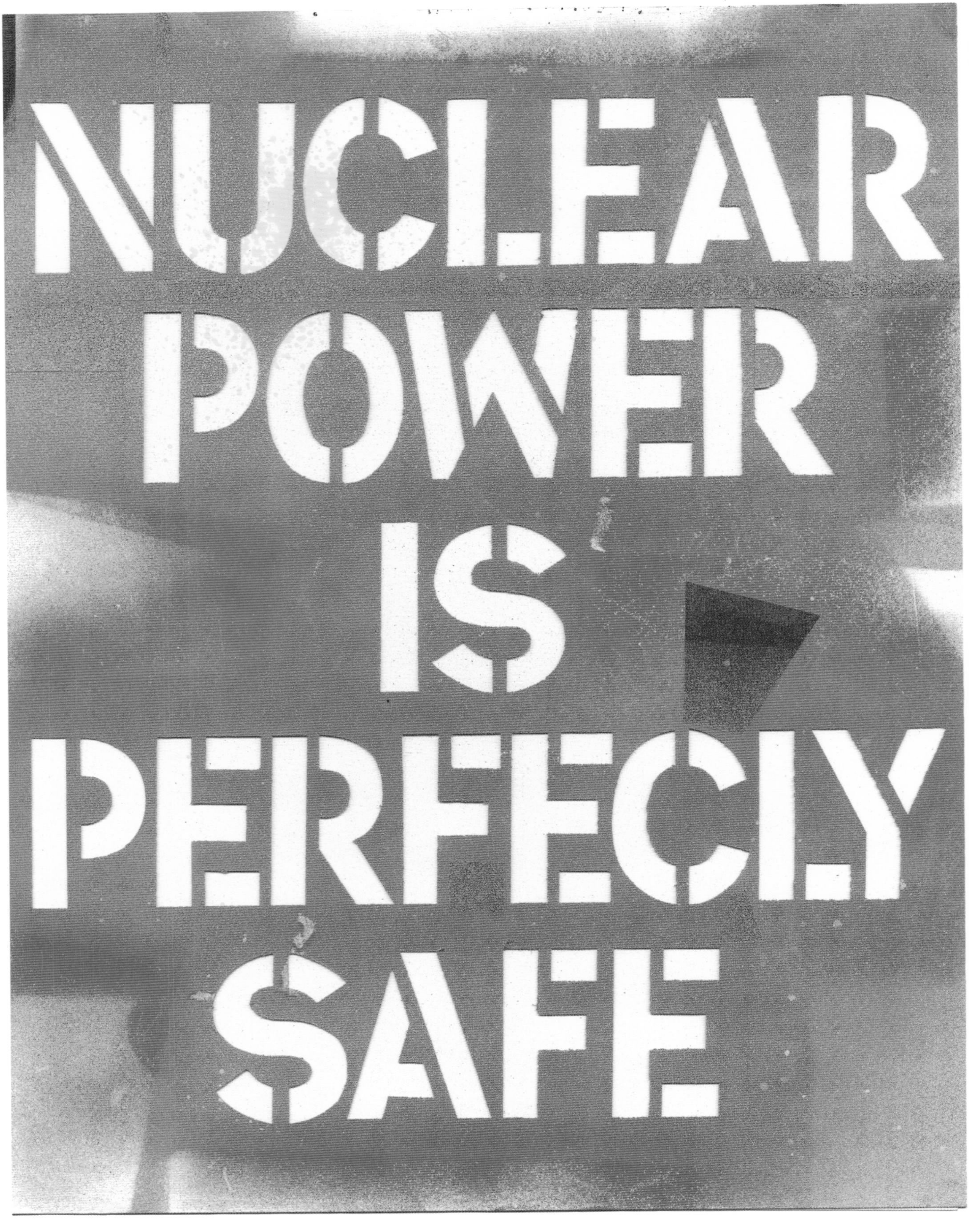
NUCLEAR
POWER
IS
PERFECLY
SAFE

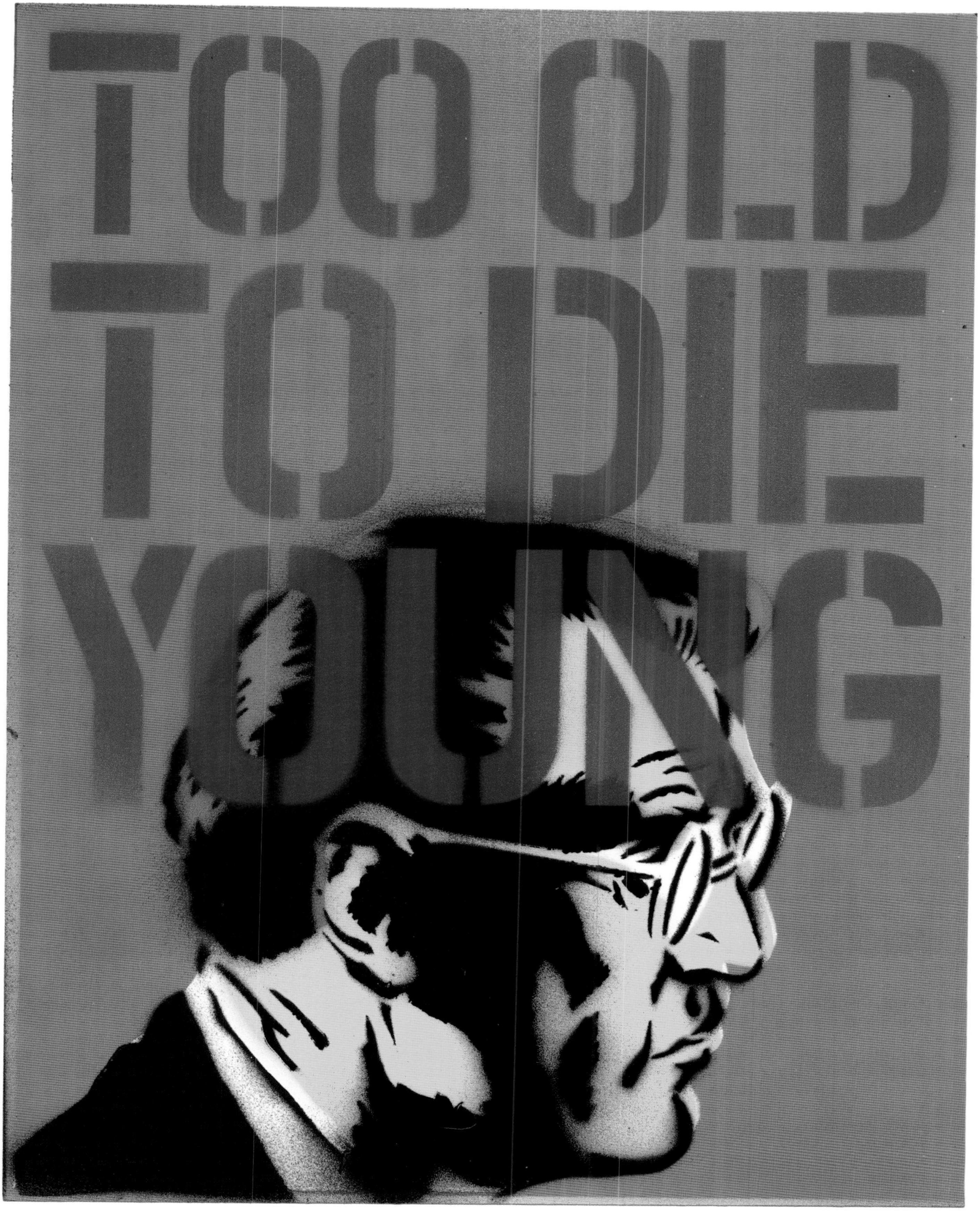
TOO OLD
TO DIE
YOUNG

THROUGH THE LOOKING GLASS

BK'11

THE 70'S WERE NOT COLORFUL   DK'11

CRASS RECORDS LOGO

SIERRA TANGO BRAVO

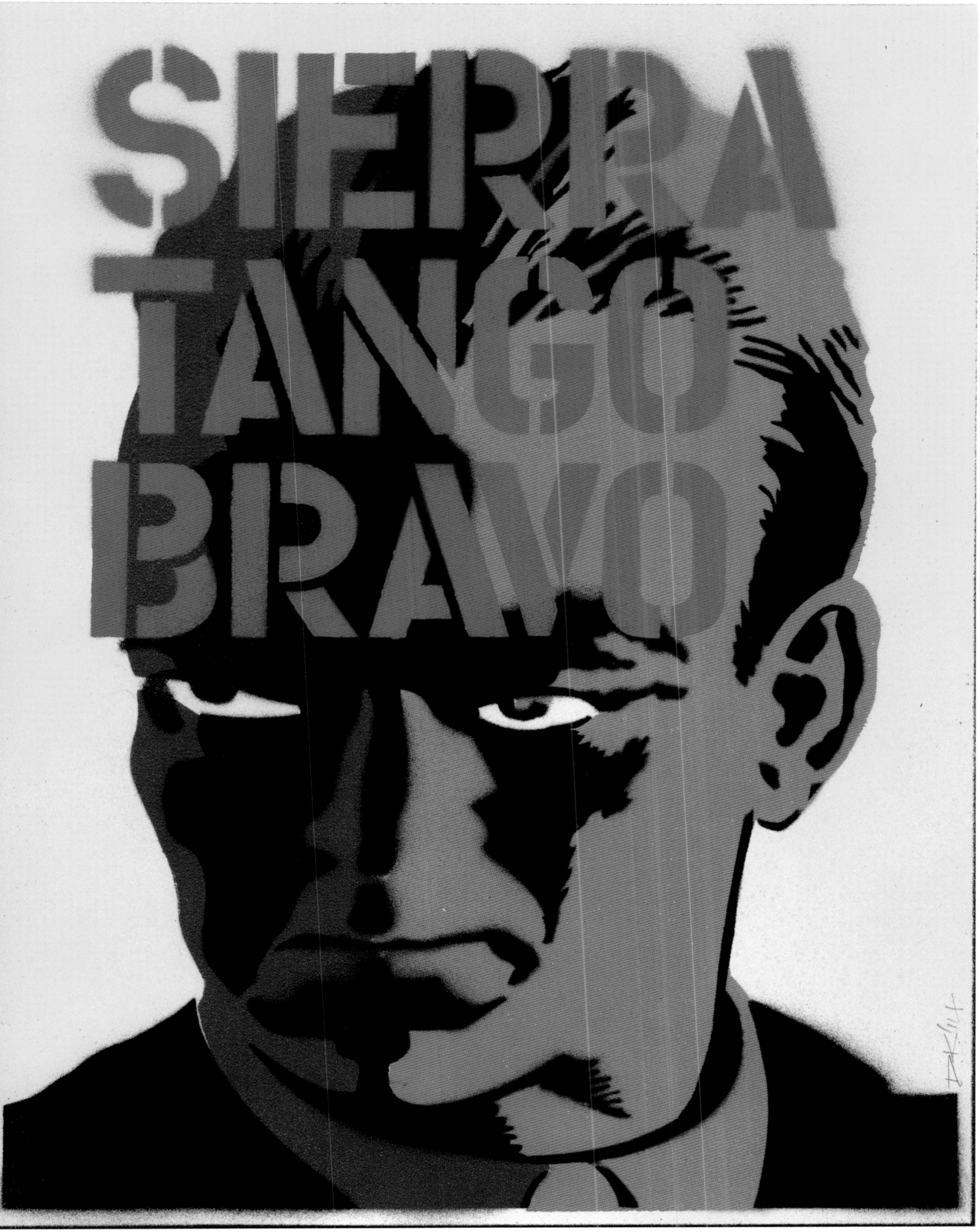
SIERRA
TANGO
BRAVO

HIDDEN PEACE   DK'11

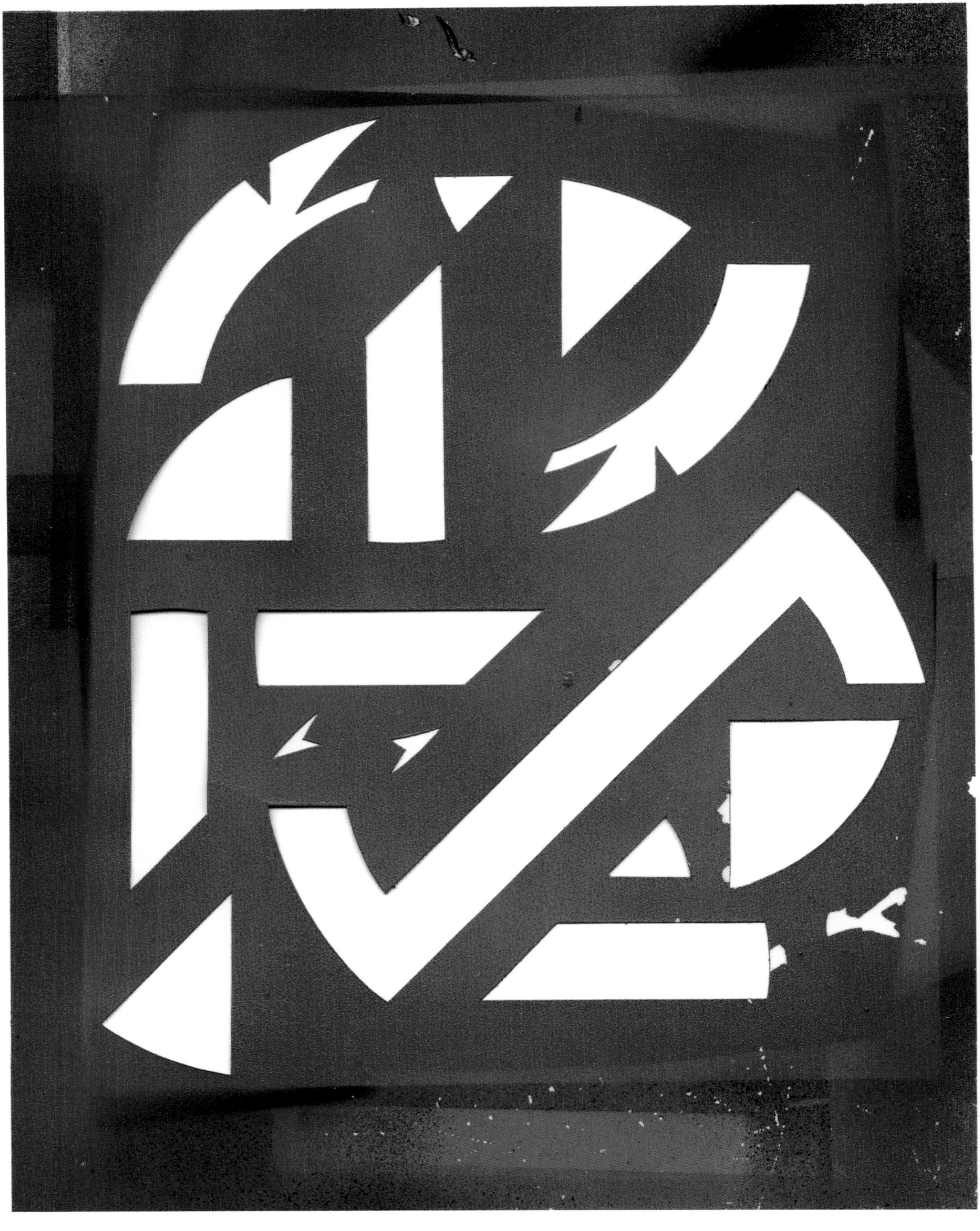

SYMBOL KIT

DK'11

REVOLT IN THE MAGIC KINGDOM

DAVE KING '12

KICK IT!

AK'12

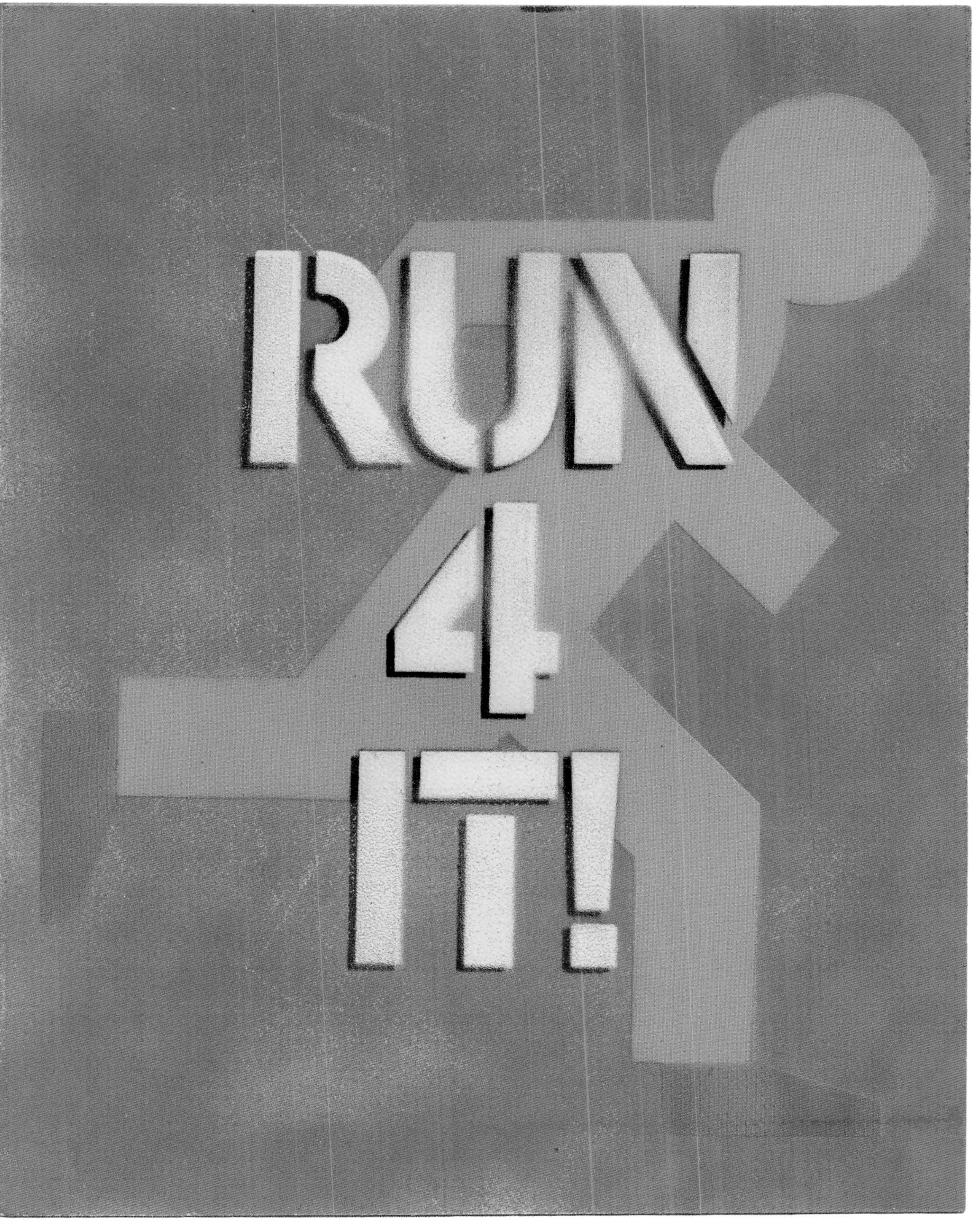
RUN
4
IT!

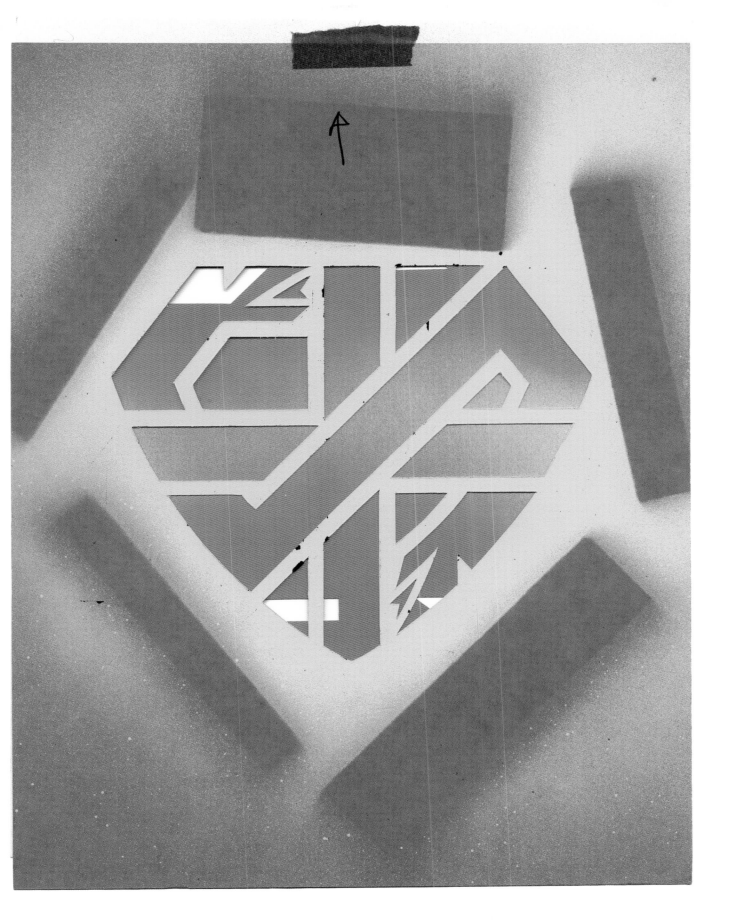

SNAKE ESCAPES

DK '11

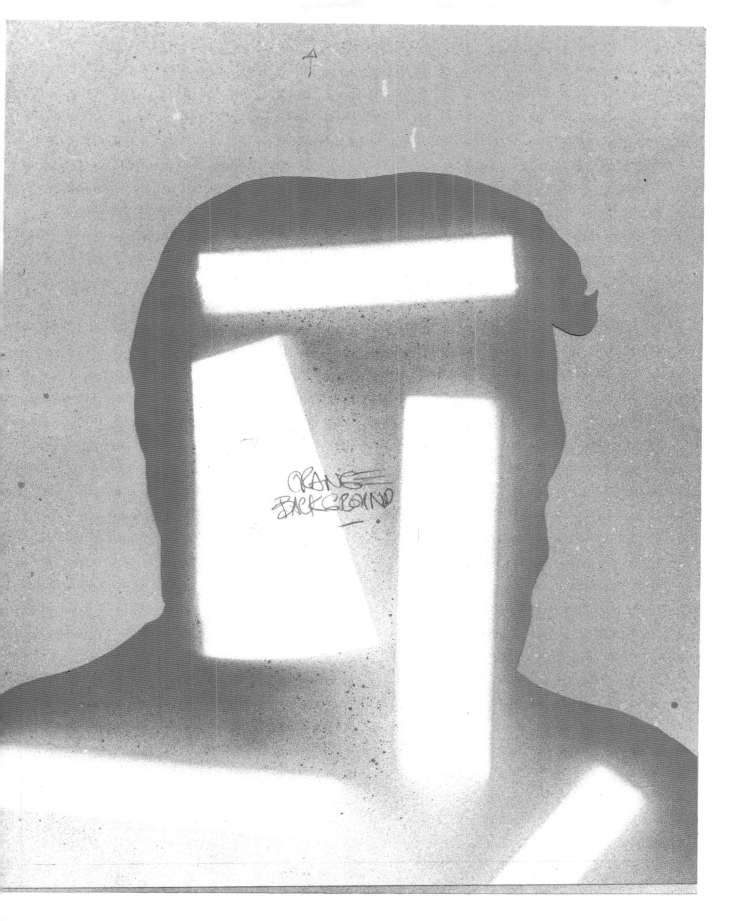

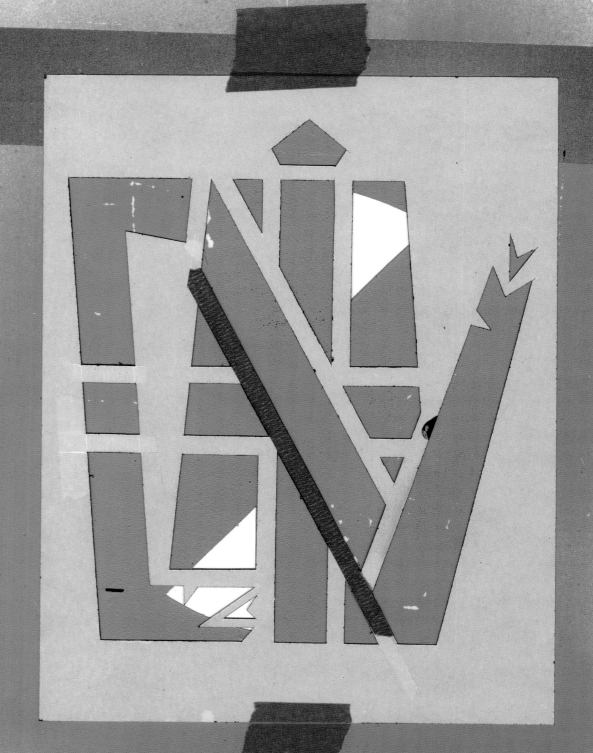

MAKE COFFEE
NOT WAR

DK13

LIVING ON TEA & CHEESE   BK'11

SLEEPING DOGS

FOR 'BASEMENT' SECTION.

ORIGINAL SKETCH FOR EXPLODED CRASS SYMBOL STAGE ONE   DK'13

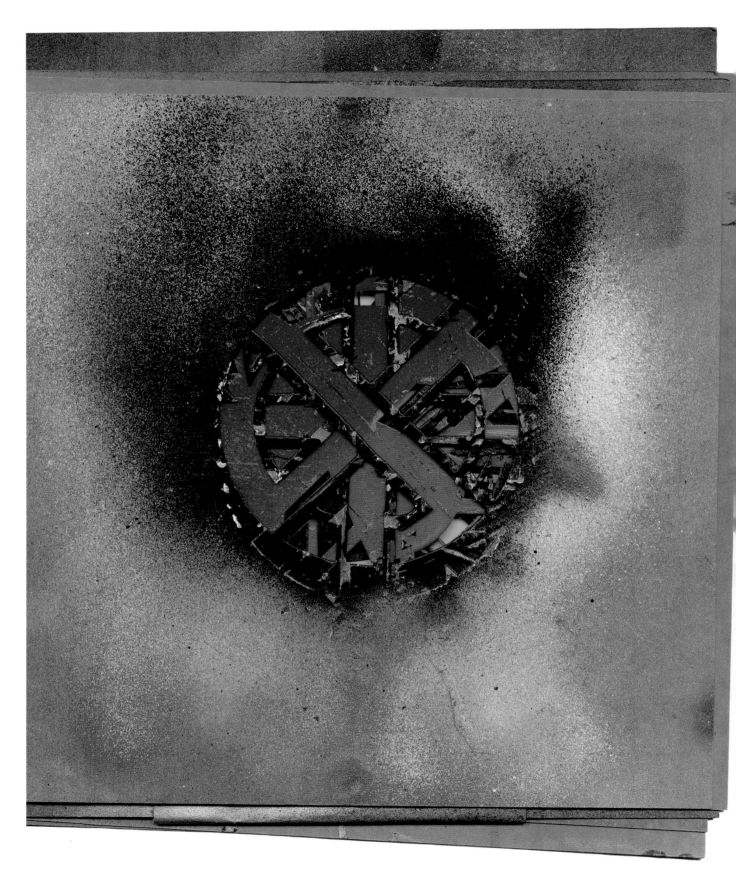

FIRE DOOR

2018

BLUEBIRD   DK'11

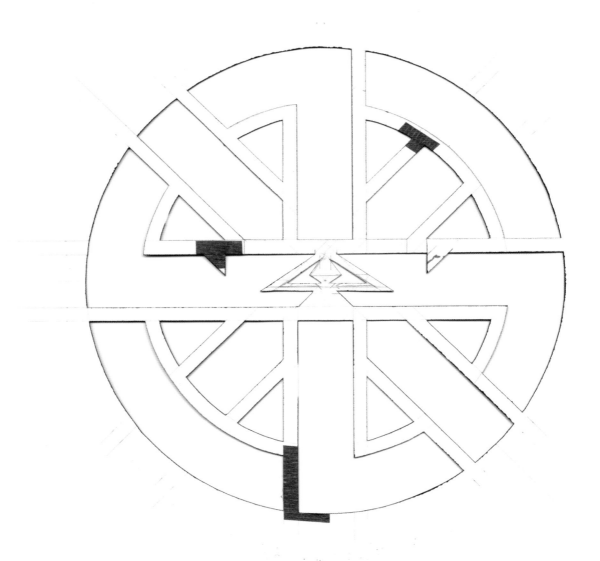

NO!#1

DK13

ANOK?   DK'11

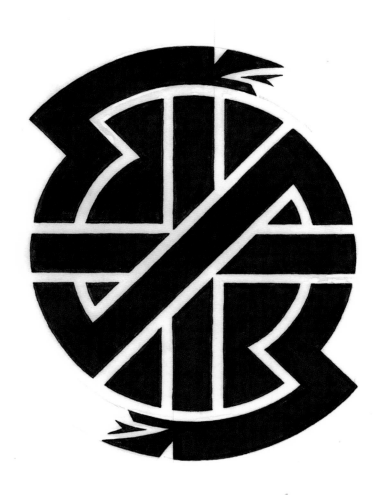

F IS FOR FANTÔMAS 2011

BURN

DK'11

FREE
SPRAY-DAY
DEC 3RD.

FREE

STRAY-CATS

SPRAY-DAY

DEC 3RD

12-5

ORIGINS

MANY THANKS

Matt Borruso, Steven Heller, Barry McGee and Howard A. Rodman for their generous forewords. To Michael Millet, an early San Francisco supporter of my work and our bands. To Matt Wobensmith for first exhibiting many of the pieces herein. To Clint Woodside and Bryan Ray for the rhythmical, mixtape-like layout and design of the book. Also to Jeremy Gray for peerless technical support and creative contributions.

DEDICATED TO
DEAREST DIONE

The first stencil lettering I was aware of was on a sign that said "WAR DEPARTMENT. KEEP OUT." The sign hung on a barbed-wire-topped fence erected to keep people out of an abandoned air base. The vast stretches of buckling concrete were limned with wild grasses: a perfect poetic playground for postwar baby boomers. During the war, stray bombs or downed fighter planes would obliterate a house or two, blasting a gap into an otherwise intact row of homes. We called these violently created spaces bombsites. There was one a few doors down from my grandmother's house, and another at the end of our street. Overgrown with tangled vegetation, these were our unstructured adventure playgrounds. One even had at its center what seemed to be a bottomless pit. The boys re-fought the war there with airguns and pea shooters.

Those ruinous gardens and ragged holes in the otherwise orderly neighbourhood stayed undeveloped until the 1960s, when the economy finally revived and made Swinging London possible. I purchased a floral tie on Carnaby Street, the mod fashion Mecca. This was a previously unimaginable item in the dominant sartorial realm of dull, striped ties for school or army regiment. Colour had entered the culture.

I attended art school from 1964 to 1967. The school library was remarkably comprehensive, and there I discovered for the first time the collage art of Hannah Höch and John Heartfield, and the stencil-centric paintings of Robert Indiana and Jasper Johns. After school I went straight into the commercial art world and worked as an art director and designer for ten years.

Then came punk rock. Punk was the essential do-it-yourself movement; what could be better suited for its graphics than the stencil alphabet? The tools were simple and cheap: a piece of cardboard, a scalpel in the UK (or a craft knife in the US) and a can of spray paint. What worked to command attention for the War Department worked just as well for a Peace Department (or Movement).

After designing the Crass symbol in 1977, I moved to New York, where I did graphics for clubs like Danceteria and the Peppermint Lounge and for the Museum of Modern Art.

I joined a band called Arsenal. Later the whole band (Dione, Charley and I) relocated to San Francisco where there was a fine, furious, thoughtful, angry and influential punk scene. We played the legendary venues on Broadway, the obscure basement clubs and the dive bars. We toured up and down the West Coast from Los Angeles to Vancouver. In time, the band changed its name to Sleeping Dogs and then to Brain Rust. Arsenal and Sleeping Dogs appeared on Crass Records; San Francisco's Broken Rekids released a collection of Sleeping Dogs and Brain Rust.

After about ten years I stopped playing in these bands and began attending the San Francisco Art Institute. There I studied media that I hadn't in the UK: painting, sculpture and photography. Since that time, I've made short films, designed more logos for bands and record labels and published a number of photo books. Along the way there have been great friendships and grand journeys through landscapes both mundane and magnificent.

I still make stencils. The act of simply folding and cutting paper and drawing with markers remains an unalloyed joy.

STENCILS?

DAVE KING

PHOTO: DIONE KING 2018

VERY FIRST TRACING OF SYMBOL 1977